ECONOMIC APPROACHES TO INTELLECTUAL PROPERTY

ECONOMIC APPROACHES TO INTELLECTUAL PROPERTY

Dr Nicola Searle
Martin Brassell frsa

OXFORD
UNIVERSITY PRESS

OXFORD
UNIVERSITY PRESS

Great Clarendon Street, Oxford, OX2 6DP,
United Kingdom

Oxford University Press is a department of the University of Oxford.
It furthers the University's objective of excellence in research, scholarship,
and education by publishing worldwide. Oxford is a registered trade mark of
Oxford University Press in the UK and in certain other countries

First Edition published in 2016

Published in the United States of America by Oxford University Press
198 Madison Avenue, New York, NY 10016, United States of America

British Library Cataloguing in Publication Data
Data available

Library of Congress Control Number: 2016935075

ISBN 978–0–19–873626–4

ACKNOWLEDGEMENTS

The authors wish to thank their helpful (and patient) Oxford University Press editors Ruth Anderson, Emma Taylor, and Gemma Parsons. We would also like to thank our reviewers, Professor Iwan Davies, Chris Davies, Aloke Siddique, and our anonymous reviewers for their helpful suggestions. We are grateful to Kelly Williams of The Admin's Niche for her help in managing files and formatting. Any omissions or errors are entirely our own.

In addition, Dr Nicola Searle would like to thank Jeremy Philips for encouraging her writing on IP and economics; Goldsmiths, University of London, for allowing her the time to write this book; and her former colleagues at the UK Intellectual Property Office for teaching her so much about policy and economics.

Martin Brassell would like to thank his patient (not patent) family.

PREFACE

Intellectual property (IP) is big business. It permeates all aspects of modern commercial practice. It is transforming, and being transformed by, the digital age. The way in which companies use it, enforce it, and locate it have become hotly debated topics.

Traditionally, IP rights have been interpreted mainly from a legal standpoint; after all, they are legal constructs. However, the growth of IP prompted by technological and social change and recognition of its importance for innovation require this approach to be reconsidered. Since economics can provide insights into the evolving role of IP and question traditional approaches, it is time IP debates and practice shifted to economics.

In the past, economists have largely developed analysis for other economists. This book adopts an interdisciplinary perspective and seeks to bridge the gap between policy, economics, law and IP. It aims to provide the reader with the foundations to critically analyse economics arguments, especially in terms of the impact and value IP delivers.

This book details key economic approaches to IP, breaks down the economics of each IP right and details the theory and practice of determining the value contribution IP makes to today's markets. From the fascinating role of status in counterfeiting, to the strategic use of intellectual assets in company valuation, the reader will derive a comprehensive understanding of the economics of IP.

This book is intended to be useful for lawyers, decision makers, and scholars, not only to inform and educate but also to be used as a point of reference and a set of inter-related arguments. The book covers a wide array of topics in IP and economics. Where readers are interested in learning more, further reading is suggested in the footnotes. Every discipline has its own lexicon and, given the interdisciplinary nature of this work, readers may find familiar terms used in unfamiliar ways. We ask that the reader keep an open mind to the language of economics.

We wrote this book because we saw that economics has something valuable to offer IP, but that important dimensions were being lost in translation between economists, lawyers, companies, and policy decision makers. We want readers to be able to tie together their understanding of IP and view it through the lens of economics by examining what creates value and why. It is our hope that this approach will provoke further debate on IP and its role in innovation, and allow firms to better understand the context in which they operate and the (often hidden) sources of the true value they own and control.

The co-authors of this book each bring a key piece of economics and IP to the reader. Dr Nicola Searle applies her academic, government, and investment banking background to explain the basics of economics and then take the reader through key economic understandings of IP theory and policy. Martin Brassell combines his knowledge of business support, corporate finance, IP identification, and valuation to detail the ways in which IP value can be realized now, and to anticipate the development of future IP markets. Collectively, we develop an all-round approach to economics and IP.

Overview

Economics is a fascinating combination of theory and application. As a social science, economics borrows from and contributes to other disciplines. However, the meeting of economics and other disciplines is not always congenial.

The crux of economics can be found in the analysis of choice. Markets operate under constraints, as resources are limited. Economics examines how these choices are made, what the outcomes are, and how to influence them.

In the past few decades, the political focus has been on innovation-enabled economic growth. Economics fundamentally views IP as an incentive to innovate. Under this view, IP is a policy that grants innovators rights over their innovation for the benefit of the greater good, namely long-term economic benefit.

However, as this book details, things are not that simple. Competing viewpoints suggest that the economic standpoint may neglect the intrinsic right of innovators to own the fruits of their labour. There is also a growing movement questioning both the process of innovation and the need for rights over knowledge. As markets and IP develop, so does the economic understanding of IP and innovation.

Further complicating the picture is economic dependency on good data. Robust economic analysis, particularly for use in the development of evidence-based policy, is hard to come by. IP's intangible nature, the unregistered status of a number of rights and the proprietary nature of some data mean that good empirical analysis of IP is rare. However, as IP offices publish more data and their abilities to collect data in digital environments improves, so too will empirical analysis.

The heterogeneity of economic analysis of the various IP rights also highlights some of the challenges a one-size-fits-all approach to IP rightly faces. While patents, copyrights, and design rights suggest relatively straightforward incentives to innovate, the picture is murkier when trade marks, trade secrets, and *sui generis* rights are considered. These differences highlight the strengths and weaknesses in understanding IP's economics in general, and the process of innovation in particular.

The chapter on competition addresses the economics of competition and its application to IP. The depth and detail of this chapter is a response to readers' feedback that competition is an area of interest. *Prima facie*, IP introduces a monopoly and therefore is bad for markets. However, this chapter details how a combination of market structure, the behaviour of firms and the performance of the market determine where IP, or any anti-competitive behaviour, is problematic.

Combining practice and theory, the last five chapters of the book move to a consideration of how IP creates value. Lifting the lid on the otherwise hidden world of IP valuation, these chapters explain how registered and unregistered rights deliver value for business. Taking the reader through the case for associating value with IP, the ways in which value gets created and key valuation practices, the section concludes with the practical accounting aspects that have led to IP value often remaining well hidden.

Guide to the Book

The book is divided into three main Parts. Each of the three Parts begins with a summary.

The first Part, Chapters 1–2, begins with an overview of economics and the economics of IP. Readers comfortable with their understanding may not need to pause for long on the first chapter, or may prefer to refer back to it as needed for explanations of key principles in economics. The second chapter details the innovation focus of economics and anticipates key themes of economic analysis of IP.

The second Part, Chapters 3–7, first delves into the particulars of each IP right. It starts with the more mainstream rights of patents and copyrights and then addresses trade marks, trade secrets, and a number of *sui generis* rights. It then spells out economics of competition and the interaction of competition and IP. These chapters are written independently of each other to accommodate readers' interest in specific topics.

The third Part, Chapters 8–12, brings these theoretical aspects together, giving detailed consideration to when, why, and how IP delivers value. It begins with discussions on the role IP has in generating value at a macro- and micro-economic level, then describes the aspects that determine the value of IP and the contexts in which it most often delivers value. It then details key methodologies and techniques for IP valuation before concluding with the reporting and accounting of IP and intangibles.

CONTENTS

PART I INTRODUCTION TO THE BOOK

Part I

INTRODUCTION TO THE BOOK

These first two chapters introduce principles of economics and their application to PI.01
intellectual property (IP). The first chapter examines markets and principles of economics, providing a general introduction for those less familiar with the concepts and terminology involved. The second chapter delves into economic frameworks for IP.

Summary

Economics is the study of choice. Given that resources are finite, who gets what, PI.02
when, where, and how shapes economic performance and the economic approach to IP. Economics analysis provides insights into how markets, firms, and individuals choose their consumption and production.

Markets and Other Considerations

In a world where resources are limited, individuals and organizations must make PI.03
choices as how to allocate budgets, time, production, etc. Economics examines how these choices are made and how incentives can influence these choices. Key concepts are supply and demand; the preferences of consumers and producers determine the price and quantity of goods in the market.

The structure of markets is key to the performance of the market and the need for PI.04
government intervention. These structures range from markets with high levels of competition to monopolies. Where markets are dysfunctional (market failures), government and policy may be able to nudge decisions towards a better outcome. IP is one such nudge. Government policy, grants, incentives, disincentives, and regulation may affect choices, costs, and benefits.

PI.05 A common goal for societies is economic growth. Most government economic policy emphasizes production and money as measures of economic success, although alternate approaches focus on utility (happiness) and environmental resources. Innovation is an important way to increase economic growth without having to use increased resources. Economists combine theory and statistics to create the systematic approach to economic analysis. Innovation and innovation policies are at the heart of the economic approach to IP.

PI.06 Evidence-based policy, which seeks to develop policy based on objective evidence, relies heavily on the empirical side of economics. The development of evidenced-based IP policy is challenged by the dearth of good IP data. Registered intellectual property rights (IP rights) benefit from the relative richness of data available. However, unregistered IP rights are particularly difficult to study empirically. To account for this, empirical analysis of IP often includes techniques such as surveys.

Innovation and the Social Contract Theory

PI.07 The classic economic interpretation of IP is as an incentive to innovate. IP introduces a property right over intangible assets. It provides innovators with a means to realize the returns of their investment and supports this process.

PI.08 One way to consider IP is the social contract theory. This is an agreement between innovators and society. Innovators receive a temporary monopoly (IP rights) for their innovations; the protected innovation then becomes part of the public domain. Under these monopoly conditions, society initially pays higher prices for lower quantities, but eventually receives the long-term benefit of the innovation. The social contract is a balancing act between the interests of innovators, society, and future innovators. It accepts higher costs for society in the short term, in exchange for long-term continued innovation.

PI.09 This incentives-to-innovate path of economics is in contrast to other approaches. A second, common interpretation of IP is to consider it an intrinsic right. This approach, sometimes called the labour desert theory, ties an individual's ownership of their labour to the fruits of their labour; innovative works are intrinsically the property of the innovator. A third way questions the value of property rights over innovation. Instead, a variety of alternatives range from the outright rejection of property rights to open innovation approaches. This third nexus continues to evolve.

PI.10 Innovation, which may be defined by economists as an applied invention, can be viewed in different ways. One popular model is creative destruction, which posits that innovation is a series of disruptions of the status quo. Technology is disruptive to existing business models, markets, and firms. Innovations are classified as either process or product innovations. A process innovation typically reduces the costs of production, whereas a product innovation introduces a new product.

Conclusion

Economics contributes much to IP; however its contributions are targeted towards an innovation-focused approach. This focus is not always consistent with alternative approaches. The empirical analysis, however, provides an objective means to evaluate economical hypotheses. As both the understanding of innovation and the available evidence develop, economics will further contribute to the refinement and optimization of IP. PI.11

1

INTRODUCTION TO ECONOMICS

Economics, like most other subjects, makes use of phrases with particular mean ings that are not always apparent from, or perfectly aligned with, their literal sense. Accordingly, this first chapter takes the form of a 'primer' setting out, in straightforward terms intended to be accessible to non-economists, the key concepts of greatest relevance for the discussion on intellectual property (IP) that follows. **1.01**

By focusing on the meaning of common economic terminology, the chapter is unavoidably a little technical in nature in order to clarify the concepts featured throughout subsequent chapters. **1.02**

Economics has been described as 'the dismal science'.[1] It is a discipline that is often focused on quantifying the unfortunate and forecasting the unpleasant, and this darker side of economics does not sit well with those less inclined to objectify life. But in fact, economics is neither dismal nor a science: instead, it is fundamentally about choice. Economics studies the production, consumption, and distribution of goods and services, and the underlying choices that dictate these. **1.03**

Economics approaches choices in IP with these principles in mind, examining reasons why economic interpretations of IP differ from those of other disciplines. The economist's underlying approach to IP, and indeed any subject, stems from a very specific analytical, logic-based framework. This can be very useful in creating consistency and reducing subjectivity in conclusions, but leaves economic approaches open to criticism as the specificity may come at the cost of flexibility if incorrectly applied. **1.04**

---

[1] The origins of the phrase 'dismal science' are disputed, but they are generally agreed to be a reference to the collective and pessimistic works of Thomas Robert Malthus, who predicts starvation as a consequence of population and economic growth, and David Ricardo, who argued the natural state of wages is subsistence level.

The Basic Principles of Economics

Supply and demand

1.05 A fundamental principle in economics is that of scarcity. Scarcity is the concept that humans have unlimited wants in a world with limited supplies. Without scarcity, everyone's demands could, in theory, be met. This scarcity then gives rise to core concepts of supply and demand.

1.06 Demand is the want side of scarcity. Consumers, who drive demand, have wants and willingness to pay for goods and services. Goods are typically things consumers can touch such as computers or cars;[2] services are things that cannot be touched, ranging from haircuts to legal representation. These are generally measured by two key values: quantity and price. Depending on their wants, a consumer will buy less (a lower quantity) if the price is high, and will buy more (a higher quantity) if the price is low. The maximum amount a consumer is willing to sacrifice for a given good or service is that consumer's willingness-to-pay.

1.07 Supermarket shoppers faced with changing price may find themselves buying more or less. Taking cheese as an example, should their favourite camembert suddenly become more expensive, shoppers may buy less. For example, if the maximum amount a shopper is willing to pay for one brie round is £5, then their willingness-to-pay is £5. If the brie is £6, the shopper will not buy that round. If the brie is less than £5, the shopper may buy more rounds. If all of the demand from cheese shoppers is added together, it is possible to determine the aggregate demand for cheese.

1.08 On the other side of the market is supply. Supply is the goods and services on offer in the economy. Put slightly differently, it is availability and quantity of goods and services. The quantity is the amount of goods and services offered by producers (suppliers). The price is the payment asked by the supplier in order to part with the goods and services.

1.09 On the supply side, as prices go up, the quantity supplied increases and vice versa.[3] The more a producer can charge, the more they are willing to sell. If price decreases, producers will be willing to sell less. For example, the more a law firm can charge its clients, the more legal services it will offer. Suppliers may be willing to sell ten tonnes of cheese at £5, but will want to sell less if the price is only £4 and more if the price is £6.

[2] Rather than list individual goods, economists often use the handy term 'widgets' as a generic example of a good.

[3] This is a simplification and assuming nothing else has changed.

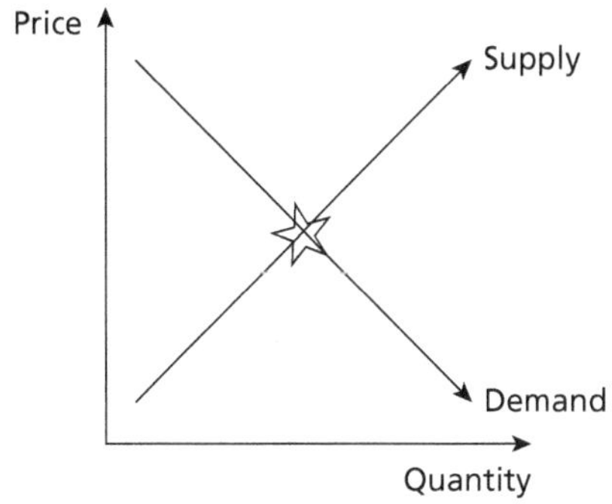

Figure 1.1 Supply and demand

The principles of supply and demand form the fundamental graph of economics: the supply and demand curves (see Figure 1.1).[4] This graph, with its cross-shape,[5] represents a quasi-religious symbol for economists as it visually demonstrates the paragraphs above. As such, it is one of only a few graphs in this book. **1.10**

On the vertical axis (often referred to as the y-axis) is Price and on the horizontal (x-axis) is Quantity. The curves are Supply and Demand. Where the vertical and horizontal axes meet is zero. The supply curve slopes up, which shows the positive relationship[6] between price and quantity for producers. The demand curve slopes down, which shows the negative relationship[7] between price and quantity for consumers. **1.11**

Where the supply and demand curves meet is the magical point (indicated by the star) economists call equilibrium. This is the point where the price and quantity supplied equals the price and quantity demanded. Consumers and producers are both happy in this equilibrium. Back to the cheese example, assume the price, in this case, is £5 and the quantity is ten tonnes. In this case, cheese shoppers willing to pay up to £5 are all buying cheese, the suppliers willing to sell at £5 are selling, and ten tonnes of cheese are being traded. Problems arise when markets stray from this point. Economists lie awake at night pondering these problems,[8] wondering why the market is not in equilibrium, and contemplating how to fix it. **1.12**

---

[4] The lines are referred to as curves as they are often not straight. However, in the simple model shown here, straight lines suffice.

[5] To be more specific, the cross is the Saltire or the St Andrews cross.

[6] A positive relationship is the term used to denote a relationship between two values (in this case price and quantity) where as one increases, so does the other, or, as one decreases, so does the other.

[7] A negative relationship is the opposite of a positive relationship, as price increases, quantity decreases and vice versa.

[8] This could be considered the dismal part of the dismal science.

1.13 Many economic considerations in IP arise from the fact that markets in IP struggle to find this equilibrium. In real life, demand and supply curves can change, producers may over or under produce and demand may rise or fall. The next sections will discuss these challenges further.

Supply

1.14 Producers who supply the goods and services in the economy are assumed to do so with the goal of making money, known as the profit motive. Profit is the difference between the money coming into the firm (i.e. the producer) and the money going out (i.e. the costs). Money coming into the firm is known as revenue and is equal to the price of the good or service multiplied by the quantity sold. Producers are assumed to be profit maximizing[9] and have three ways of increasing profit: increase price, increase the quantity, and/or decrease costs.

1.15 Costs[10] can be broken down a number of ways. Fixed and variable costs account for the fact that some costs can change with the quantity produced and others do not. If the good is a cup of coffee, then the mug, water, coffee, and effort (labour) are the variable costs and the coffee machine is the fixed cost. Another key cost is the marginal cost, which, as the name suggests, looks at the margins. This is the cost per each additional unit of good or service. The marginal cost of the cup of coffee is the difference in costs between making one cup of coffee and two cups of coffee. Without going too far into the theory, a common assumption in economics is that competition (generally considered a good thing) results in price equalling marginal cost.

1.16 Costs are a very important concept in the supply of goods and services associated with IP. In the music industry, a sector dominated by copyrighted goods, the fixed costs of setting up a recording studio are relatively high. At the same time, the marginal cost of each additional MP3 or CD is relatively low. This creates further complexities in obtaining the magical equilibrium between supply and demand.

Demand

1.17 Consumers, unlike profit-driven suppliers, are assumed to be utility maximizing.[11] Utility is an abstract concept that encompasses all the preferences, wants, and needs that result in satisfaction. Utility encompasses many things: pleasure, nutrition,

[9] The profit-maximizing characteristic of firms is a form of utility maximizing (see discussion later) where the utility is profit. Firms are profit-driven. While this is generally the case, there are exceptions such as charities.

[10] Costs may not necessarily be money-based (monetary). For example, time, health, and 'hassle' can be costs.

[11] Consumers are often construed as individuals, but firms, groups, and other agents are also considered consumers when they are on the demand side of the market.

security, love, status, and people's endless needs, wants, and desires.[12] However, as much as the consumer seeks to maximize utility, they are ultimately constrained by their own budget. Each consumer will have a limited amount of some resources such as time and money. The goal of the consumer is to maximize their utility given their budget. Therefore, the consumer must trade-off between quantities of camembert, football tickets, and yoga classes, as they only have a set amount of time and money.

Incentives and disincentives

Incentives and disincentives are the carrots and sticks, the push and pull, or the punishment and reward systems of economics. They help explain the motivations behind the decisions made in an economy. Incentives are the reasons to engage in a specific behaviour whereas disincentives are the reasons not to engage. Annual bonuses for employees and reduced car taxes for fuel-efficient vehicles are examples of incentives. Examples of disincentives are jail terms for criminal behaviour and fines for late payment of bills. **1.18**

Incentives are a fundamental argument for IP. For economists, IP exists to incentivize innovation (see Chapter 2 for a more detailed discussion). In general, economic approaches discourage regulations that interfere with markets. However, in cases where the market fails to achieve certain objectives, regulation can be warranted. For innovation, the market often fails to provide innovators with sufficient rewards in the form of profit. This means the economy produces less innovation than is desirable. Hence, regulations such as IP intervene to increase the incentives to innovate. **1.19**

Disincentives also play a large role in IP. The enforcement of IP is achieved primarily through a series of legal constructs that serve to discourage certain behaviours. Damages in infringement cases are a prime example. Discouraging letters, limiting internet access, and fines are all disincentives used to increase the cost of, and, therefore, discourage consumption of copyright-infringing online content. **1.20**

Market structures

As much as the basic supply and demand, with its magical equilibrium, is an ideal, the reality is often murkier. Different market structures affect the supply and demand curves and where they meet. Two basic structures relevant to IP are perfect competition and monopolies. **1.21**

[12] Interested readers can find more on these by the psychologist Abraham Maslow and his hierarchy of needs in his 1943 paper 'A Theory of Human Motivation' published in *Psychological Review*, 50, 370–396.

1.22 Perfect competition is the 'gold standard' of economics. It is where there are unlimited suppliers and consumers, and conditions are so flexible that the market is always in equilibrium. It is the utopian dream of economists. Whilst it is highly unrealistic as an objective, consideration of perfect competition serves a useful purpose as a benchmark for comparison purposes. It allows the flaws in other markets to be identified, and highlights why economists like competition as it is efficient and the market is in equilibrium.

1.23 On the other hand,[13] economists are not big fans of monopolies in general.[14] In a monopoly, there is only one producer on the supply side of the market. Monopolies grant firms a high level of market power that allows them to raise the price above the marginal costs. This is nearly the opposite of competition, and results in higher prices and lower quantities of the good or service. Monopolies tend to benefit producers at the cost of consumers. Like perfect competition, pure monopolies are rarely observed in practice. Between monopolies and perfect competition fall variations on the two.

1.24 IP creates a legal monopoly in which the owner of the IP has a monopoly mandated by law for that particular piece of IP. This is not the same as an economic monopoly (as discussed above) as the legal status of IP does not, by itself, create a market. For example, simply owning a patent does not mean that its owner will automatically have market power, as the market for the products of that patent may not exist. However, a legal monopoly can translate into an economic monopoly and limit competition in practice.

1.25 For example, if a patent is for an obsolete piece of mobile phone technology, then the legal monopoly is not accompanied by an economic monopoly. However, a patent for an essential piece of mobile phone technology in current use means that the owner of the patent (the legal monopoly) will also enjoy the market power stemming from the economic monopoly. This market power will allow the patent owner to charge higher prices. Thus, there is a cost to using IP as a means to provide protection for innovation. The reduction in competition leads to higher prices and lower quantities.

1.26 Consider a pharmaceutical market where there are drugs that cure a common cold. The drugs have slightly different side effects and overall efficacy, but one drug is preferred. If the preferred drug is under patent protection, the owner of that patent will enjoy a legal monopoly over that particular drug but will still compete with other

---

[13] U.S. President Harry Truman is quoted as saying, 'Give me a one-handed economist. All my economists say, "on the one hand... on the other"'.

[14] There are cases in which monopolies may be desirable such as patents, which are detailed further in Chapter 7.

drugs. This is not a pure monopoly situation, but the patent owner will still be able to command higher prices at lower quantities.

Therefore, the market structure forms another piece of the puzzle. The creation of IP rights necessarily distorts markets. However, this is balanced against other considerations such as incentivizing innovation. **1.27**

Market failure

Following from the discussion on market structures, another key concept is that of market failures. Markets may not always reach an efficient equilibrium. All sorts of challenges may stand in the way, including monopolies (both the legal and economic ones discussed above), negative externalities and information asymmetry (discussed below). All of these can create market distortions that lead to market failure. **1.28**

Negative externalities are when transactions or choices impose costs on others outside the transaction. They can create markets that do not account for the costs imposed on others. For example, consider an individual's choice to use a private car instead of public transportation. The cost of the petrol used does not include the costs to society as a result of the pollution created. The choice creates a negative externality in the form of pollution. Positive externalities also exist where those outside a transaction receive benefits. For example, a neighbour's beautiful garden may increase the value of the house next door to it. **1.29**

Information asymmetries occur when one party engaged in a transaction knows more than the other. For example, the seller of a used car will know significantly more about the quality of the car than the buyer. The used car market failure resulting from this information asymmetry is known as the market for lemons (a 'lemon' being a popular term for a defective used car). While sellers know whether their car is a lemon, the buyer is unable to distinguish between a defective and a good car. Knowing this, the buyer will assume all cars are of average quality and will not be willing to pay more for a good car. Sellers of good quality cars, therefore, may be faced with selling at a price for a lower quality car and choose instead to not sell. Thus, the average quality of a used car available for sale is driven down and lemons eventually dominate the market for used cars. The information asymmetry creates a market failure. **1.30**

Market failure is often given as a rationale for government intervention. In the case of used cars, possible solutions may be government mandated service records, laws protecting the accuracy of odometers, and consumer protection regulations. In the markets for innovation, as discussed later, IP is introduced as a means to create property rights to correct the market failure. However, as discussed earlier, IP itself may introduce another type of market failure, that of monopoly. **1.31**

Costs and benefits

1.32 A useful framework for analysing the incentives and disincentives of any situation is the cost–benefit analysis. A cost–benefit analysis is a standard analysis technique used to weigh up the pros and cons of a particular choice. The cost–benefit analysis is used across many disciplines, but in economics, it provides a structured approach to model factors such as costs, revenues, profits, incentives, disincentives, and utility. This logical approach argues that if the costs of a decision outweigh its benefits, then agents do not proceed with the decision. Likewise, if the benefits outweigh the costs, then the decision goes ahead.

1.33 Consider a consumer's decision to download copyright-infringing music from the internet. In this case, the consumer of the music weighs the costs of being caught or fined for infringement, against the benefits of consuming the content and decides to infringe. Changes to government policy and IP law often take into account a cost–benefit analysis as they seek to tip the balance to discourage infringement. Theoretically, every economic decision made has incorporated some form of cost–benefit analysis.

Money and time

1.34 Even economics standards recognize that 'money isn't everything'. In fact, in economics, money is simply a proxy for value. Value is the consumer's calculation, or perception, of utility. Money is a way of creating a relatively concrete measurement of an abstract concept. In economics, money is a universal language. It allows disparate values, utilities, goods, and services to be compared and contrasted. Money is vital to modern economies as it facilitates payment and stores value. The bartering days of carrying around a chicken in case you need a jug of milk are long gone.

1.35 'Time is money', so goes the saying. In economics, this is partially true. A key concept, shared with other disciplines such as finance, is the time value of money. The time value of money says that money today is worth more than money tomorrow; interest rates and inflation mean that £100 today is worth more than £100 in a year's time. Time value of money is important to remember when comparing money across different time periods, as all things are not equal. The phrase might more aptly be 'time costs money.'

1.36 A further concept of time is the economic ideas of the long and short run[15] for firms. In the long run, anything can change. In the short run, the firm may have three options: increase production, decrease production, or cease production.[16] For

---

[15] The short and long *run* differ from the short, medium, and long *term*, as the latter is a measurement of time and the former a concept of time.

[16] This is an oversimplification but covers the general options typically available to firms.

example, in the long run, a pharmaceutical company can build a new laboratory, downsize an existing laboratory, enter or leave a new industry. In the short run, the company can hire more workers, lay off workers, buy more or fewer chemicals, or cease to operate entirely. These concepts are important in considering how quickly firms can respond to changes in market conditions, and not all businesses are equal in this respect; for example, a software development firm is likely to have the capability to respond more quickly to market changes than an aerospace firm.

The long and short run for economies as a whole is also important. In the long run, **1.37** economies are completely flexible. Labour moves and adapts and capital travels the world. In the short run, the economy is less flexible. For example, in the short run, the increase in demand for specialized software skills may lead to shortages and higher wages. In the long run, the labour supply will adapt as more people, attracted by the higher wages on offer, will be incentivized to train in these areas. This concept of the long and short run for economies is important as one of the fundamental economic justification for IP rights relies on a trade-off between the long and short run (as detailed in Chapter 2).

Risk and uncertainty

Appetite for risk is another important concept in economics, although rather disap- **1.38** pointingly, economists are not the risk-seeking, Gordon Gekko[17] bankers they might be considered to be. Is a firm risk neutral, risk-seeking, or risk averse? The appetite for risk helps to predict a firm's behaviour. Risk is a cost–benefit analysis in which potential gains are weighed up against potential profits. Litigation in IP involves a fair amount of risk. Any patent owner suing for infringement has to balance the risks of incurring heavy legal fees and inviting invalidation proceedings against the possibility of damages awards and injunctions. For a small, likely risk-averse firm, IP litigation may place the firm's future at risk while a larger firm will have the resources to absorb losses from litigation and be able to engage in risky strategies.

Economics makes a distinction between risk and uncertainty. Risk, as noted be- **1.39** fore, is a calculation and is relatively known. Uncertainty, in contrast, is entirely unknown. In uncertainty, outcomes and possibilities are unknown. Uncertainty is a common feature in industries relying heavily on copyright. In the creative industries, where the copyright for creative content is important, there is great uncertainty about the success of any particular work; predicting how well a book or television programme will fare is difficult.

In general, uncertainty is not a good thing for firms or economies as it may result in **1.40** wasteful avoidance behaviour. For example, decisions may be postponed until the

[17] An avaricious, fictional stockbroker played by Michael Douglas in the 1987 movie *Wall Street*.

uncertainty is reduced. However, until the crystal ball is invented (and doubtless subsequently patented), uncertainty will exist. Risk is less of a problem, as being quantifiable, it allows firms to adopt risk management strategies.

Innovation and growth

1.41 Innovation is a fundamental concept for the economics of IP. For economists, IP rights serve to incentivize innovation. The definition of innovation is rather specific; an innovation is an applied invention. An invention is the creation of a new product or process; whereas innovation is the use or application of the new product or process. Innovation is important for the primary goal of modern economics: growth.

1.42 Economic growth is the increase in production in an economy. Typically this is measured as GDP.[18] There are two ways to increase productivity: increase inputs (labour and capital) or increase their efficiency.[19] Innovation increases the efficiency of inputs. Therefore, even if capital and labour do not change, innovation can increase production. It is, therefore, a very attractive way to increase economic growth when labour and capital are constrained.

1.43 Related to economic growth is the idea of economic development. This is particularly a concern for developing[20] countries. Developing countries are those with lower standards of living, lower levels of industrialization, and lower GDP per capita when compared to developed countries. Developing countries can often be resource-rich (in inputs) in both labour and natural resources. However, they often lack capital and technology. Again, innovation can improve the efficiency of these inputs and lead to economic growth, which can result in further economic development. This is viewed as desirable at it can raise living standards and address humanitarian concerns.

1.44 However, the focus on GDP growth attracts a lot of debate. Is more necessarily better? GDP is a measure of production, but there are a lot of other potential measurements in an economy. Natural resources and environmental degradation are not counted in GDP; utility is also not captured. As an alternative, economists have put forward the idea of GNH—Gross National Happiness. If utility via happiness is the goal, could GNH be a better measurement? Innovation can also address such

[18] GDP is Gross Domestic Product and is the sum of monetary value of all goods and services produced within a nation over a year.

[19] This is a very simplified version of this discussion; interested readers may want to read further on production functions, the Solow model, and related topics. For more, see Weil, D. N. and Sharma, A. (2013). *Economic Growth* (Harlow, Pearson Education).

[20] The terminology for differentiating between economies has varied over the years and includes rich/poor, first/second/third world and developed/developing/less-developed/least-developed countries. There is a lot of debate over these terms as some imply inferiority or superiority.

issues by decreasing demands on natural resources, reducing environmental degradation, and promoting happiness.[21]

The focus on growth and GDP is unlikely to change anytime soon as it is entrenched in popular concepts of economies. Fortunately, innovation can offer more than just growth by reducing negative aspects such as pollution[22] and improve positive ones, such as happiness. **1.45**

Economics as a Discipline

A social science

Economics is a social science.[23] This is very important to remember, as aspects of economics sometimes resemble a natural science.[24] The statistics and modelling used by economists are also used by natural scientists and there is a lot of overlap in the training. However, economics examines societies, not nature. Societies and their economies are necessarily more fluid than the scientific laws used by natural scientists. Therefore, economics, as a social science, has a high degree of uncertainty (hence the long-standing joke that an economist who is right 50% of the time is the world's best economist). The economics of IP is perhaps even more fluid than other areas of economics. IP is an intangible good[25] and less amenable to quantitative techniques favoured by economists. **1.46**

A second point is that economics is not business studies. The two overlap in areas of interest, but economists tend to be more theoretical. Fundamentally, economics analyses choice and business studies analyses organization. Economics examines the production, consumption, and distribution of goods and services from both the transaction, microeconomic perspective and the wider, GDP, macroeconomic perspective. Business studies examines the organizational, financial, managerial, and marketing aspects of firms. **1.47**

The two areas also differ in their methods. As academic disciplines, economics focuses on theoretical models and quantitative methods while business studies **1.48**

---

[21] For example, innovation may allow us more leisure time or new forms of cultural expression. Interested readers may wish to read Professor Andrew Oswald's work on the economics of happiness or Frank, Robert H. (1999). *Luxury Fever: Money and Happiness in an Era of Excess* (United States, New York, NY, The Free Press).

[22] However, the relationship between innovation and pollution is complex as the industrial revolution, for example, increased pollution. Conversely, innovation in green technologies may reduce pollution.

[23] Social sciences look at societies and include economics, sociology, political science, and related disciplines.

[24] Natural sciences look at nature and include chemistry, biology, physics, and related disciplines.

[25] As discussed elsewhere, IP is intangible as it is, unlike other goods and assets, not physical.

focuses more on theory and qualitative methods. In practice, there is a competition between the two camps and the lines are blurring. Economists argue that business studies is too subjective; in response, economics is criticized for being too abstract and attempting to quantify the unquantifiable.

1.49 The definition of an 'economist' is ambiguous. Unlike accountants, lawyers, and similar professions, there is no professional regulation of economists. Typically, an economist will have at least one degree in economics. It is not uncommon for economists to have more interdisciplinary backgrounds incorporating other social and natural scientists. The three main employers of economists are business and industry, academia, and government.

Economics in practice

1.50 Within economics itself are at least two main axes: macroeconomics versus microeconomics, and applied versus theoretical.

1.51 Macroeconomics, as suggested by the suffix 'macro', looks at the economy as a whole. This includes unemployment, inflation, exchange rates, and development. Microeconomics focuses on individual (micro) interactions and examines firms and individuals. Popular topics in microeconomics are prices, supply, demand, and policy. In practice, the two overlap but generally macro is associated with big and micro with small. This book focuses primarily on microeconomics as it provides a transactions-based analysis for immediate debates in legal disputes, day-to-day business, and specific policy questions. Macroeconomics is also very important to IP and is discussed in sections considering wider innovation and growth concerns, and the market focus of the book's third Part of IP in practice.

1.52 A second axis is theoretical versus applied. Economic theory typically starts with an economic model. This is expressed in mathematical terms, often with Greek letters. These theoretical models predict behaviour. An economist using a model will develop its assumptions, change one or two parameters, and then predict the outcomes. As an example, the effects of the introduction of criminal sanctions for design rights infringement might be predicted using a model. In contrast, applied economics uses empirical data. This type of data is typically quantitative but may also be qualitative. For the design rights example, applied economics could examine the impact of the change in law using data on convictions. Again, in practice the two overlap, as theoretical models provide the theory to be tested by applied methods.

1.53 Economics of IP analyses IP as an incentive to innovate, and its impact on choices. In addition, in the specific area of 'economics of IP', economic analysis of IP can be found in the economics of innovation, industrial organization, the economics of law, development economics, and, increasingly, health economics. These sub-disciplines look at a wide range of topics, including the valuation of IP, policy analysis, investment in IP as part of the global economy, the economics of copyright, and analysis of the generics market for pharmaceuticals.

Economic Analysis and Research Techniques

Economics attempts to adhere to the scientific method. In the scientific method, the hypotheses stemming from theoretical models are empirically tested via applied analysis. As discussed earlier, economic research largely falls into two categories: theoretical and applied. More completely, economists using the scientific method ask questions, make hypotheses, test these hypotheses empirically, analyse them, and draw conclusions. The testing of hypotheses can be considered an experiment; in theory, this experiment should be clear and replicable so that any researcher asking the same questions with the same data will reach the same conclusions. However, not only is this utopia rarely true in the natural sciences, it is non-existent in the messy world of the social sciences. **1.54**

This leaves economic analysis in a difficult position. The utopia of the pure scientific method is unreachable; yet stopping the analysis at the point of positing hypotheses is unappealing. The challenge lies mainly in the difficulties associated with empirical testing of any given hypothesis. As discussed later, in the section on data, data in IP is particularly problematic and ill-suited to empirical testing. Collectively, these challenges mean that all economic analysis in IP comes with significant caveats. This is not to say that economic analysis cannot provide insight into questions on IP, but to highlight that there are no sure answers. **1.55**

With that fairly substantial caveat, there follows a discussion on the types of theoretical and empirical tools available for economic analysis. **1.56**

Theoretical tools

The primary tool for economics is that of the theoretical economic model. The supply and demand model described earlier is an example of such a model. Evans (1997) categorizes these models as visual models, mathematical models, empirical models,[26] and simulation models. **1.57**

Visual models can be useful in the first steps of the scientific method. At this stage, questions are asked and answers are hypothesized. Visual models, as the name suggests, are visual representations of economic thought. The graph used earlier to demonstrate the interactions of supply and demand curves is a classic example. **1.58**

[26] In this chapter, empirical models are discussed separately as they are data-driven, unlike the other models.

Movements along, in, or out of curves can be used to demonstrate changes in economic conditions or market equilibria.

1.59 Mathematical models are the models with the Greek letters and squiggly lines, often off putting to the casual reader. Evans describes these as the most formal and abstract of economic models. They can be very complex and typically require a good knowledge of algebra and calculus. Commonly, a mathematical model will include a set of equations with the goal of solving particular variables. Mathematical models may complement visual models. For example, a mathematical model may have equations for supply, demand, and equilibrium in order to solve for price and quantity.

1.60 Simulation models are relatively new[27] in economics, as they require computers. Fans of artificial intelligence and computer programmers may be drawn to these models as they use computer programming to simulate the interaction between variables. The user of the model need not understand the workings of the system (the 'black box') but can grasp its inputs and outputs. Given the current interest in financial markets and crashes, programs such as the Minsky economic stimulator[28] have been developed in the hopes that they will better predict changes in the market.

Assumptions

1.61 All economic models begin with a series of assumptions. These are the conditions in which the model can operate. These assumptions are necessary in order to isolate and test the questions posited. However, assumptions can be problematic as clarity and simplicity often come at the cost of completeness and depth. Economists' reliance on assumptions is so renowned that the classic economic joke is as follows:

> An economist, an engineer, and a chemist are stranded on a desert island. They have plenty of food, but it is all tinned. Each of them proposes a solution. The engineer suggests a contraption using coconut fibres and rocks to open the cans. The chemist identifies a number of chemicals that could be used to dissolve the cans. The economist, having thought at great length about the problem, finally states, 'Assume the can opener'.

1.62 Common assumptions in economic models are those of perfect information and perfect rationality. As a starting point, perfect information implies all agents in the model (e.g. all firms or people) have complete information. In the case of selling a car, this implies both the seller and the buyer know exactly the quality, cost, and lifespan of the car. When there is imperfect information, where different

[27] At the time of writing, the authors are not aware of any IP research using simulation models.

[28] An open source software which takes a non-mainstream approach to the modelling of markets based on the theories of Hyman Minksy.

agents have different information, things get interesting. In the case of used car sales, it is clear that the seller likely knows more about the car's condition than the buyer.

Despite being a useful starting point, the assumption of perfect information rarely holds true, in particular for IP. Copyrighted goods, for example, are typically 'experience goods' where the quality (value) is difficult to ascertain in advance. For example, consumers of movies do not know the quality of the movie when they purchase their ticket. Trade marks, discussed later, serve to improve the challenges associated with imperfect information. **1.63**

The second common assumption is that of perfect rationality. This assumes that the agents in any model will behave in a way as to maximize their utility. This is a challenge, as observation and experience demonstrate that perfect rationality is unrealistic and agents often behave in an irrational manner. If a model is too narrow in scope, then what may look like irrational behaviour on the part of an agent may actually be rational within the bigger picture.[29] Again, it is a challenge to model all the potential influences that may affect rationality. Wherever irrational behaviour is observed, further investigation is required. **1.64**

Collectively, the series of assumptions deployed in an economic model provide a basis for investigating particular relationships. A common phrase deployed in economic analysis is *ceteris paribus*, the Latin term for 'all things being equal'. In an economic model, this means keep all, but one, variables and assumptions fixed. The one assumption or variable that changes allows the analyst to investigate a particular relationship. **1.65**

For example, an economic model of patents may assume that patentees will apply for patents if the benefits outweigh the costs and assume certain levels of applications, the number of claims per patent, patent fees, and legal costs. *Ceteris paribus*, what happens if patent fees are lowered or raised? An economic model may give insight into how a change in fees will affect the number of claims or other variables. **1.66**

The challenge to these assumptions is that they may not be observed in practice. This removal from the reality of the actual economy can limit the insights economics offers. Additionally, the series of assumptions required to make a model work may be so specific that the model is unable to work without them. Again, this **1.67**

[29] For example, a (hypothetical) writer may maximize their short term utility by eating tonnes of chocolate in the process of writing a book, at the loss of overall utility in terms of health. Thus, not eating chocolate while writing may look irrational in a model of writing/chocolate consumption, but rational in the larger context of health.

limits the findings from the models. So, while an economic model may suggest that protecting smaller innovations via patents and larger innovations via trade secrets, the innovator may find that this does not work in practice. This is not to say that these insights from these models are not useful, but to remember that they must be sufficiently caveated.

Empirical models

1.68 Empirical models are driven by data; they combine mathematical models with data. Empirical models seek to put numbers against relationships. For example, an empirical model can offer predictions, such as (hypothetically) that a 2% increase in fines for counterfeiting trademarks will result in a 5% decrease in customs seizures of counterfeit goods. These models will again be subject to the challenges associated with other models but face the additional challenges of accessing the data needed to drive them. Data in IP is a challenge, especially in respect to unregistered IP rights.

Types of data

1.69 Economists tend to prefer quantitative[30] evidence. Where quantitative data is not feasible or flawed, economists often work with qualitative evidence and towards generating metrics. Although it is based on numbers, it is important to remember that quantitative measurement is fallible. Data, when it is possible to access, collect, and analyse them, are often far from perfect. Failures in data collection, measurement methodology, and the use of proxies may result in flawed data. Even good data is still subject to interpretation and manipulation. As the adage goes, data don't lie, people do.

1.70 There are many types of quantitative data available, such as counts, prices, scales, or temperature. Time-series data are collections of data of certain variables and how they vary over time. For example, it may be interesting to examine the number of patents against the performance of the economy as a whole using time series. Cross-sectional studies, on the other hand, analyse data sets which contain different observations of the same variable across different cases. For example, cross-sectional studies may look at how the stock prices of listed companies are impacted when they lose a patent case.

1.71 A second option is qualitative evidence. Qualitative data is often described as being richer than quantitative data. Instead of measurements and numbers found in quantitative data, qualitative data is more descriptive.[31] Examples of qualitative

---

[30] Quantitative is numerical and measurable, thus quantitative data is numerical data.

[31] To confound things, qualitative data can be converted into quantitative data. However, for simplicity we shall assume the two are separate.

data include case studies, interviews, and opinions. While qualitative data can provide more detail, it is criticized as being subjective; researcher bias is difficult to detect and data is typically quite resource-intensive to collect. The skills set to properly conduct qualitative research can be very different from that of quantitative research.

The challenges faced by applied economic analysis of data may lessen. The online environment offers an overwhelming amount of data and the possibilities for insights using data mining are tremendous. For example, data allow retailers to predict, with great accuracy, whether a particular customer is pregnant.[32] **1.72**

Econometric analysis

Econometrics is the application of statistical methods to economic analysis. It is primarily used for statistically testing relationships between economic factors. Econometrics encompasses a vast array of statistical techniques. Perhaps the biggest challenge for good econometric analysis is having sufficient data. If an econometric model is missing key data, the results will be weak. For example, a model attempting to measure the impact of counterfeits on the sales of legitimate goods would need a vast amount of data to account for consumer preferences, actual sales of both counterfeits and legitimate goods, changes in the overall economy, and other possible influences. **1.73**

A classic error in econometric analysis is the confusion of correlation with causation. In correlation, it may appear that one variable influences another, but in reality the two variables are simply observed to occur at the same time. This is known as a spurious relationship. For example, the number of deaths in American swimming pools correlates with the number of Nicolas Cage movies.[33] In reality, while the deaths and films are observed at the same time, there is not a relationship between the two. A causal relationship, on the other hand, would be one where one variable affects another. For example, an increase in the number of fences around swimming pools may cause a decrease in swimming pool deaths.[34] **1.74**

In contrast, causation describes cases in which there is a causal relationship. For example, an increase in the number of cars on the road causes an increase in air pollution. Robust, in-depth econometric analysis should investigate causation and not correlation. **1.75**

---

[32] There is a wonderful anecdote as to a large retailer in the United States predicting the pregnancy of a customer and sending relevant marketing materials before the customer had announced her pregnancy. Duhigg, C. (2012). *How Companies Learn Your Secrets* The New York Times Magazine, Available at: http://www.nytimes.com/2012/02/19/magazine/shopping-habits.html

[33] Vigen, T. 'Number of people who drowned by falling in a pool correlates with films Nicholas Cage appeared in'. Available at: http://www.tylervigen.com/spurious-correlations.

[34] Statistically identifying a causal relationship as opposed to a correlation is not straightforward. There are tests to reduce the likelihood of this confusion, such as the Granger causality test, but there remains room for error.

Surveys

1.76 Surveys are often relied upon in economic analysis, particularly in IP. Survey analysis is a combination of data collection and statistical analysis. Surveys can encompass both qualitative and quantitative data. However, surveys face their own challenges in sampling, response rates, response bias, and question formation, among others. The choice of the sample surveyed can greatly alter results. In most cases, only a minority of those invited to participate in the survey will do so. The response rate (the rate of those who respond versus those who are invited to) may suffer from bias as those with particularly strong feelings on a survey topic are more likely to respond. Recent evidence suggests that survey response rates are decreasing at the moment due to a variety of factors including potential respondents' ability to block unsolicited telephone and online survey requests.[35]

1.77 Surveys are based on reported behaviour instead of actual behaviour. Respondents may adjust their responses to please the interviewer, support a particular position, conceal information they deem confidential or otherwise undesirable, or simply make errors. Responses using Likert scales[36] typically have a positive bias.[37] Even offering an even versus odd number of response options can create a positive bias. The very act of participating in a survey can influence responses. These can be compounded by the design of questions as subtle differences in wording can influence outcomes ('Of course, anyone with any sense would understand: don't you agree?')

1.78 Methodologies and structures of surveys vary. Two classic types of surveys are questionnaires and interviews. Questionnaires allow survey respondents to answer a determined set of questions and often a determined set of options to answer (such as 'Yes' or 'No'). By comparison, interview surveys, which can be conducted in person or over the phone, allow more flexibility in both question content and answers. There are pros and cons to each type of survey. Questionnaires are more likely to provide consistency but may over-limit respondent's answers; interviews may provide more detail but be less consistent as interviewers vary.

1.79 A specific type of survey analysis is the use of willingness-to-pay as introduced in the section on demand. In IP disputes, this is a useful technique as it allows the researcher to approximate market prices by asking, via a survey, how much potential consumers would be willing to pay for a good or service. However, this technique

[35] See NSF. 2015. *Survey Says?: Questionable Future.* Available at: http://www.nsf.gov/news/special_ reports/survey/index.jsp?id=question.

[36] A scale for answering questions based on a scale. A common example is options ranging from 1 to 5 where 1 indicates strongly agree, 5 is strongly disagree, and the interim numbers represent degrees along the scale between 1 and 5.

[37] A positive bias is where respondents are more likely to say yes or agree to statements, independent of their true opinion.

often overestimates the actual price participants would pay. 'What people say is different from what they do' and their accuracy is akin to election polling where outcomes vary as elections progress, suggesting initial positions were malleable (Hausman, 2012).

Surveys are an excellent way of collecting data for economic analysis. Survey data may simply be reported in summary statistics, such as that '10% of firms use patents for defensive reasons' (not a real statistic). Survey data may also be inputted to econometric models to test relationships between variables. **1.80**

Despite the challenges, survey analysis is a popular option in the analysis of IP. Behaviours, attitudes, and use of IP can be measured via surveys. In the absence of observable data sources for other aspects of IP, surveys allow for empirical data and provide fodder for analysis. **1.81**

Other empirical techniques

Another area of economic analysis, one that has been popular amongst other social sciences, is experimental economics, featuring techniques such as randomized control trials (RCT). Experimental economics is an applied sub-discipline of economics that uses experiments to create data sets. For example, an economic experiment might involve asking thirty participants to play a game in a computer laboratory under different rules while being observed. RCTs, experiments in which participants are randomly assigned to a control or treated[38] group, are considered a gold standard in experimental methods. The differences between the outcomes for the control and treated groups can be analysed to provide insights into the treatment. **1.82**

RCTs may be useful for licensing and consumer approaches to IP but are less useful for policy settings where randomly assigning participants to different policies may not be possible. These methods are growing in popularity but are yet to be widely applied. **1.83**

Evidence-based Policy

In policy environments, analysis of the evidence can be framed as an impact assessment. The concept of an impact assessment is a weighing up of the pros and cons, winners and losers, costs and benefits of a policy change. In government policy, different governments have different formats and formalities for impact assessment. **1.84**

[38] The 'treated' group receives some form of intervention (treatment). In medicine, the control group would receive a placebo and the treated group a particular medicine. In economics, the difference may be companies who receive a particular grant and those who do not.

In the United Kingdom, impact assessments are a formal means of providing an unbiased analysis of the evidence and consequently making a policy recommendation. Similar analysis exists at the European Union (EU) level where the European Commission may issue impact assessments.

1.85 As an example, the UK[39] process typically goes as such: before a policy change, an impact assessment will be issued to start a public consultation phase. During the consultation phase, the public is invited to submit evidence to further inform the policy analysis. After the consultation is complete, a second impact assessment is issued reflecting the evidence gathered. Evidenced gathered during a consultation can change the ultimate policy recommendation. Formal impact assessments are useful documents for the public as they are a window into the economic analysis and political environment of a policy.

1.86 Evidence-based policy has long been popular in the medical profession.[40] The use of evidence by doctors has brought improved patient outcomes and a better understanding of the cost–benefit of existing treatments. Evidence for IP policy promises the same. Yet, failures in evidence-based medicine highlight flaws with this approach.

1.87 Medical theory says that beta-blockers ease hypertension. However, evidence shows that beta-blockers are actually problematic.[41] Here, good evidence trumped theory. However, evidence can be flawed. In theory, hormone replacement therapy (HRT) is meant to benefit patients. The evidence shows that HRT reduces the risk of bone fracture, but initial studies failed to pick up on the fact that it increases the risk of cancer and heart disease.[42] The data were flawed but still HRT still became recommended practice until later studies proved its harmful effects. Both evidence-based and theory-based approaches can result in failings and what counts as proof can be a matter of opinion.

1.88 However, the parallels with evidence in science and evidence in economic policy are limited. Evidence in science is more concrete, as in measurements of blood pressure or salt content, whereas all measurements in IP policy are abstract, such as money and job satisfaction. It is not possible to measure many economic concepts directly as they are often theoretical constructs. Instead, economic data tend to involve the

---

[39] This is correct at the time of writing but procedures in governments are often subject to change.

[40] Economists and doctors have many things in common (this includes the ability to walk on water).

[41] The NHS removed beta-blockers as the first line or second line treatment for hypertension in 2006 and the guidelines continue to change as evidence emerges. See Kristensen, S. D., Knuuti, J., Saraste, A., Anker, S., Bøtker, H. E., De Hert, S., Ford, I., Gonzalez-Juanatey, J. R., Gorenek, B. and Heyndrickx, G. R. (2014). '2014 ESC/ESA Guidelines on Non-cardiac Surgery: Cardiovascular Assessment and Management' *European Heart Journal* 35: 2383–2431.

[42] Grimes, D. (2002). 'Reflections on the Women's Health Initiative Trial of Postmenopausal Hormone Therapy' *World Health Organisation (WHO)*, Available at: http://apps.who.int/rhl/Reflections_on_Womens_Health_Initiative_Trial.pdf.

use of proxies for concepts such as value, sustainability, and development. In addition to its abstractness, economic data is subjective, in the same way as the same conditions for two employees may result in different levels of job satisfaction. The ambiguities arising from the abstract and subjective states of economic data further cloud its application.

One non-economic approach in evidence-based policy is anecdotal evidence. **1.89** Anecdotes can be powerful as they are often emotive and appealing. Economists are not fans of anecdotal evidence as it is too subjective and influenced by individual experience. The parable of the elephant and the blind men illustrates this:

> Once upon a time, there lived six blind men in a village. One day the villagers told them, 'Hey, there is an elephant in the village today.'
>
> They had no idea what an elephant is. They decided, 'Even though we would not be able to see it, let us go and feel it anyway.' All of them went to where the elephant was. Every one of them touched the elephant.
>
> 'Hey, the elephant is a pillar,' said the first man who touched his leg.
>
> 'Oh, no! it is like a rope,' said the second man who touched the tail.
>
> 'Oh, no! it is like a thick branch of a tree,' said the third man who touched the trunk of the elephant.
>
> 'It is like a big hand fan,' said the fourth man who touched the ear of the elephant.
>
> 'It is like a huge wall,' said the fifth man who touched the belly of the elephant.
>
> 'It is like a solid pipe,' said the sixth man who touched the tusk of the elephant.
>
> They began to argue about the elephant and every one of them insisted that he was right.[43]

Anecdotal evidence may be inappropriate when it is biased and contrary to the **1.90** quantitative evidence. At the same time, quantitative and other qualitative evidence poorly gathered or interpreted can be equally inappropriate. Anecdotal data can be useful for identifying potential areas of research or highlight particular cases.

Even where evidence is imperfect, it is likely better than policy based entirely on **1.91** opinion. As policy itself represents a second-best solution, evidence must always be a compromise.

Further Underlying Concepts in Economics

In addition to the concepts already addressed in this chapter, some further underly- **1.92** ing assumptions are deployed across economic approaches to IP.

[43] The origins of this parable are unclear. This quote comes from Jain World, J. (2015). 'Elephant and the Blind Men'. Available at: http://www.jainworld.com/literature/story25.htm.

1.93 It is important to remember that the mere concept of IP, indeed property, is not universally accepted and varies between markets. IP is fundamentally a capitalist construct which is not acknowledged by all cultures or market structures. Communism, for example, argues against private ownership of means of production. IP is not accepted in traditional communist theory. In practice, however, predominantly communist societies do have IP rights regimes as discussed in Crane's (2008) analysis of China.

1.94 A simplistic, colloquial guide to the primary market structures of capitalism, socialism, and communism is illustrated with cows. Assume you have two cows: under communism, the state takes both and gives you milk. Under socialism, you give one cow to your neighbour and keep the other. Under capitalism, you sell one and buy a bull, multiple your herd, and get rich. However, in practice no economy exhibits a pure structure based on such models; all markets are mixed.

Approaches to Economic Analysis

1.95 Economic analysis of policy such as IP often looks at impact across whole economies. It asks what positive and negative externalities are generated and how this impacts social welfare. These analyses stem from an initial framework, often an ethical framework, to enable the weighing up of pros and cons.

1.96 A basic economic analysis of markets considers both producer and consumer surplus. As in the earlier supply and demand discussion, suppliers are assumed to be profit maximizing and consumers utility maximizing. In equilibrium, there often exist consumer and producer surpluses, which are collectively known by a variety of names including total welfare, social welfare, economic surplus, or Marshallian surplus. This book will use the term social welfare to indicate the collective benefits (surpluses) enjoyed by consumers and producers in a market.

1.97 Consumer surplus is the area under the demand curve, but above the equilibrium price (the star shown in Figure 1.1 on page 7). It represents the extra utility all the consumers gain from paying a price lower than they were willing to pay. To present a simplified example, imagine there are only two consumers (you and your friend.) You are willing to pay £4 for the widget, but your friend is willing to pay only £3. If the market equilibrium results in a price of £2, then you are £2 better off and your friend is £1 better off. Added together, this represents the consumer surplus. In Figure 1.2, this is represented by the lighter area.

1.98 Producer surplus is the area above the supply curve but below the equilibrium price. It represents the extra revenue producers gain from selling at a price higher than they were willing to. The logic is the same, but the benefits go to the one willing to sell at a lower price. If there are two producers, one willing to sell at £1 and the other

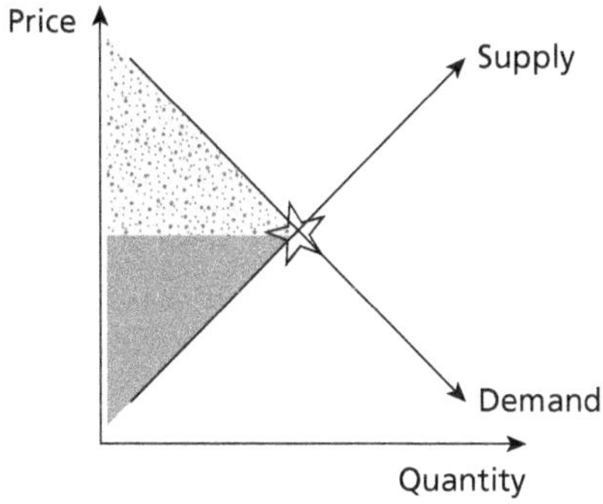

Figure 1.2 Social welfare = consumer + producer surplus

at £2, then at a market price of £2, the producer willing to sell at the lower price is £1 better off and the second is neutral. Added together, this is a producer surplus of £1. In Figure 1.2, this is represented by the dark area.

In practice, the supply and demand curves are made up of many producers and consumers with many different price and quantity points. The important thing to focus on is the economic goal of maximizing social welfare—the sum of the light and dark areas (consumer and producer surplus). **1.99**

This approach is essentially a utilitarian approach. That is, its goal is to maximize total utility[44] by maximizing social welfare. The goal is simply the greatest good for the greatest number. It is a rather blunt framework and is criticized for its Machiavellian implications. A similar concept to utilitarian approaches is that of Pareto efficiency, also known as Pareto optimality. Pareto efficiency is achieved when no individual in an economy can be made better off without making another worse off. However, these approaches represent only starting points for economic analysis and the full picture, presents a more nuanced interpretation. **1.100**

In practice, efficiency is not simply about maximizing utility but also considering the distribution of utility. An economy where ten people have ten units of utility has the same total utility as an economy where nine people have one unit of utility and one person has ninety-one units. However, clearly the second economy has an unequal distribution of utility.[45] Economics often considers utility and income distribution[46] in addition to measurements of social welfare. **1.101**

[44] In this case, utility encompasses both consumer utility and producer utility (profits).

[45] This book will not delve into the economic and political consequences of income inequality. For more on this, readers may wish to read Piketty, T. (2014). *Capital in the Twenty-first Century* (Cambridge, MA, London: Belknap Press).

[46] Two key measurements in income distribution are the Gini coefficient and the Lorenz curve. Pitketty (n 46) discusses income distribution in more detail.

1.102 The implication of the combination of utilitarian and income equality approaches mean that economic analysis must consider both the total and individual impact of a change. In IP, this means that analysis of changes to copyright, for example, must consider both the impact on consumers and on producers. Furthermore, a complete economic analysis should consider how smaller groups within consumers or producers are affected. Typically, changes in policy result in winners and losers and economic analysis can provide insight into who these may be. Furthermore, analysis should consider both the short and long term.

Conclusion

1.103 This chapter has provided a primer on some of the key principles in economics with relevance for IP for readers who are not themselves economists. It has covered a wide variety of material that should provide sufficient knowledge to understand the fundamentals of the economics of IP. Like all disciplines, the devil is in the detail and this chapter has necessarily presented a simplified explanation.

2

ECONOMICS OF INTELLECTUAL PROPERTY

This chapter presents the economics of intellectual property rights (IP rights), examining their rationales, evidence, and use. The chapter begins with a discussion on the broader theories of the economics of IP rights and innovation. This should give the reader an improved understanding of the economics of these rights and their practical uses, and insights into the thinking behind IP policy measures. **2.01**

The fact that IP rights are legal and separable aids their usefulness, because it enables them to operate like other forms of property rights, including their suitability for being transferred by way of assignment or licence. However they are vastly more mobile than most other types of property asset, and more likely to appreciate in value over their lifespan if they are appropriately managed and commercialized. For this reason IP rights are sometimes called, 'the currency of the knowledge economy.' **2.02**

Economic Theories of IP

In this section, we look at the philosophical underpinnings of the economics of IP rights and the principles that dictate economic debates over them. The justifications for IP rights have a long history and one that has considered the ethical approaches discussed in the previous chapter. There are three main schools of thought in the economic justification for IP rights: these are incentives to innovate, labour desert theory, and the rejection of IP rights. **2.03**

In economics, the incentive to innovate is the primary justification for the creation of IP laws. The creation of any monopoly in economics is typically considered an anathema because monopolies create markets with higher prices and lower quantities, and in doing so, they reduce social welfare because the reduction in consumer surplus does not correspond to an equal increase in producer surplus. A typical **2.04** monopoly is, therefore, inefficient. Thus, economics would expect further justification for the creation of an IP monopoly. This justification is perhaps best expressed in social contract theory, which frames IP rights as a form of contract between society and innovators.

2.05 In social contract theory, the temporary monopoly granted by IP rights is tolerated in exchange for the longer-term interest of sustained innovation. An IP right represents an agreement, a social contract, between society and innovators. In the short term, the monopoly created by IP rights comes at the cost of consumers through the higher prices and lower quantities of the protected innovation. The innovator uses the monopoly to recoup the costs and risks associated with the development of the IP for which rights have been granted, and appropriate the rewards of their innovation. In the long term, the monopoly expires; the protected innovation becomes part of the public domain; and consumers and subsequent innovators benefit from the availability of the innovation. Innovation also improves productivity, stimulates investment, and facilitates growth, which contribute to wider, macroeconomic benefits. Innovators continue to innovate and society, as a whole, benefits from the incentives created by IP rights. This principle is further developed later in the chapter.

2.06 A second school of thought frames IP as a natural or intrinsic right whereby an innovator should automatically own the innovation. This can be expressed via labour desert theory, also known as the labour theory of property, labour theory of ownership, or principle of first appropriation. In this theory, it is assumed that an individual (in this case the innovator) owns their labour and consequently owns the fruits of their labour.[1] For example, the person who plants the tree owns the apple. The seventeenth-century philosopher John Locke was a proponent of this argument. However, as IP is intangible, as opposed to tangible, property, special rights to protect IP must be created. It is relatively easy to protect an individual apple, but less easy to protect a method to improve apple yields. Thus, the natural right of ownership over innovation requires IP rights.

2.07 Many of the recent policy debates surrounding IP can be plotted on an axis stretching between the incentive to innovate and natural right approaches. If IP is a natural right, then strengthening IP rights to protect the owners of, for example, music, is a positive thing. However, if IP is an incentive to innovate, then strengthening existing rights at the expense of consumers or other innovators is a negative step. Striking the balance between these two poles is an ongoing challenge in IP systems.

[1] This approach can be extended to consider moral rights, which are addressed in the section on copyright.

A third school of thought differs dramatically. This school of thought views IP rights as an obstacle to the free flow of information and even as theft. A common objection is the framing of IP as a property right and that this framing creates undue restrictions on the use of the protected knowledge. Given its intangible nature, IP lacks two main characteristics of property: scarcity and rivalry. Scarcity is the condition in which unlimited demands are placed on limited resources. This is easy to see in the case of physical goods such as clean water, in which quantities are relatively fixed, but less so in the case of intangible goods like song lyrics or a formula as the quantity cap can be easily increased (copies). Rivalry[2] is a second condition often associated with physical goods in that the consumption by one affects the consumption of another[3]. However, my consumption of the song lyrics does not affect your consumption, whereas my consumption of clean water does. Again, this is difficult to apply to the ideas and expressions of ideas often protected by IP rights. Based on these and related arguments, there is a growing movement of thought against the legal protection associated with IP. **2.08**

Throughout this book, these approaches will be explored in an effort to understand whether it is possible to strike an optimal balance in the case of IP. In essence, the goal of economics is to have an IP system that supports a healthy innovation system. However, this is much easier said than done as problems arise due to technological disruption (consider the effect of the internet and digitization on long-standing copyright models), moral concerns (the importance of moral rights), humanitarian concerns (e.g. pharmaceutical innovation), and strategic use of the system (often by non-practising entities). **2.09**

Fitche (1793) encapsulates these various arguments in his description of the defence of an alleged infringer of a patented medicine. **2.10**

> I like to proceed in a principled way. As everyone knows, the only true measure of the excellence of our actions is their utility. The more widespread and significant the benefits of an action, the more virtuous that action is. . . . But is it really necessary to show that my actions have the most beneficial of consequences for the public? I sell the nostrum much more cheaply than the plaintiff; the lowliest man can thus afford to procure it, unlike at the high price demanded by the monopolist. . . . What a service to humanity! Could I but paint a vivid picture for Your Majesty of the groans of the suffering, the rattling throats of the dying, who have been saved by the physic they bought from me! . . . Just calculate all the work which everyone whose life has been extended by several years through this miracle

[2] Rivalry is not found in all physical goods as, for example, in public goods. Public goods are non-excludable (individuals cannot be excluded from consuming the good) and non-rivalrous (consumption by one does not affect consumption by another.)

[3] IP is sometimes cast as a 'club good' in that it differs from public goods as it is excludable but non-rivalrous.

medicine can perform for the culture of the land in these years; just imagine the even greater culture that will thereby become possible, and so on ad infinitum. . . . figure the total growth of humanity and culture which results from all of this and which would have been absolutely impossible had I not stolen those miraculous drops from the plaintiff.[4]

2.11 With the rising profile of IP generally, the tensions between competing schools of thought on IP rights may increase. While economists (particularly microeconomists) tend to cluster on the innovation/social contract end of the spectrum, the relative lack of economic evidence and analysis of IP rights, compared to the wealth of analysis of tangible property rights, provokes anxiety[5] amongst economists. IP, as an innovation-related area of policy and a system with important economic implications, warrants further investigation, and so each of these three principal theoretical approaches will be examined in turn.

Social contract theory

2.12 Social contract theory is the predominant theoretical approach to IP rights as an instrument to encourage innovation. The social contract is a philosophical and political approach to the relationships between individuals and societies. It argues that individuals will voluntarily surrender rights and freedoms in exchange for protection and preservation from society/governments. This exchange is the contract. Applying social contract theory to IP rights frames IP systems as a contract between innovators (the individuals) and society.

2.13 There are two key players in the social contract theory: the innovator and society. Innovators are those that create, invent, and innovate. They spend resources to create their output of innovation. Society is everyone else (although generally considered to be consumers). Society is interested in innovation as it leads to better and/or cheaper products and services. Innovators incur costs to innovate from which society benefits.

2.14 In an ideal system, the costs associated with each innovation would be perfectly offset by the benefits of each innovation. That is, society would reward (pay)

[4] Fitche, J. (1793). 'Proof of the Illegality of Reprinting: A Rationale and a Parable' as translated by Martha Woodmansee. Available at: http://www.case.edu/affil/sce/authorship/Fichte,_Proof.doc

[5] The reactions of economists when they first confront IP can be rather amusing. This ranges from shock that such a wide-arching policy can exist with so little evidence, to confusion as to why society actively creates these legal monopolies. In a meeting the author of this chapter attended, a well-known economist, new to IP, expressed perplexity at the government's interference in private contracts where IP is concerned. The same does not happen in other private contracts. He then compared the enforcement of copyright to the equivalent of using a steamroller over consumers' rights to the benefit of copyright owners. The point is that IP, *prima facie*, does not conform to standard economic theory.

innovators exactly the value of the innovation which would generate an appropriate level of return on their investment. In practice, this is nigh-on impossible. Instead, what exists is a compromise or second-best[6] solution in the form of the IP regime.

The costs associated with each innovation are borne by the innovator. The innovator incurs these costs in the hopes of being rewarded with appropriate benefits. For example, in the successful development of new song lyrics, a writer will have invested their skills (obtained through time and education) and a variety of other costs. These are the sunk costs associated with the innovation. However, once created, the innovation of the lyrics can be copied very cheaply. As discussed earlier, in efficient markets, the price of a good falls to its marginal cost. Therefore, the price of the song lyrics will eventually fall to nearly zero—the cost of making a photocopy or additional electronic copy. **2.15**

Given the relatively high costs of developing an innovation compared to the price commanded by the market, without IP rights, the innovator will struggle to recoup their costs. In this case, the expected value of innovating becomes zero. The intangible quality of knowledge means that it is difficult to prevent others from making use of it. In this sense, knowledge is often referred to as a public good. Public goods are goods that are non-rival rous and are non-excludable.[7] IP roughly fits this description as, to a degree, one person's consumption of the knowledge does not affect the consumption of another (non-rival). IP is also non-excludable as it is difficult to prevent others from consuming knowledge. In this context, IP rights serve as a means to construct protective barriers around knowledge by creating a property right with the aim of preventing copying. **2.16**

The property right created by an IP right creates a legal monopoly for the innovation. This may translate into a market monopoly in which the innovator is able to achieve monopoly profits, as discussed in the introductory chapter. The monopoly profits, in theory, allow the innovator to appropriate the returns from their investment in innovation as the legal monopoly protects the innovator from having to compete against copies. This satisfies the innovator's preference for profits. **2.17**

However, this monopoly implies higher prices and lower quantities for society. Society knowingly grants innovators such rights because the contract exists in two time periods. The first time period is short-term in which the monopoly situation exists as described above. It is a static period and essentially presents a snapshot of **2.18**

[6] In some economic situations, the optimal solution cannot be reached, as it would decrease overall efficiency. In this case, the practical costs of calculating the value of each innovation and rewarding the innovator would outweigh the benefits of appropriately distributed rewards. Instead, what exists is called a second best solution, which is the feasible, efficient solution.

[7] Other examples of public goods range from clean air and attractive views to lighthouses and national defence.

the innovation. The innovator recoups their investment and society accepts the higher prices and lower quantities.

2.19 The second period is long-term in which society's goal of continued investment in innovation becomes realizable. Instead of focusing on a snapshot, the long-term looks at the dynamic, ongoing environment in which the formerly legally protected IP can encourage repeated innovation. If the short-term bargain was to fail, and an innovator did not recoup his or her initial investment, then innovators would cease to have the funds and incentives to innovate. Thus, society is willing to accept the relatively disadvantageous conditions of the short term in order to have the long-term advantages.

2.20 However, the bargain does not end there. Innovation is cumulative in the sense that one innovation nearly always builds on another. For continued innovation to happen, previous innovation must be freely available. Thus, rights expire. Society grants innovators these legal monopolies on the condition that there are limited, made public (disclosed), and eventually fall into the public domain. The social contract creates conditions in which knowledge is shared and innovators have continued incentives to innovate.

2.21 A third player in this theory is government, which acts as an intermediary between innovators and society. Governments are motivated by the demands of innovators and society, and by a wider goal[8] of economic growth through innovation. Government sets the policy and provides a number of key services, such as registrations and court systems, as enablers of a functioning IP system.

2.22 In brief, the short-term, static inefficiency of the temporary monopoly is granted in exchange for the long-term, dynamic innovation that it incentivizes. Clearly, this is a difficult balance to strike. If the temporary monopoly is too strong, society pays too much and/or other innovators are unable to build on the innovation. If the temporary monopoly is too weak, then innovators may not recoup their investments and may cease to innovate.

2.23 Social contract theory presents a neat framework for interpreting IP. However, various assumptions associated with the theory are not necessarily evident in practice. For example, innovation certainly occurred before the advent of IP rights, and profits and continued innovation are apparent in areas with relatively weak IP rights protection (such as the fashion industry). In the creative industries, creators are often intrinsically motivated with little regard for IP. Numerous studies have suggested that many innovative businesses view marketing, timing, and

---

[8] The theory does not require that governments be motivated by a desire for economic growth, but this motivation is often the case.

other strategies as relatively more important than obtaining IP rights. There is also growing concern that this social contract is now tilted in favour of existing innovators, rather than innovation. These themes will be explored further throughout this book.

Interaction with other theories

In contrast to the innovation-based, social-contract theory of IP, there is the labour desert theory. Individuals are assumed to own their own labour and, therefore, own the fruits of their labour. Consequently, innovators have intrinsic ownership of the fruits of their efforts—the innovation. Having ownership via IP rights provides an incentive to continue these efforts. However, it fails to fully account for the wider societal interest in innovation. If innovations are owned by their creators, full stop, how does cumulative innovation occur? This also becomes a problem for creators as, in the process of innovating, they may need to use other people's innovations. Labour desert theory struggles to balance the interests of the one-off, individual innovation with the wider innovation and societal environment. **2.24**

However, an innovation approach, *prima facie*, is less able to deal with non-innovation concerns associated with IP. A good example of this is provided by moral rights in the realm of copyright. Moral rights, unique to copyright, go beyond the traditional concept of ownership of property. Moral rights include the right to attribution or anonymity, the right not to have work falsely attributed, and rights to safeguard the integrity of the work. Labour desert theory can easily include moral rights as they are compatible with the intrinsic rights stemming from ownership over the fruits of one's labour. Yet moral rights are likely very important innovation motivators for creators of copyrighted content; a lack of control over creative output would be a disincentive to creativity and innovation. Therefore, moral rights can also be considered an incentive to innovate and one that fits with social contract theory. Other concerns, addressed in subsequent chapters, are challenges associated with human rights (pharmaceuticals), traditional knowledge, and the limits of the public domain. **2.25**

A third cluster of theories of IP, and one that is still developing, is the concept that the limitations IP rights impose on the flow of information and knowledge does not solve challenges to continued innovation, as discussed earlier. Instead, knowledge should be more freely shared. This free sharing of knowledge ranges from the complete rejection of IP rights altogether to the concept of open innovation, in which innovators collaborate and information flows more freely. The anarchist view of 'property as theft' has also reached the realm of IP and consumer attitudes to IP rights have changed with the advent of the internet. There are also business models based on open innovation, free software, creative commons, and concepts of free culture. **2.26**

2.27 Indeed, this third nexus of approaches to innovation and knowledge is a very heterogeneous set of theories.[9] It should be noted that open innovation or 'knowledge-is-free' is not inherently in opposition with IP. IP can serve as an important enabler for collaboration by defining collaborators' foreground knowledge at the start of the co-creation process.

2.28 In summary, viewing IP rights primarily as incentives to innovate is only one of many ways to consider its role. It is, however, the predominant economic approach to IP and will likely remain so given the continuing focus of national economic policy on innovation and growth. Accordingly, the following section uses the innovation framework to structure an analysis of IP rights and highlight debates, weaknesses and strengths of IP systems.

IP laws as innovation policy

2.29 Despite growing interest in and awareness of IP, as demonstrated (for example) in the increasing numbers of registered rights, there is plenty of evidence to suggest that it is easy to overestimate the role of IP rights in stimulating innovation and achieving business success. Numerous studies have suggested that IP is not the preferred means for innovators to recoup their investment: a study by Cohen, Nelson & Walsh (2000), for example, notes that market strategies such as branding, access to markets, and economies of scale are preferred. In research on business models (Searle, 2011), creative businesses did not cite IP rights as a primary concern. Given that IP is only one aspect of a complex set of economic measures within a wider policy environment, the nature of innovation itself provides other means to create profits. The next section will examine the economics of innovation further.

Economics of Innovation

2.30 As noted earlier, it is in the interest of society to encourage innovation because it enables members of society to have better healthcare, enjoy new media, do things better and at lower costs, and benefit from new technologies. Innovation allows people to do more with existing resources or do the same using fewer resources. It's all very exciting. Innovation is popular politically as it is a way to grow an economy without necessarily increasing consumption of natural resources and may provide a comparative advantage against other nations. This makes encouraging innovation an important component of economic policy.

[9] The nuances of open innovation are outside the scope of this book. For more, see the works of Henry Chesbrough, the main theorist for open innovation, in particular his 2003 book, *Open Innovation: The New Imperative for Creating and Profiting from Technology* (Harvard Business School Press, Boston, MA).

There are various concepts of innovation, but one that is particularly prominent is that of Schumpeter (1934, 1939). In economics, an innovation is an applied invention. Schumpeter posits a theory of 'creative destruction', in which innovation occurs through the destruction of the status quo. This implies that creativity leading to a new technology may necessarily be highly disruptive, because such innovation comes at the cost of existing models. Other theories focus less on the destruction of the status quo and more on the creative elements: Kirzner (1979) for example, focuses more on the role of innovators discovering opportunities for gain. 2.31

A long-standing and continuing example of creative destruction and technological disruption is provided by the internet and its impact on the music industry. The music that began as live performance of compositions has been partially replaced by recorded music, which has itself evolved from wax discs on gramophones via vinyl records and cassette tapes to compact discs and DVDs. This continued development of technology has long challenged the music industry's business models, though until recently, it was at least still able to control the higher quality physical formats, enabling some market structures to be retained. Recently, this has been revolutionized by the internet, allowing new formats, new process, and reduced distribution costs for music. Whilst this has been highly disruptive to the existing industry, it has delivered substantial opportunities for new entrants to the market, such as Apple, who have able to gain large market shares in a short period. 2.32

Innovations are broadly divided into two types: process and product innovation. Product innovations work towards introducing new products (automatic transmission, for example, created cars that were easier to drive), while process innovation is generally directed towards reducing the costs of production.[10] For example, the American industrialist Henry Ford reduced the costs of manufacturing cars by introducing the assembly line; instead of one or two workers building an entire car, each worker specialized in one area, and the cost per car fell. 2.33

The system of innovation is also very important. Basic models of innovation present a linear model that begins with basic research and invention that is then developed into an innovation and finally is launched to the market. This can be a 'push' or 'pull' model in which innovators either introduce innovation and generate demand (push) or innovate to fill existing demand (pull). More complex models acknowledge that innovation is rarely linear and instead is a messy, iterative process. 2.34

[10] Economic models often use process innovations, as a decrease in costs is relatively easy to model.

2.35 A classic model of innovation in economics is that of the innovation race. In this race, competitors seek to innovate first as success means monopoly profits. According to Shy (1995), there are a number of scenarios of innovation races based on the relative costs of innovation, the probability of success, and the expected payoffs (profits and innovation). If too many firms engage in costly innovation with a low probability of success, then duplicate efforts are wasted. If the probability of successful innovation is very low, then no firms may engage in innovation (this is one argument cited in discussions on antibiotic development; see Chapter 3 on patents). If innovation is relatively cheap, then the duplication of efforts may not be wasteful. To avoid potential waste, models of cooperation and licensing may be practical.

2.36 However, those who innovate first are not necessarily those who reap the largest rewards from their creativity. There also exists the 'second mover advantage' in which competitors are able to learn from the mistakes or setbacks experienced by first movers and overtake them. An example of this is the Apple iPod, introduced in 2001, some years after the first MP3 player entered the market. Apple developed a product that was more user-friendly, compact, attractive, and aspirational than its predecessors and was able to capture the market quickly.

2.37 A similar phenomenon, known as leapfrogging, occurs at a country level where developing countries skip ahead in innovative products and services. This can occur because a country may invest in wider intervals, skipping interim technologies, rather than continually investing. An oft-cited example of this is telephone technology, where countries may go from having limited access to land telephone lines to a much broader distribution of mobile telephones.

2.38 The practice of licensing, discussed in following chapters, is very important for the diffusion[11] of information and innovation. It allows for continued innovation and can also create value for existing innovations. For example, the song 'A Little Less Conversation,' performed by Elvis Presley in 1968, was remixed and became a chart-topper in 2003. The remix, licensed from the original, revived a creative piece that had otherwise limited value to consumers at the time. The creators of the remix also benefited from the ability to use the modified work commercially via licensing.

2.39 The role of governments in subsidizing research and development (R&D) is also a key component of innovation. Popular innovations that began as military technologies include computers and microwaves. Government funding of R&D ranges from

[11] In some cases, compulsory licensing may be used. Compulsory licensing, instigated by government, obligates a rights holder to licensing their innovation. This may occur in instance of social health needs (pharmaceuticals) or for practical reasons (some aspects of copyright).

tax breaks, direct subsidies, higher education funding, and government research itself. Public and charitable funding also helps to support an innovative climate for the creative and cultural industries. The impact of government funding of R&D has hugely contributed to advances in medicine, the iPhone, and a host of other innovations (Mazzucato, 2014).

The government may also intervene in innovation when the market is unable to provide sufficient incentives. Mazzucato also argues that the private sector only enters into R&D areas once the government has already undertaken the high-risk investments. In IP, the patent box, a tax break on profits associated with patents, is a form of government subsidy for R&D, discussed in more detail in Chapter 9. **2.40**

Of course, whilst being perceived by governments as a societal benefit, innovation is not universally welcomed by society, as is illustrated by the story of the Luddites. In the early 1800s, faced with the mechanization of their jobs, some English textile workers took to destroying the offending machinery. The term 'Luddite' is now emblematic of a reluctance to embrace, or to actively oppose, progress in the form of new technologies and points to a different aspect of innovation which economic constructs of IP rights fall victim to non-economic social and psychological pressures. This theme is nicely captured in a quote from the novel *Player Piano*, a dystopian view of an entirely mechanized future: **2.41**

> 'Of course you're right. It's just a hell of a time to be alive, is all—just this goddamn messy business of people having to get used to new ideas. And people just don't, that's all. I wish this were a hundred years from now, with everybody used to the change.'
>
> — Kurt Vonnegut (1952), *Player Piano*

Luddites aside, innovation is generally considered beneficial for society. However, interpretations and justifications for IP systems surrounding innovation vary significantly. Innovation itself is a messy process and one that does not always have clear outputs. **2.42**

Economic analysis and IP policy

Evidence-based policy

Economic analysis of IP rights informs IP policy. Analysis provides evidence[12] and scrutiny to suggest policy changes and measure the impact of IP rights. Policy, and the policy-making process, is a convoluted drama in which economics plays only **2.43**

[12] It is important to note that evidence in economics and policy is different from the evidence used in legal disputes. Evidence in economics is fairly broad and includes examples, arguments and data supporting a particular view. The legal understanding of what constitutes evidence is much narrower and more specific.

one part in a cast of many actors. However, the economic approach can provide a wider perspective to policy and, in an ideal world, may act as a neutral approach balancing consumer and supplier welfare.

2.44 In accordance with the economic approaches discussed in Chapter 1, economics offers two main ways to analyse to IP policy: applied and theoretical. In the case of applied economics, economic analysis can measure the impact of a current policy or a policy change, the economic performance of IP-centric industries, consumer preferences, levels of investment in IP, the contribution of IP to the economy, the impact of IP on trade, and a variety of other measurements. All of these applied analyses are based on empirical data, often described as 'evidence' in the policy realm. In the era of evidence-based policy, economics is popular.

IP data

2.45 In practice, 'measuring' IP impact is extraordinarily difficult, and quantitative measurements are elusive. How can a trade secret be measured? Yet some evidence may be better than no evidence.

2.46 IP data is not plentiful and useful data is scarce. For registered rights, such as patents and trade marks, some data exist. Patents are associated with a relative wealth of data gleaned from patent registries[13] that include names of inventors, previously cited patents, dates, and locations, and combined with the fact that, of all IP rights, patents are generally regarded as offering the best proof that some degree of innovation has occurred,[14] it is no surprise that economists have focused much of their attention on patents. The data for trade marks is improving but still suffers from the lack of availability. Yet the official registries for registered rights, even patents, can only provide a limited amount of insight. They rarely include economically interesting variables such as firm size and licensing information, and they cannot be relied upon to be 100% accurate or up to date. Nonetheless, a worthwhile amount of economic and business insight can be gained from analysis of registered right data.

2.47 Unfortunately, non-registered rights do not benefit from the standardized, systematic information collection process that benefits registered rights. Copyright is perhaps the most extreme case,[15] and measuring copyright is as difficult as

[13] There is a large body of literature on the use of patent data that the interested reader may want to pursue. A good starting point is Jaffe and Trajtenberg (2002).

[14] This is not the same as saying that patents are proof that innovation has occurred, but they are considered a better indication than other rights. There are competing schools of thought which argue trade marks may be a better measurement as they indicate when (as a minimum) an innovation may be in the development stage.

[15] In some jurisdictions, such as the United States, registered copyright exists. However, registration is optional and official records will likely cover only a minority of copyrightable materials.

answering the familiar question regarding the length of a piece of string. Unlike registered rights, copyright has a low threshold for inventiveness and is highly heterogeneous. As relatively data-poor areas, the economics of copyright, trade secrets, and other forms of non-registered rights have been largely neglected; indeed, copyright only became a 'hot topic' with the transformation of the market by digital technology.

Economically interesting data for both registered and non-registered data is also elusive. As intangible property cannot be directly observed, direct measurement of the incorporeal that is IP is impossible. Couple that with further abstract concepts such as value, and it becomes apparent that good, observable data in IP will be very limited. Interesting, related data such as licensing revenues, copyright collections, IP strategies, and so on are often held privately. It is often not in the commercial or lobbying interests of private owners of such data to make them public. **2.48**

Due to the difficulties surrounding IP-relevant data, a common approach is to generate data sets via surveys. This allows for analysis of areas in which it would otherwise be a struggle to provide quantitative results. Other potential areas of data include the creation of data in laboratory experiments or simulation data, as discussed in Chapter 1. The use of proxies, which indirectly measure IP, may also be used. However, these techniques are limited in their application compared to data-wealthy areas of economic analysis such as finance. **2.49**

Thus, while economists may prefer observable, quantitative data, in practice this is not always possible in IP. However, as the digital environment develops, the collection of IP data may improve. In the era of 'Super Crunchers',[16] a revolution in evidence for IP may be possible. **2.50**

Theory-based analysis

Theoretical approaches to IP offer insight into the potential for a particular policy to achieve both its intended effects and consider what unintended consequences may result. The theory is useful as it creates propositions, provides predictions and suggests solutions. Theoretical models can, for example, suggest strategies to influence the consumer decision to download unlicensed copyrighted content.[17] IP policy as an incentive to innovate is based on the economic theory detailed in this chapter. **2.51**

[16] Reference to Ian Ayres (2007), *Super Crunchers* (New York, NY, Bantam Books) which provides analysis and predictions of the use of data and statistical analysis in areas not traditionally the domain of statisticians.

[17] For example, McCorkle et al (2012).

2.52 However, a challenge to economic theory is its application. What may work in theory may not work in practice. Theoretical models often require a set of assumptions[18] and inflexibilities in order to isolate the particular question of interest. These assumptions and fixed properties can over-simplify the position or be unrealistic. A common, oft-criticized economic assumption is the idea of rationality. For many models to work, the participants in the model must be perfectly rational. Essentially, economic models are based on logic but we operate in a sometimes illogical world. Additionally, expecting a single model to encompass the entire world that any particular policy will face is unrealistic.

2.53 Despite the limits of theoretical approaches, they are very useful tools for developing IP policy. Without theoretical models, there would be no applied analysis. Theory creates the questions and predictions that shape economic analysis and its usefulness to policy.

2.54 Economics can, from both theoretical and applied approaches, suggest, inform, and evaluate IP policy. Evidence-based policy places an emphasis on the 'evidence' generated by data-heavy approaches. While theory can suggest and analyse, it is the applied, empirical analysis that is preferred for the development of policy. This can occur at any stage of policy development as in the introduction of a new policy, change in an existing policy, and evaluation of the impact of existing policies. However, as this section has detailed, both theoretical and applied approaches are imperfect.

Case Studies: Economic Analysis

2.55 This section presents two IP case studies to highlight the role of economics in policy. The first is an academic example on tobacco consumption and advertising and the second is a policy example on EU copyright. The tobacco paper is an example of applied economic research and uses consumption and advertising data to assess the impact of advertising on tobacco consumption. The EU copyright report is a combination of theory and applied analysis to inform policy decisions on exceptions and limitations to copyright.

Academic example: Investigating the relationship between advertising bans and tobacco consumption

2.56 Given the link between tobacco use and cancer, governments often seek to limit marketing of tobacco products. One potential policy solution is the concept of plain

[18] As discussed in Chapter 1. Theoretical models are also subject to researcher bias in that the economist begins with a particular view and then sets up an assumption to prove this view. This is compounded by the fact that theoretical models are not accessible to non-specialists and therefore difficult to critique.

packaging. Under a plain packaging law, tobacco products would have standardized packaging. Tobacco firms object to this as an unfair limitation on their trade marks. However, the question remains whether this limitation actually has its desired impact. This example demonstrates how economics can measure the impact of policy, and the potential greater issues surrounding IP.

In their 2000 paper entitled, 'The Effect of Tobacco Advertising Bans on Tobacco Consumption,' Saffer and Chaloupka develop empirical data on the effect of tobacco advertising on consumption. As with most academic economics papers, the paper begins with an introduction to the subject, then provides a literature review of existing research, presents their new research, and finishes with conclusions. **2.57**

In their literature review, Saffer and Chaloupka present a visual model of how counter-advertising (e.g. public service campaigns highlighting the negative effects of smoking) and advertising bans should shift consumption of cigarettes downwards. They then provide a list of relevant empirical papers in the field, categorize them by type of study (time series, cross-sectional) and their conclusions. The literature itself is an important piece of analysis as it provides context and suggests potential answers to the question posed. **2.58**

The empirical section of their paper is where the real meat of the economic analysis lies. In this case, the researchers collected data from twenty-two countries for 1970 to 1992. They gathered data on per capita consumption of cigarettes and a series of dummy variables[19] on advertising bans. To capture wider effects in the economy, they also include data on price, income, a percentage of filtered cigarettes, and unemployment. The percentage filtered variable is included as the literature review suggested that smokers who smoke unfiltered cigarettes smoke more than those who smoke filtered. The other data provide economic context to demand and how much money is available to spend on cigarettes. **2.59**

The analysis then proceeds with a mathematical model. In this case, in the authors' structure, their model predicts tobacco consumption based on the type of ban and the other data noted above. They then use the data to test this model. They find that limited bans, bans where only some media types are excluded, have only minimal effect in reducing tobacco consumption. They further hypothesize that this is due to advertising switching to non-banned media. However, when examining comprehensive bans, they find a clear reduction in consumption. **2.60**

As this is an empirical study, the authors offer figures against their findings. 'The data indicate a 5.4% reduction in tobacco use and about a 7.4% reduction in **2.61**

[19] Dummy variables are categorical variables. They are a binary indication of whether a particular observation belongs to a category. For example, if the dummy variable were economists, a value of 1 = economist and 0 = not an economist.

cigarette use if all OECD countries had enacted Comprehensive Bans.'[20] They then apply their findings to the potential effects of a European Commission directive to phase out tobacco advertising and 'predict that the new legislation will reduce tobacco consumption by 6.3% and cigarette consumption by 7.9%'.[21]

2.62 This paper presents a classic approach to academic economic analysis. For IP, the analysis could be used to support the total ban of branding on cigarette packages. This would constitute a new IP and advertising policy limiting the use of trade marks. However, the study, like all empirical studies, looks at a particular set of observations in a particular time frame. It is possible that these findings would not apply in other countries. Given that the study looked at advertising, rather than packaging specifically, it could be that packaging functions in a different way from, say, television commercials. Nonetheless, it provides empirical evidence to suggest that the policy of comprehensive banning of tobacco advertising can reduce consumption. This example looks less at incentives to innovate, and more at policy impact.

Policy example: European Commission's impact assessment of exceptions and limitations to copyright

2.63 In assessing the economic impacts of adapting certain limitations and exceptions to copyright and related rights in the European Union (EU) (MARKT, 2014), the European Commission presents commissioned analysis of potential policies for the exceptions and limitations to copyright. The report is authored by consultants at the Charles River Associates consulting firm and published by the DG Markt (Internal Market and Services Directorate General, which was reorganized by Commissioner Junker so that the copyright remit largely falls under DG Connect). This example combines incentives to innovate and impact analyses.

2.64 The report, a follow-on piece of a wider research project examining copyright in the EU, assesses the various policy options associated with copyright and related rights with regards to exceptions and limitations. It focuses on five areas:

1. Preservation by cultural heritage and educational institutions;
2. The provision of remote access by cultural heritage and educational institutions to their collections for the benefit of their patrons;
3. E-lending by publicly accessible libraries;
4. Text and data mining for the purpose of scientific research;
5. Reproductions made by natural persons for private uses.[22]

---

[20] Saffer and Chaloupka (2000) 1135.

[21] ibid.

[22] MARKT, D. (2014) 1, assessing the economic impacts of adapting certain limitations and exceptions to copy-right and related rights in the EU.

The methodology of the report is a literature review to examine transaction costs, market power, and externalities associated with each exception and limitation. **2.65**

A section on e-lending illustrates the report's structure. The analysis begins with a description of the policy question and the market. E-lending, or the electronic lending of books, by libraries is not developing at the pace expected. This is a concern as it suggests a potential market failure and questions the future role of libraries. Libraries would like to lend more electronically, although rights holders of these works are concerned about the impact on their revenue and policy makers question the long-term impact. Copyright, as a key policy lever for creative digital works, may be one way of addressing this challenge. The policy in question is the possible introduction of a copyright exception allowing libraries to e-lend. **2.66**

Using key pieces of literature, the report describes the market and notes differences between EU countries. It proceeds to examine the creation of value and market structure, business models, and supply and demand considerations. This background information is then assessed using the transaction cost, market power, and externalities methodology. On transaction costs, the report finds that transactions costs are not the main impediment for library e-lending but the market failure may, 'simply [be] that the willingness-to-pay for the service is lower than the opportunity cost of providing it'.[23] The analysis finds that rights holders hold significant market power. In terms of externalities, an e-lending exception would create positive externalities in improving access to existing content (books) but negative externalities in the incentive to invest in new content. Overall, it is a rather murky picture. **2.67**

The report notes that there is no 'clear-cut conclusion' on the subject of e-lending. As the perceived market failure stems from a variety of issues, a single policy is unlikely to have its desired impact and the researchers conclude that 'the case for a constrained e-lending model appears to be weak'.[24] The report instead recommends that libraries and rights holders be encouraged to negotiate a Memorandum of Understanding. **2.68**

This report illustrates the challenges associated with policy-oriented research. The researchers cover a very wide array of topics and produced a roughly 100-page report investigating and analysing various options. The analysis addresses the Commission's specific need to inform evidence-based policy. The wide scope and likely short timescales of the report restrict its analysis to existing literature. The report also focuses on impact and makes recommendations to maximize the positive impact of the potential policy options. **2.69**

---

[23] ibid. 51.
[24] ibid. 4.

Comparison of economic policy reports and academic papers

2.70 The two case studies highlight another aspect of the application of economics. Economic analysis occurs in a wide range of sectors and in different forms. Goals, funding, and other processes differ. This section compares the two examples to explain the differences between these approaches.

2.71 In the academic example, the researchers generally would have independently decided the question, research method, and analysis. The research may or may not be funded and typically there are no fixed deadlines. Research with interesting findings is far more likely to be published. For papers published in peer-reviewed academic journals,[25] a draft of the research would have been distributed to typically anonymous peers (often other academics in the field) who would have reviewed the research's quality and contribution to the discipline.

2.72 In published government-sponsored, policy-related research, research questions are typically targeted and findings are often presented as normative statements or recommendations. If a government body has commissioned the research, then an external researcher, such as an academic or consultant, will perform the research. If instead, the government body produces the work internally, an internal team of analysts will perform the research. The research will usually have tight deadlines and a need for findings and recommendations. When peer-reviewed, reviewers may include stakeholders, policy makers, academic researchers, and others, and will often focus on consistency and accuracy.

2.73 Government and academic research in economics is not without its controversial aspects. In principle, the independence of the academic should result in the impartiality of results. In practice, academics often publish research that does not contradict their previous findings. Likewise, policy research should also result in the same impartiality of results as in academic research. In practice, maintaining the impartiality of commissioned reports is challenging as the selection of researchers is difficult and there are pressures to not contradict policies.[26]

Conclusion

2.74 This chapter has detailed the main economic approaches and philosophical justifications for IP. There are a number of competing, sometimes contradictory

[25] A peer-reviewed journal is a journal in which experts in the area have independently reviewed content. These experts are independent from the editors. The main benefit of peer review is that generally published work will be of a high standard. However, a disadvantage is that the process is often long-winded and may be subject to personal biases of the reviewers.

[26] See Saunders, L. (2007). 'Educational Research Commissioned by/for Policy Audiences' (London, TLRP) for an interesting analysis of commissioned policy research in the education sector.

approaches between IP as an incentive to innovate, an intrinsic right, and open innovation. Evidence-based policy in IP attempts to provide economic evidence to inform decision-making in the midst of these competing approaches. As this chapter has detailed, the data-based evidence in IP is particularly challenging. The two case studies of tobacco and copyright exceptions highlight the strengths and weaknesses of economic analysis in IP.

Part II

ECONOMICS OF INDIVIDUAL PROPERTY RIGHTS

This Part of the book provides detailed analysis of individual property (IP) and competition. The dominant economic approach to IP is that of its impact on incentives to innovate. However, not all IP fits nicely into this approach. Instead, the economic analysis of patents, copyright, trade marks, design rights, trade secrets, and related rights have different rationales and impacts. PII.01

Summary: Patents

Patents are a quintessential fit for IP as an incentive to innovate. A patent grants the innovator a twenty-year legal monopoly over the innovation. During this period, the patented innovation may enjoy monopoly profits, which reward innovators and provide incentives for future innovation. At the same time, society incurs higher prices and lower quantities under the monopoly. However, upon the patent's expiry, the innovation becomes part of the public domain where it may be used freely and may generate further innovation. The short-term monopoly conditions fund the longer-term goal of ongoing innovation. The result is a *quid pro quo* in which innovator and society benefit from continued innovation. PII.02

A growing area of economic interest is that of the strategic use of patents by firms. The use of patents as both a defensive and offensive tool is changing the economic impact of patents. Non-practising entities (NPEs, Patent Assertion Entities, or patent trolls) exploit a patent system that favours existing patent owners. These strategic uses of patents increase litigation and legal costs and consequently increase the cost of doing business. However, the question remains whether this is a natural consequence of the patent system. PII.03

PII.04 Economic policy considerations address how patentability, patent scope, and a number of other policy measures can tweak incentives to better suit desired outcomes. There are debates around pharmaceuticals and developing countries in which IP, rewards to innovation, and economic development clash. Patent harmonization may reduce costs for patent owners and increase patenting. However, more patents are not necessarily better as patent thickets or dense areas of patents limit the space in which new innovation can occur.

Copyright

PII.05 Copyright is also a good fit for the innovation approach of IP. With copyright, creators are granted protection of lifetime plus up to seventy years or more for their creations. As per the social contract theory, society pays higher prices during the term of the copyright, to reward the creator, in exchange for the creation becoming part of the public domain.

PII.06 However, the economic quirks of industries dominated by copyright make the innovation argument less straightforward. The creative industries, which include copyright-intensive sectors such as music, publications, and film, are characterized by an unpredictable, hits-driven market. In addition, the business models of the creative industries have been seriously disrupted with the advent of digital media. Creators may be intrinsically motivated rather than financially focused. These unusual characteristics, coupled with a dearth of data, make the economic analysis of copyright challenging.

Trade Marks

PII.07 The classic economic argument supporting trade marks is their important role in providing information for consumers. Trade marks signal important aspects such as quality and origin to consumers. This is efficient as it saves consumers time in identifying a particular product and information about how the product is expected to satisfy their needs and desires. As brand owners spend money on marketing to develop their brands and signal brand aspects, trade marks allow them protection against copying.

PII.08 Trade marks may also be economically justified based on a combination of innovation and information considerations. As trade marks protect signs and marks associated with the origin of a good or service, they do not fit with a classic interpretation of innovation. Instead, a wider definition of innovation suggests that trade marks may provide increased utility for consumers and may grow markets. Trade marks may also enable the development of innovation and serve as an indicator of other innovative activities.

Design Rights

Design rights are another classic fit as an incentive to innovate. Designers are granted a temporary monopoly that protects their designs from copying and allows them to appropriate the returns from their design activities. Upon expiration, these designs become part of the public domain. The registered and unregistered system of design rights accounts for the trend-driven market for designs. As designs may go out of fashion quickly, the three-year unregistered right provided in Europe offers cheap protection. Designs with longer market duration can instead opt to incur the costs for a registered design with longer protection. This two-tiered system provides flexibility to account for these market conditions. **PII.09**

Trade Secrets

Trade secrets, which, by definition, are secret, are an unusual fit for the standard economic understanding of IP. While trade secrets grant innovators the means to protect their innovation, they do so in terms which do not require the innovation to become part of the public domain. While this does appear to be a rejection of the *quid pro quo* of innovators and society, it is a necessary complement to IP systems. As other IPR recognize an innovator's right to disclose, there is an implicit understanding of the right not to disclose, that is, trade secrets. In addition, trade secrets are an important complement to other IPR such as patents as they may cover non-patentable innovation. **PII.10**

Traditional Knowledge and Geographical Indications

Traditional knowledge is the skills, know-how, and practices held by traditional communities. It is innovation that is collectively held and often not written down or documented in a manner recognized by mainstream IP systems. This poses challenges for rewarding innovators. In particular, cumulative innovation may inappropriately reward subsequent innovators if IP fails to recognize the contributions of traditional knowledge. **PII.11**

Unlike other IP, geographical indications are defined primarily by their geographical location. Similar to trade marks in their justification, geographical indications provide consumers with information about the origins of a good. Like traditional knowledge, a primary function of geographical indications is to dissuade copying **PII.12** and free riding on the goodwill of a particular region. Both geographical indications and traditional knowledge often seek to encourage the economic development of rural and indigenous communities.

Competition

PII.13 The interaction of IP, competition, and economics raises doubts about the innovation aspects of IP. Competition is generally considered beneficial for markets. In contrast, IP actively reduces competition by introducing legal monopolies. This can leave room for anti-competitive behaviours in which firms may take advantage of market structures to their benefit. Analysis of market structure, firm behaviours, and the overall performance of the market can illuminate when IP becomes a problem for competition. When there is a competition problem, consumers may face higher prices, lower quantity, less variety, and/or lower quality. Competition problems may also unfairly disadvantage existing firms and potential entrants to markets. Government intervention can intervene to improve competition and, ultimately, a market's performance.

Conclusion

PII.14 While economics approaches IP from a holistic, innovation basis, in practice economic justifications and functions of IP vary. While patents, trade marks, design rights, and geographical indications are registered, whereas copyright, trade secrets, and traditional knowledge are largely unregistered, some similarities end there. Innovation arguments nicely support patents, copyright, and design rights. In contrast, trade marks and geographical indications instead focus more on signalling and communicating information between producers and consumers. Trade secrets can be framed as a necessary complement to the wider IP system while not directly fitting into a classic innovation argument. Finally, traditional knowledge, which is very loosely defined, may be better justified as recognizing existing rights rather than incentivizing innovation.

3

PATENTS

Patents are the classic example of intellectual property as an economic tool, and the quintessential IP right for the social contract theory. Innovator innovates; consumers benefit; short-term costs are incurred for long-term benefits. However, patents are also one of the most controversial IP rights in that they are used strategically, are subject to high profile litigation, and have implications for human rights. This chapter will investigate these topics and consider some of the economic implications of patent regimes. **3.01**

Economists have been enamoured with patents for some time,[1] although empirical studies of patents are relatively new. The registration requirements of patents provide a rich source of data with possibilities for economic investigation. Economists have used patents to track knowledge flows, mechanisms for cumulative innovation, valuation of IP, and evaluation of patent policy. A highly flawed, yet common, use of patent data is its use as a measure of innovation. Unsophisticated analysis of patents can lead to poor conclusions, as patent data may reflect patent strategies and bureaucratic quirks that limit its application in economic analysis. Yet patent data stands out as an attractive source for insights in an otherwise data-poor area. **3.02**

This chapter covers key areas in the economic research of patents and then provides more targeted analysis in pharmaceuticals, economic development, the Unitary Patent and other policy areas, and patent litigation strategies. **3.03**

Economic Constructs of Patents

The dominant economic approach to patents is that they serve as an incentive for innovation. Patents are the classic example of the social contract theory discussed **3.04**

---

[1] For example, Smith, C. (1890). 'A Century of Patent Law' *The Quarterly Journal of Economics* 5: 44–69, which was written in a time when neo-classical economics was only just emerging and economics was still closely related to philosophy and sociology, from which it has since moved away. Recent economic studies of patents have a much more empirical or mathematical model basis. In part this is due to computing power and the availability of patent data.

in Chapter 2. Society grants the innovator the patent, which is published and lasts twenty years. Upon expiration, the patent falls into the public domain. Society enjoys the benefits of the innovation and pays higher prices for lower quantity in the short term, in exchange for the long-term benefit of continued innovation. In its perfect form, the patent policy represents a *quid pro quo* in which everyone wins.

3.05 However, a pure incentive to innovate, in the form of a perfectly functioning patent and innovation system, is not found in practice. Litigation, cumulative innovation, human rights, and firm strategy mean that the reality of the economics of patents is not the predicted utopia. In addition, there are concerns about the quality of patents granted, the quality of the examination process, and the high proportion of patents that never make it to market. This gives rise to a number of interesting questions that economics can interpret.

Patents as an innovation lever

3.06 Without patents, it is argued, innovators would struggle to reap the rewards of their innovation, as it would be freely copied. Innovation would grind to a halt, as innovators would have no financial incentive to innovate. The case of pharmaceuticals, discussed further later in the chapter, presents a tidy example of the arguments supporting the idea of patent policy as an important incentive for innovation. Whilst it is clear that innovation is not contingent on patents (humankind has long innovated while patents are a relatively new addition to our economies), such an argument does not disprove the view that patents act as an incentive by providing rights holders with limited monopolies over their innovation.

3.07 Economics is particularly interested in the various policy options and characteristics of the innovation that can affect the incentive aspects of patents. For one, the legal duration of patents may differ from its effective duration (its market duration.) As markets change, demand for a particular innovation may rise or fall. Equally, new innovation may render a previously patented innovation obsolete. These changes will influence how effective a patent is in providing monopoly protection in practice. Effective patent duration may be relatively short as technology and market cycles are often shorter than the twenty years of legal protection. This point is considered further in Part III.

3.08 There are good arguments for keeping patent length relatively short. Gallini (1992) argues in favour of shorter patents, as longer terms require that other innovators unnecessarily devote resources to inventing around existing patents. She further argues that longer patents may actually dissuade innovation, as the longer legal monopoly provided does not necessarily accompany a longer market monopoly. For example, in fast-moving industries such as mobile phone technologies, patents can become market obsolete quickly and, therefore, longer durations would be inefficient.

In addition to the length of patents, policy can influence the relationship between existing and potential future patents by adjusting patent scope and breadth.[2] Patent scope determines what other innovations are patentable and patent breadth determines what other innovations are considered infringing or not. **3.09**

Patent scope is the policy lever that defines what a particular patent covers and is identified by its claims. Once granted, the claims in a patent become part of the prior art for future patent applications. Patent breadth is the 'size' of a granted patent's contribution to this prior art and, therefore, influences the threshold relating to the inventive step. **3.10**

If a patent's scope is interpreted as wide, then the inventive step required to distance a patent application from existing patents will be greater; if narrow, then the inventive step is also narrower. This question of scope is key in determining the cost of inventing around existing patented innovations, since wider patents will be more expensive to invent around, and narrower patents cheaper. **3.11**

By contrast, patent breadth determines the distance required for a substitute to be non-infringing. A wide breadth will mean that competing innovations (substitutes) will have to be very different to the patented technology in order to be patentable themselves, and a narrower breadth will mean that closer innovations will not be considered infringing. **3.12**

To manage the incentive effects of patents, longer patents can be offset with narrower breadth. Alternately, if all patents were decreased from twenty years to fourteen, economic theory would argue that their monopoly power could still be maintained by widening their scope. **3.13**

Cumulative innovation

A core concept in innovation is that of cumulative innovation. To use Newton's 1676 cliché, it is the concept of 'standing on the shoulders of giants'. Alternatively, to take the hyperbole, it is the statement attributed to former Commissioner of the United States Patent and Trademark Office (USPTO), Charles Duell in 1901 that, **3.14**

[2] Scotchmer (2006) presents a more nuanced view of scope and breath where scope can be broader or narrower and the inventive step can be larger or smaller. For the sake of simplicity, this text assumes that the inventive step is held constant but the scope can change.

'everything that can be invented has been invented'.[3] The concept is that there are no completely new, independent innovations. Instead, every innovation builds upon existing innovation. Therefore, innovation is not a breakthrough process, but a cumulative one in which innovation is incremental. In fact, the modern patent policy itself is a cumulative innovation that builds on centuries of policy innovations.

3.15 The challenge of combining the concept of cumulative innovation and patents[4] is ownership. When one innovation builds on another, it is difficult to determine how each should be rewarded. If patents weigh in favour of the original innovator, then the incentives to develop subsequent innovations are reduced. If instead patents favour the following innovation, then the original innovator may be under-rewarded, which additionally reduces incentives to innovate. Either way, inappropriate rewarding of one innovator over another reduces the incentive effects of patents.

3.16 Furthermore, cumulative innovation makes the 'one-size-fits-all' structure of patents a challenge. One potential mitigant is the use of licensing and collaboration. If the original innovator grants a licence to the follower, then the innovators may achieve an efficient outcome. Another option is for the follower to simply infringe the original patent. In the event the original innovator and follower engage in litigation, a court finding for damages in favour of the original innovator has a similar economic outcome to that of a licensing deal. The follower still pays the original innovator but in the form of damages instead of royalties,[5] at least initially. Alternately, the innovators could jointly develop the subsequent innovation that again would allow for sharing of rewards.

3.17 However, models for innovation vary. Just as no innovation is entirely independent, neither is it likely that innovation follows a linear model in which subsequent innovations rely solely on a single original innovation. Since innovation is messy and patent policy is messy, it follows that striking the balance of patent policy between rewarding existing innovation and allowing sufficient room for new innovations will be messy.

Knowledge diffusion

3.18 Another core concept in economic interpretations of patents is the role of patents in encouraging diffusion of knowledge. The disclosure aspect of patents, by which

[3] The word 'attributed' is intended to reflect the fact that the accuracy of this quote is a topic of debate.

[4] This argument is equally true for copyright, as in discussion of derivative works.

[5] Schankerman, M. and Scotchmer, S. (2001). 'Damages and Injunctions in Protecting Intellectual Property *RAND Journal of Economics* 199–220. Note a circularity whereby reasonable royalty is determined by a theoretical willing licensee and by the damages situation in which licensing is coerced.

patent applications are published, signals the knowledge associated with the innovation. For the patent owners, this may come at a cost as disclosure may reveal firm strategies. For other innovators, the patent contributes to the stock of publicly available technological knowledge. The publication aspect of patents should reduce duplication of efforts and wasted research and development (R&D) expenditures as innovators can identify that which has already been invented.

Patent data also provides a fascinating window into the diffusion of knowledge. As patent applications require that prior art be cited, insights into cumulative innovation and research collaboration can be identified. This information can be important for assessing the impact of patent policy and identifying areas for improvement. For example, firms or governments interesting in developing their innovation strategy may look to patents[6] to identify research partners and areas of reference. **3.19**

Patent costs

Another economic consideration is the cost of patenting. Patenting is generally considered to be an expensive endeavour, even without accounting for enforcement costs. From an economic perspective, the cost of patents should be commensurate with the legal monopoly and potential economic monopoly they provide. If patents are too cheap to obtain, then society is essentially unnecessarily subsidizing[7] innovation. If, on the other hand, patents are too expensive, then their role in incentivizing innovation is diminished as innovators find the costs outweigh the benefits. **3.20**

The challenge, as is often the case with IP policy, is finding the right balance. While users always argue that patent fees are too high, economists are split on the subject (see De Rassenfosse and Van Pottelsberghe de la Potterie (2013) for a discussion). However, it is difficult to use patent policy as a lever to adjust these costs. The vast majority of patent costs are private legal costs and not the renewal, filing, and associated fees under the control of patent policy. Instead, tax policies such as the UK's patent box, where patent owners receive tax breaks on profits stemming from patents, reduce the costs of patenting (provided it is successfully commercialized). **3.21**

---

[6] The use of patents as a measure of innovation, research productivity, and impact is a tempting but inappropriate use of the data. Patents data is an indication of patents, not innovation, productivity, or impact. Again, it is important to separate the IP rights from the underlying innovation. Great caution should be exercised when using patent data as a proxy for innovation.

[7] 'Subsidizing' is here used in a general sense. As patents provide a means to appropriate the rewards from innovation, if innovators are over-rewarded then the surplus reward element acts a subsidy rather than an incentive. The patent box, a policy in which profits stemming from patented innovation qualify for tax breaks, provides double incentives and could be construed as a subsidy. The patent box provides incentives over and above the incentives provided by patents. However, the patent box could merely be incentivizing patents and not innovation. See Chapter 9 for more on the patent box.

Theoretically, policies that reduce the costs of patenting may increase innovation, but in practice they may simply increase patenting.[8]

3.22 Overall, patents offer a number of policy levers to affect their innovation impact. As markets and technology evolve, so does the shape of patents. The next sections will focus more on the strategic use of patents and key topics in their applications.

Strategic use of patents

3.23 There is a vast array of available strategies for the use of patents. High-profile technology cases in the last decades have highlighted some of these strategies as large technology firms sue, counter-sue, and amass patents for defensive and offensive reasons. The licensing and cross-licensing of patents is big business.

3.24 The scope and quantity of patents are also increasing. 'Recent court decisions and patent-office rule-making have made software the fastest growing patent category, and companies are rushing to patent the most basic methods of doing business. This is a disaster,' says Lawrence Lessig, a Harvard law professor and cyberspace expert. He continues: 'This is a major change that occurred without anybody thinking through the consequences. In my view, it is the single greatest threat to innovation in cyberspace, and I'm extremely skeptical that anybody's going to get it in time' (*Gleick*, 12 March 2000).

3.25 As patentability changes and innovation continues, new patent strategies are developing. The following section examines these further.

Non-practising entities

> I'm a troll, foldy roll,
>
> ...
>
> And I'm getting very hungry
>
> (Mitton, 2007)

3.26 While they have not always been characterized as 'patent trolls' exemplifying the troll characteristics noted by Mitton, non-practising entities (NPEs) have always existed. The strategy of owning patents, but not using them to produce goods and services, is implicit in the IP system. A patent is a right to exclude, it is not a right or obligation to produce. Owning patents and licensing them or asserting rights through litigation is a legitimate business model. It is, however, one that has come

[8] As discussed extensively in Chapter 5 on trade marks, the separation between the IP right and the subject of the IP right—in the case of patents, innovation—must be remembered. Therefore incentivizing patenting is not necessarily incentivizing innovation.

to the forefront of patent and innovation policy in recent years, particularly in the United States, and has demonstrated that litigation can itself provide a means of generating value from IP in which the owner has no other interest.

Lawsuits have been getting rather expensive. A 2013 estimate from the American Intellectual Property Law Association (AIPLA) puts the costs of discovery for a patent infringement dispute under USD 1 million at USD 530k and through a trial at USD 970k. This would imply that the court costs are, on average, at least 50% of the value in dispute and in some cases will exceed them. Defending against an NPE for a dispute over USD 25 million is estimated to cost USD 2.9 million through discovery and USD 4.4 million through a trial. **3.27**

As a cost of doing business and innovating, these lawsuits are considered transfers. Transfer payments are simply redistributions of income and do not contribute to innovation or create output. In these litigation circumstances, transfer payments arising from litigation costs benefit legal service providers. Transfer payments arising from damages simply redistribute income to patent owners, away from users of the patented innovation. While this increases the rewards associated with patenting, it also increases the costs of doing R&D and innovating. If the goal is growth and innovation rather than a change in the distribution of wealth, transfer payments can be seen as counterproductive.[9] **3.28**

Opinions vary on the rationale behind the growth in NPEs and associated lawsuits. It could be as simple as market sophistication and the development of higher profile licensing practices. However, NPEs in the modern era are characterized as firms that acquire rights, not with the intention of using the rights, but with the express intention of litigating. The threat of litigation is changing firm behaviour as firms acquire arsenals of patents for primarily strategic means. **3.29**

The aggregation of patents can be divided into defensive and offensive strategies. Under the offensive strategy, patents are acquired with the intent to pursue licensing. In defensive aggregation, the acquisitions of patents is done with the purpose of warding off potential lawsuits and preventing competitors or NPEs from acquiring them. Like many aspects of the patent system, this strategic aggregation by firms is a consequence of the system. **3.30**

The prevalence of the NPEs in the United States in comparison with the United Kingdom is often attributed to the 'loser pays' system in the United Kingdom, under which the losing party pays the costs of the lawsuit. This may discourage speculative lawsuits by NPEs as they may not have the resources or risk tolerance to **3.31**

[9] However, if wealth is concentrated in the very few, then the redistribution of wealth from the wealthy (big firms) to the poor (smaller firms) could increase growth and innovation as the scope of R&D widens. This is an argument that some NPEs have used.

pay both parties' legal costs in the event of losing. In the absence of loser pays, legal firms may take on lawsuits on a contingency basis, and as the risk of losing is spread between the law firm and the NPE, the expected costs of losing are lower for the NPE. Additionally, there are arguments that legislation such as the 2011 America Invents Act, the use of injunctions, and the pro-patent stance of the US District Court, Eastern District of Texas have all increased the quantity and success rates of patent infringement cases.[10]

3.32 NPEs in their latest and most widely discussed incarnation started as small entities with comparatively limited resources. As non-producing firms, they are not vulnerable to accusations of infringement and have no interest in cross-licensing, but still have the ability to target larger firms. The risk of counter-suit is therefore limited. However, as the business model evolves, NPEs are growing and changing. VirnetX, an NPE holder of security-related patents, is a publicly traded company which has been valued at as much as USD 1.2 billion.[11] Additionally, large technology companies, such as BlackBerry have been amassing their own patent portfolios and are taking more aggressive stances. Litigation as practised by NPEs is now a business model in its own right.

3.33 For economics, NPEs highlight the flaws of the patent system. A system that encourages business models based entirely on litigation clearly has consequences other than the intended incentives to innovate. In addition, the threat of trolls distorts firm behaviour as patents are acquired with the goal of protection[12] from litigation rather than protection for innovation. While enforcement, and hence litigation, of IP rights is necessary for a functioning patent system, vexatious or unnecessary litigation disrupts the balance between enforcement as an IP-supporting system to enforcement to exploit IP rights.

Business model patents and the scope of patentability

3.34 With the increase in the scope of patentability comes the greater potential for strategic use of patents. An interesting example is that of the expansion of patents to business models. While the precise patentability of business models is debated, they serve a useful illustrative purpose as they expand the scope under which rivals may sue or force licences on each other. This behaviour is predominantly seen in the United States, though the fact that this is concentrated in one market may be irrelevant as developments in the United States have international impact; the US

[10] Gerardi (2014); the Eastern District of Texas is discussed further in this chapter.

[11] As cited in Kerstetter (5 April 2012), although, at the time of writing, the stock price of the VirnetX had fallen 75% from June 2014 to June 2015.

[12] A typical defence in a patent infringement suit is to counter-sue, alleging infringement of patents by the accuser. Claiming that the original patent is invalid is also common.

market is sufficiently large and its policies sufficiently influential that litigation in the United States may impact a firm's global activities. For example, a firm threatened with an infringement lawsuit has the option to license, change business model, or exit the US market. In this case, the size of the US market makes licensing or changing a business model more attractive. The firm may also decide that it is more efficient to change its business model globally as maintaining heterogeneous models, as opposed to a single model, is relatively expensive.

Patent thickets

Further strategic use of the patent system can be seen in the use of patent thickets, also known as patent floods, patent clusters, and other density-related nouns. The concept of patent thickets is the idea that patents can be generated to 'surround' a technology with a dense cluster of legal rights. Shapiro (2001) notes the idea in his oft-quoted description: 'Mixing metaphors, thoughtful observers are increasingly expressing concerns that our patent (and copyright) system is in fact creating a patent thicket, a dense web of overlapping intellectual property rights that a company must hack its way through in order to actually commercialize new technology. With cumulative innovation and multiple blocking patents, stronger patent rights can have the perverse effect of stifling, not encouraging, innovation.' **3.35**

These thickets occur in a variety of forms. A single company may patent a particular technology and then patent extensively in the innovation 'space' around the patent. This potentially wards off competitors and will force them to license in the event of subsequent innovation. Likewise, competitors may patent around a competitor's original innovation so that the original innovator is compelled to license in order to further develop the innovation. Either way, patent thickets saturate an innovation space to make further innovation in that area more difficult or costly. **3.36**

The challenge is that patent thickets may undermine the innovation aspects of patent policy and disproportionately benefit larger firms. Thickets may also discourage further patenting in that area. There is also a general fear that patent thickets are growing. Hall et al. (2012) identify six factors contributing to the growth in patent thickets: **3.37**

1. Changes in enforcement of patent rights in the United States during the 1980s;
2. Cumulativeness of innovation and the increasing complexity of technology;
3. Shifts in technological opportunity in some areas;
4. Strategic patenting by large corporations and the rise of NPEs;
5. Lack of resources and misaligned incentives in patent offices faced with a flood of patent applications;
6. Growth in trade of high technology products, leading to an increase in the demand for patents worldwide.

3.38 Patent pools and cross-licensing can address some of the concerns raised by patent thickets. Patent pools, where a number of patents, potentially owned by different entities, are grouped together for licensing, can reduce the costs of licensing and may encourage more widespread adoption of common standards which can facilitate economic growth. For a particular technology, the availability of a patent pool negates the need to negotiate individual licences and the hold-up power of an individual patent owner. Cross-licensing allows patent owners to license patents to each other. This again potentially reduces costs. That said, the NPE challenges already presented suggest that patent pools and cross-licensing do not solve these problems.

3.39 Patents act as an incentive to create property rights over innovations. However, the creation of property rights can create opportunities for exploitation. It is difficult to see how a one-size-fits-all patent system will ever fully address the challenges created by strategic, and potentially detrimental, use of patents.

Development and Global Health—Questions on Generics, Pharmaceuticals, and Developing Countries

3.40 The pharmaceutical industry is perhaps the classic example of how IP can create economic conundrums. It is an industry where the private benefits of successful medicines can be vastly outweighed by the public benefits. However, it is the private sector that typically bears the cost of creating new medicines. At first glance, a basic economic analysis would argue that, given the social benefit (social welfare) is maximized when the medicine is freely available, private parties should not enjoy patent protection. However, the lack of patent protection may mean that the private innovator of the medicine is unable to recoup their costs. Freeing an essential medicine from patent protection may work once, but innovators are unlikely to continue innovating in the future without financial reward. This section covers development questions of pharmaceuticals followed by an analysis of the economics of drug development.

3.41 This is especially the case in diseases of poverty and neglected diseases. This analysis is less applicable to lifestyle diseases[13] and conditions that do not affect overall health (such as baldness).[14] Instead, diseases of poverty and neglected

[13] There are a number of other terms similar to these: preventable diseases, disease of affluence, diseases of longevity, and diseases of civilization.

[14] Even in the case of baldness, it is possible that the social benefit from the cure for baldness outweighs the private benefit under patent protection. The globally aggregated increased happiness of formerly bald people could outweigh the profits of the innovator of the cure. Perhaps unfairly, baldness is often used to highlight the disparity between research investment in medicines as significantly more is spent on baldness research than on malaria research. However, the contrast is stark, 'Androgenetic alopecia, or male pattern baldness, affects 6.5 million men in the UK and 35 million in the US.... By comparison, malaria affected an estimated 219 million people in 2010 and killed

diseases can have huge negative welfare impact on countries. This is particularly the case in diseases predominantly found in developing countries (e.g. malaria), but also applies to diseases found globally (e.g. HIV) and underfunded medicines (e.g. antibiotics).

International debates over pharmaceuticals typify debates in IP. Competing interests between developed and developing countries, capitalism and other economic systems, different concepts of property, and long- versus short-term considerations create tensions over how patents, generics, and compulsory licensing should be treated. Ultimately, though, the goal is singular: sustainable development of medicines that improve global health. **3.42**

Development and global health

The economics of health, development, and IP meet in the analysis of the economics of pharmaceuticals for diseases of poverty, and neglected diseases. The health of a country's population can have profound impacts on its economic growth and development. Countries with a high disease burden[15] face a large cost to the economy without a corresponding benefit. Diseases such as malaria and tuberculosis weigh down populations and economies. The humanitarian impact easily translates into economic impact. **3.43**

One means to estimate the impact of disease is the economic concept of a statistical life. This is known as the Value of a Statistical Life (VSL). It is a rather uncomfortable calculation that associates monetary values with measurements of life. For example, a VSL may tell you that the loss of one hand for one year is worth £20k. This is useful when governments decide policies and insurers calculate payouts. It allows for a relatively objective decision-making process, when, given a limited budget, deciding between saving one hand for one year and saving four toes for two years. **3.44**

Developing countries have particularly limited budgets and often have high disease burdens. Cost becomes a focus in improving access to essential medicines. As economic theory suggests, the legal monopoly created by a patent translates to higher prices and lower quantities of the medicine than without the patent. Therefore, enacting IP regulations that are economically beneficial in countries with lower disease burdens and higher budgets for healthcare may not be in a developing country's best interest. However, these IP regulations are often presented as part **3.45**

660,000—mostly children in Africa, where a child dies every minute from the disease.' Chu, B. "Bill Gates: Why do we care more about baldness than malaria?" The Independent, March 16, 2013.

[15] The total cost of a disease. In this case, the disease burden for a country is the total cost, across its population, of the lives, years of life, loss of productivity, expenditure on healthcare, and other factors, of a disease.

of a wider trade and political package, which may be in a country's best interest as a whole.[16]

3.46 Reducing the burden of disease not only addresses humanitarian concerns but also frees up economic resources to be used in more productive ways. Populations not encumbered by disease will be more productive, achieve higher[17] levels of education, and in general improve economic growth and development.

Economics of drug development

3.47 Drug development in general is a complex economic situation. R&D for these drugs will involve highly specialized labour, advanced laboratory equipment, expensive clinical trials, and a variety of other factors that makes drug development a very expensive business. For every successful drug, there may be ten other failed drugs, or one hundred. Long-term sustainability of pharmaceutical companies demands that successful drugs must be sufficiently financially successful to cover the losses on unsuccessful drugs. Therefore, the price of a single pill may not reflect the relatively low cost of producing that individual pill, but the costs of the R&D of that drug and the other, failed drugs.

3.48 At the same time, once a successful drug has been developed, it is often relatively straightforward to determine the chemical structure of the drug and reverse engineer it. In the absence of patent protection, the firm reverse engineering the drug will have the ability to produce the drug without incurring the costs of R&D. In the marketplace, this means that the original innovator would not recover its costs as it competes with a lower-cost reverse engineered equivalent drug.

3.49 Herein lies the argument for patent protection. With patent protection, the pharmaceutical company has tools to legally prevent the reverse engineering and use of its drugs. The company, in theory, will enjoy a monopoly and charge higher prices. This allows the company to remain profitable and continue its R&D for new drugs. Patents allow for the sustained development of new drugs.

3.50 This argument is not without its critics. In addition to the development and humanitarian concerns addressed earlier, costs not directly related to drug research, such as marketing, inflate development costs. Additionally, many

[16] For example, Trade Related Aspects of Intellectual Property (TRIPS) is the 1994 agreement that is required for membership in the World Trade Organisation (WTO). In this case, the costs associated with enacting TRIPS may be outweighed by the benefits of membership in the WTO.

[17] Higher is generally considered better when considering economic growth and development. There is some debate on this matter as alternate ways of measuring growth, including measurements of happiness and environmental impact, suggest that higher growth as measured by money is not necessarily desirable. See Chapter 1 for further details.

successful drug-enabled health outcomes have occurred in the absence of patents. Economists Boldrin and Levine (2007) are particular proponents of these arguments. They calculate that only two of the top fifteen medical and pharmaceutical discoveries[18] were patented.

Diseases of poverty and neglected diseases

If we assume that firms are profit-driven, then pharmaceutical companies will naturally be drawn to potentially profitable markets. Profit equals total revenue minus total costs. As discussed earlier, costs are relatively high in the pharmaceutical industry and the emphasis then becomes maximizing revenue. Revenue is price multiplied by quantity. Thus markets with wealthy consumers who will consume high quantities of a particular drug are particularly desirable. In contrast, markets where consumers are poor and will not consume large quantities are less desirable. Diseases associated with poverty, by definition, fit the latter description. The market for diseases of poverty fails to provide sufficient incentives to encourage drug development. The result is neglected diseases. **3.51**

The case of antibiotics highlights these failings. The social benefits of new antibiotics are potentially very large. However, compared to other drugs, antibiotics are largely out of patent protection, prices are low, and the quantity demanded low. Unlike other medications that are taken over a sustained period of time, antibiotics are often only taken for short courses. Over-use of antibiotics is said to be increasing the prevalence of drug-resistant bacteria. New antibiotics may not be widely used due to health policies that discourage their use and reserve them for a limited number of cases. Thus, the potential market for antibiotics is less lucrative. **3.52**

These economic conditions of the market for new antibiotics are readily apparent. According to Aglionby and Ward (2014), 'No new classes of antibiotics have been discovered since 1987 and only six in the 24 years before that'.[19] It is likely that government intervention in the market for these drugs will be required. **3.53**

Other examples can be readily seen in neglected tropical diseases. As most countries with tropical climates are poor, diseases and infections in these countries have limited markets outside poor countries. Thus the markets for new medicines for these diseases suffer from significant failings. **3.54**

[18] List of the fifteen discoveries calculated by a survey of the *British Medical Journal*'s editors, readers, and colleagues. Boldrin and Levine (2007) also cite other, similar estimates in Chapter 9 of their book.

[19] Aglionby, J. and Ward, A. (2015). 'David Cameron Calls for Action to Fight Antibiotic Resistance', *FT.com*.

Potential solutions

3.55 In the face of significant failings in both the markets for new drugs, what are potential solutions? Patent protection serves as a means to incentivize innovation. However, as noted earlier, patents do not solve the market failures for drugs. Yet patents are not the only solution to incentivizing innovation. Other options include prizes, government funding (or other incentives that address development risk and assist profitability), and non-governmental organizations (NGOs).

3.56 Prizes are a long-standing means to provide financial incentives for innovation. For example, in 1714, the British Government created the Longitude Prize, a £20,000 prize to improve the precision and ease of calculating a ship's longitude. The 2014, £10 million update to the prize targets antibiotics.[20] The advantage of a prize is that it allows the prizegivers to target a specific area of interest. Depending on the prize structure, the innovation also becomes part of the public domain and is freely available for subsequent use and further innovation. It is also less likely to attract litigation and encourages private investment in innovation. However, it may encourage duplication of efforts as multiple teams compete for the same prize.

3.57 A more obvious way of encouraging innovation in drug development is for governments to directly fund development. This is often seen via funding of academic research. Variations on this exist as funding can be in the form of grants or commitments to purchase future drugs. With governments being large customers for pharmaceutical products and responsible for their regulation, there are significant incentives for pharmaceuticals to participate in not-for-profit programmes and collaborations and to engage in corporate social responsibility.

3.58 A non-governmental approach to encouraging innovation is shown in the efforts of NGOs such as charities. The Bill and Melinda Gates Foundation, for example, funds research in global health as part of its mandate to reduce the impact of diseases such as malaria and tuberculosis. This sector includes a number of players who fund and campaign on behalf of drug development for these diseases.

3.59 Patents, the focus of this discussion, also includes policies which can be applied to drug development for neglected diseases. One of these is to provide patent term extension[21] specifically for certain pharmaceuticals. The idea is that, by granting a longer legal monopoly for a pharmaceutical, companies will be more appropriately incentivized to invest in innovation in these otherwise neglected areas. However, this approach does not solve other questions raised here. A longer patent means

---

[20] The Longitude Prize 2014, launched by the British Government.

[21] For example, as discussed later, supplementary protection measures (SPCs) are pharmaceutical specific monopoly extensions that account for the extensive time, independent of the patent itself, to gain regulatory approval to take a drug to market.

prices will remain higher than current patent lengths which is, as discussed earlier, particularly problematic in the poor countries where the majority of sufferers of these targeted diseases reside.

The debates on these areas continue and no clear model has emerged as particularly successful. As diseases and priorities change, solutions to these problems will change also. **3.60**

Generics

Generic pharmaceuticals, which include medicines with expired patents, those that never received patent protection, and those that have been licensed for generic manufacturing by the patent owner, play an important role in global health and drug markets. Generics offer out-of-patent medicines at what is often a drastically reduced price. This often results in sales in the previously patented medicine dropping. As a result, pharmaceutical companies have incentives to seek to restrict markets for generics or prolong patent protection. **3.61**

To illustrate the fall in revenue from patented medicines upon the expiration of a patent, known as the patent cliff, Lines (2012) calculates that, 'Once drugs lose patent protection, lower-price generics quickly siphon off as much as 90% of their sales. For consumers, the savings from generics can be substantial. Drugs are granted 20 years of patent protection, although companies often do not get a product to market before as much as half of that period has already elapsed. Once a drug enters the market, however, patent protection can result in high profits, with gross profit margins exceeding 90%.' **3.62**

India is often cited in discussions on generics. In 1970, India removed patent protection for pharmaceuticals. The result was fast growth in the domestic pharmaceutical market in the production of generics.[22] Eventually, the increased skills, standards,[23] and facilities which accompanied the growth in the generics sector translated into innovation in pharmaceuticals and is now an important sector for the Indian economy. However, with the ascension of TRIPS,[24] many of the 1970s restrictions were rescinded in 2005. The future of the Indian generics market is now less certain and may have a knock-on effect for the markets it supplies. **3.63**

The debate around pharmaceuticals and the patent system is ongoing. It encapsulates a number of competing interpretations of IP systems and the ownership of **3.64**

[22] For an overview with some statistics, see Greenhalgh and Rogers (2010).

[23] As a highly regulated sector, pharmaceuticals are subject to specific high standards. Generics sold internationally must also conform to international standards.

[24] The Agreement on Trade-Related Aspects of Intellectual Property, known as TRIPS, is an international agreement on intellectual property administered by WIPO as part of the World Trade Organisation (WTO). It creates minimum standards for most intellectual property rights.

ideas and innovation. In the case of India, a generics sector not subject to patent protection spurred innovation. The relationship between innovation and IP is not straightforward. Pharmaceuticals are also where the international IP system butts up against international human rights and world health.

Extended patent life: Supplementary Protection Certificates, branding, and pay for delay

3.65 Supplementary Protection Certificates (SPCs) are a *sui generis* right associated with biologically related patents, typically pharmaceuticals. SPCs are designed to compensate for delays in achieving market authorization for products and services covered by qualifying patents. SPCs function roughly like a patent term extension in which the effective coverage of the patent includes its statutory twenty years plus the term of the SPC.

3.66 SPCs can delay the advent of the patent cliff, therefore the calculation of its expiration is very important. However, it is not the only means to extend the practical life of a pharmaceutical monopoly. Another option is the concept of pay for delay. Under this strategy, pharmaceutical companies with expiring patents will contract with competitors to pay them not to introduce generic versions of the medicines in question. The owner of the expiring patent benefits as they continue to enjoy monopoly profits, albeit at an increased cost. The competitors also benefit as they are paid not to produce. This assumes that the payment for delay outweighs any expected profits competitors would receive from producing generics. The cost of all of this is borne by patients, and in the case of national health services, taxpayers. Ethical questions aside, this market behaviour is most likely anti-competitive[25] (see Chapter 7 on competition for further discussion). Again, the patent system is open to exploitation.

3.67 A third means to extend effective monopoly rights is through branding. Effective branding and marketing of a drug to patients and doctors can create sufficient demand that, even with patent expiration, market dominance can be maintained. An example is the market power of the 'purple pill' (Wall, April 2012), a heartburn medication that has been sufficiently marketed that patients ask for the non-generic version by name by name.

3.68 Other strategies include the idea of 'evergreening', in which patent owners make small changes to a drug in order to achieve a new patent. Licensing strategies and control of inputs into drugs can all contribute to creating a longer effective monopoly over a particular innovation.

---

[25] At the time of writing, these concerns are being addressed by a number of governments.

International Systems: Patent Harmonization, Cooperation, and Convergence

Patents, as a registered right, are granted in each jurisdiction. An international patent right does not exist. In contrast, from an economic perspective,[26] an international copyright does exist. Differences between national patent systems mean that even ostensibly the same innovation patented in multiple jurisdictions will have different protection in these jurisdictions. For example, an American patent and European patent[27] may both protect the same innovation, but subtle differences in patentability, claim structure, enforcement, and policies such as grace periods will differentiate the two documents and the rights they confer. These differences lead to uncertainty and increased costs for the patent rights holder and non-rights holders operating internationally. **3.69**

The lack of harmonization (consistency) across patent jurisdictions has wider impacts on the economy. Differences between jurisdictions allow for firms to engage in strategic behaviour to 'game' the system, play into international governmental negotiations, and cause uncertainty for innovators. This section addresses topics in jurisdictional differences: harmonization, cooperation, and convergence. **3.70**

Harmonization

Harmonization arises from a variety of cultural, economic, and market structure differences. Chun (2011) categorizes types of harmonization, or the lack thereof, into, 'four categories according to the procedural–substantive and legislative–administrative standpoint'. On the procedural–substantive axis, Chun argues that harmonization is largely procedural (concerned with processes) or substantive (standards and rules). In this case, the Patent Cooperation Treaty (PCT) is procedural while TRIPS is substantive. His second axis is legislative–administrative where legislative requires law or administrative which requires practical processes. Economics largely focuses on substantive harmonization, which Chun describes as 'deep harmonization'. **3.71**

Key areas of lack of substantive harmonization are the definition of inventive step, subject matter, the definition of priority (first-to-file versus first-to-invent), and **3.72**

[26] This statement is qualified as legal scholars would no doubt argue that litigation and other limitations restrict the existence of a global, single copyright.

[27] Strictly speaking, a 'European' patent does not exist, but for convenience in this text patents granted via the European Patent Office (EPO) are referred to as 'European' patents.

grace periods.[28] These differences present costs and benefits to patent owners. For example, heterogeneity in the definition of inventive step and/or the subject matter may mean that what is patentable in one country is not in another. While recent court rulings have led to the United States's policy of permitting certain types of software patents has historically been a particularly contentious source of lack of patent harmonization.

3.73 Also contentious was the practice of the United States and other jurisdictions of using first-to-invent as the measure of priority of inventorship. While the principle of first-to-invent may seem fairer, it burdens innovators with the potentially expensive requirement to repeatedly document their R&D in the event they must prove priority. First-to-file avoids this expense by using the date of application as priority. This long debate ended in 2013 (USPTO, 2013) when the United States switched to a first-to-file system.

3.74 Grace periods are another source of lack of harmonization—again with the US system as a focal point for discussion. In the United States, innovators are granted a year's grace period between initial public disclosure of the innovation and filing of the patent right. Germany had a similar provision but, as Moy (1992) notes, removed it from its laws in 1980 as part of joining the European Patent Convention (EPC). For some research cultures, such as universities, the sharing of innovations is an important mechanism for knowledge diffusion. The grace period allows for knowledge diffusion before the patent is filed. It also potentially protects innovators from unintentionally rendering an innovation un-patentable through early disclosure. However, they cause uncertainty for other applicants, reduce knowledge mobility, and allow, as de la Potterie (2011) argues, for inventors to 'reserve' an innovation for a year without incurring patenting costs.

Impact of harmonization

3.75 Harmonization is not a new concept (as described in Moy, 1992). In 2011, the US position in favour of harmonization (as laid out in Kappos, 2010) argued,

> Harmonization—the alignment of laws and procedure among intellectual property (IP) systems to ensure consistency and clarity of rights for the world's innovators—is a prerequisite to maintaining the development and dissemination of innovation and thereby improving the quality of life for all the world's

[28] Another curious source of lack of harmonization is claim structure. This is particularly vexing for researchers as the construction and analysis of patent data may be hampered by internationally differing claim structures. This is perhaps not of a paramount concern for most patent owners, but it does keep the odd economist awake at night.

> people. Harmonization is also absolutely essential to reducing the global patent backlog and reducing the amount of time it takes innovators around the world to get a patent.

In theory, harmonization reduces uncertainty for users of patents, strategic use of the system, and barriers to flows of knowledge. In terms of cost, harmonization can reduce costs associated with repeated searches, translation costs, and legal costs. However, the precise impact of these cost reductions will vary depending on the level of harmonization.

Sceptics such as Moy argue that harmonization is largely based on self-interest. He suggests lack of harmonization exists as, 'international patent transactions therefore reallocate wealth away from the granting country and into the country of the patent owner. Prior to the Paris Convention many countries had acted on this basic economic truth.' Therefore the lack of harmonization by some countries may be protectionism and efforts towards harmonization may be self-interest. The international distribution of wealth, exports, and imports likely dictates attitudes towards harmonization. **3.76**

The potentially uneven distribution of benefits stemming from patent harmonization questions the development of bilateral and plurilateral IP agreements encouraging harmonization to standards going beyond TRIPS minimum standards (TRIPS Plus). In these agreements, the possibility of benefits to the developing countries from increased trade with the developed economies is framed to outweigh any costs stemming from increased patent strength.[29] Typically, patent harmonization for developing countries means a strengthening or expansion of domestic patent policy. As patents in developing countries are mostly from foreign applicants, the economic benefits from increased patent strength will mostly go to these foreign owners. **3.77**

Whether this benefit corresponds to an equal benefit in terms of increased Foreign Direct Investment (FDI) and domestic innovation (as discussed earlier in the context of generics) for the developing country is unclear. Adams (2010) finds that strengthened IP rights protection has a positive effect on FDI but does not estimate the wider economic impact. However, the author also notes that country-specific effects may make the relationship less direct. Rai (2008) looks at the Indian pharmaceutical industries and finds that strengthened patent protection does not necessarily result in a corresponding increase in FDI. He also notes that other, non-IP-related factors likely have more importance. **3.78**

[29] Patent strength in itself is a topic of much discussion. In general, this text refers to patent strength as being any combination of wider definitions of patentability, stronger enforcement mechanisms, longer duration of patent protection, and related provisions.

3.79 Briggs (2013) finds that harmonization of patent policies in developing countries with international policies (e.g. TRIPS) increases the number of high technology exports to those countries. However, the mere importation of high technology may not lead to the desired knowledge transfer and economic development if the developing countries do not have the capacity to absorb this new knowledge. As Mancusi (2008) notes, this 'absorptive capacity' reflects 'a country's ability to understand and improve upon external knowledge'. It remains to be seen whether patent harmonization is a precursor to domestic innovation in these circumstances. The impact of TRIPS and patent harmonization on economic development is likely long-term and it may be premature to reach any conclusions at this point.

3.80 Less economic attention has been devoted to the economic impact on developed countries of TRIPS Plus agreements. Morin (2009) argues that the 'huge impact' of TRIPS Plus on international patenting standards is unsubstantiated and, for the United States, has not produced preferred results in multilateral agreements. Largely, harmonization at any level is said to reduce transaction costs for patent owners operating in multiple jurisdictions. This stems from reduced duplication of efforts in adapting each patent application to a different jurisdiction; the more harmonized regimes are, the fewer resources will be devoted to this non-productive duplication. However, harmonization in recent years has meant strengthening IP rights. The strengthening of rights benefits existing rights holders but may come at the cost of future rights holder. Stronger IP does not necessarily mean great innovation and economic growth. Hence the overall economic impact of recent trends in harmonization is ambiguous.

The Unitary Patent: Unification and Convergence of European Patent Law

3.81 This section presents a case study of harmonization of policy in practice. Similar to patent policy harmonization, are the concepts of patent unification and convergence. In unification, legal systems merge into single systems as opposed to the principle of harmonization in which the differences between systems decrease according to predefined standards and via formal process. Convergence,[30] on the other hand, refers to the process in which legal systems move towards the same model but do not merge into single systems; convergence need not work towards a formally agreed standard.[31]

3.82 The Unitary Patent is a case of both patent unification—the creating of a patent system across a number of European countries, and the convergence of domestic

[30] Convergence here refers to the political/legal sense of convergence and not the economic principle. Economic convergence is the argument that higher growth rates in poorer countries will eventually close the gap between richer and poorer economies.

[31] For further discussion, see Andenas and Andersen, 2012.

systems[32] as a result. It also represents an excellent, modern example of the impact of differences in patent systems.

The European Patent Convention of 1973 founded the European Patent Office (EPO) and, with it, the bundled patent. Between the options of a single Europe-wide patent and many, national patents, the bundled patent allows applicants to follow a single application process for national patents. A successful patent application results in a 'bundle' of national patents for the same innovation. The applicant can select in which countries the patent is then validated (the process by which the successful application becomes a national patent). Litigation is also done at the national level, which can result in conflicting outcomes as jurisdictions take different approaches. **3.83**

Economically, the bundled patent creates a simplified application process when compared to the alternative of filing an application in each jurisdiction. This reduces transaction costs associated with patenting. For applicants, translation fees, legal fees, and other fees, and other costs generally are reduced in comparison to individual applications. For patent offices, duplication of patent examination and search is reduced. Indeed, as Blackman (1995) notes, the EPO was introduced in part to reduce the pressure on national offices. Overall, reduction in transaction costs and waste in the form of duplication of efforts is good for the economy. **3.84**

However, the bundled patent only goes some of the way to streamlining patenting in Europe. An alternative approach, by way of the creation of a Unitary Patent, a single patent with effect in all of the participating jurisdictions, further reduces these costs. Translation fees, agent fees, and uncertainty arising from multiple jurisdictions are all reduced when the process and patent are unified. For the European economy, these reduced costs are economically a good thing. Furthermore, the Unitary Patent provides Europe with a single patent able to compete with the market reach of other patent systems such as those of the United States and Japan. The Unitary Patent may also create a clearer, single repository of the knowledge contained in a patent to spur further innovation. **3.85**

[32] Put differently, unification is the introduction of the single Unitary Patent which covers the signatory states. This convergence is indirect as states may elect to change domestic patent law to reduces differences between the Unitary Patent and domestic patents. For example, the United Kingdom has a policy of making small changes to GB patents (patents processed by the UK Intellectual Property Office (IPO) and valid in England, Wales, Scotland, and Northern Ireland) to bring GB patents in line with Unitary Patents as reflected in analysis in IPO 2014. Unified Patent Court implementation: Alignment of exceptions to infringement. *In:* IPO (ed.) Consultation ed. Published by the Department for Business, Innovation and Skills (BIS), 25 July 2014 and available at: https://www.gov.uk/government/publications/impact-assessment-unified-patent-court-implementation-alignment-of-exceptions-to-infringement.

3.86 At a national level, the benefits may be murkier. The reduction in patenting costs internationally could result in reduced demand for legal services.[33] However, these costs simply represent a transfer from patentees to patent services and do not provide a net benefit to the economy. Additionally, under the bundled systems, patentees may have chosen to validate the patent only in key markets. Smaller markets, under the Unitary Patent, may find themselves with an increased body of patents. More patents are not necessarily a good thing.

3.87 Another consideration is that of strategic use of the system by both users of patents and the owners of the court. Forum shopping, in which litigants will attempt to litigate in jurisdictions perceived to be more favourable to a desired outcome, affects firms' behaviour and the perceived fairness of judgments. The creation of a court held in multiple countries also opens up the possibility of forum selling. In this case, countries hosting these courts, in which judgments are valid through the signatory countries of the Unitary Patent Court (UPC), stand to benefit.[34] The resulting forum selling could distort the court.

3.88 The Unitary Patent and UPC are emblematic of the international trend in the last fifty years towards more harmonized patent policies. As a case study, they highlight the potential benefits of harmonization but also the challenges with constructing systems that optimize innovation. At the time of writing, both the court and the patent were on track for implementation; however, the number of variables affecting the final outcomes of both implementation and success make it difficult to predict its ultimate fate.

Conclusion

3.89 As this chapter has detailed, patents nicely encapsulate the economic interpretation of IP as an incentive to innovate. Yet, the rising impact of strategic patenting behaviour and questions on global health and development highlight the considerable challenges to patent policy. Global discussions on patent policy and harmonization suggest that patents continue to evolve.

[33] The overall impact of the Unitary Patent on patenting behaviour is the subject of much debate. One interesting consideration is the choice between filing at national offices and via the EPO. The numbers of patents, filing languages, and linguistic skills of examiners, may affect the perceived strength of patents examined at the EPO. Patent claims examined by non-native speakers could be construed as weaker, and the national patent, which does not suffer the same challenge, could become relatively more attractive.

[34] Increased caseloads at a court mean increased revenue from court fees, increased employment in courts, and increased demand for local legal services. A classic case of forum selling is that of the Eastern District of Texas. As noted in Klerman and Reilly (2014), 'judges in the Eastern District of Texas have distorted the rules and practices relating to case assignment, joinder, discovery, transfer, and summary judgment in order to attract patent plaintiffs to their district. As a result of their efforts, more than a quarter of all patent infringement suits were filed in the Eastern District of Texas in 2014.' As changes in any system affect behaviour, the strategic use of the new system to its users' favour should not come as a surprise

4

ECONOMICS OF COPYRIGHT

"Guys, best site to download films online? Sorry copyright, It's gotta be done."

—Facebook friend, 2015[1]

Of all the intellectual property rights (IPRs), copyright is the most controversial in current public discourse. The unique properties of copyright and its interaction in technology are testing its resilience. Copyright is a relatively strong right; protection generally lasts a lifetime plus seventy years and does not require registration. Copyright can provide protection for simple works such as a signature to *magnum opera* such as Picasso's eight-metre long mural 'Guernica'; it encompasses a wide scope of innovativeness. Copyright is highly flexible in its coverage yet accused of being largely inflexible in the modern economy. This chapter examines the economic rationale for copyright and current economic debates including licensing, public domain and the digital era. **4.01**

Economic Rationale

Copyright fits nicely into the classic social contract theory of IP as discussed in Chapter 2; unsurprisingly, it constructs a right to copy. As an incentive to innovate, copyright provides creators with a temporary legal monopoly over their creations. Society (consumers) may pay higher prices during this legal monopoly. In the long term, this content may stimulate further creation and, once it falls into the public domain, may be freely used. Copyright exists to provide incentives for continued innovation and creation. Yet further analysis suggests that this is not the case in practice. Creators may not respond to these incentives and assertions of copyright may impinge innovation elsewhere. **4.02**

[1] In a serendipitous moment, an anonymous Facebook friend posted this while the author (Searle) was working on this chapter.

4.03 Alternately, copyright can be construed as a given right over the fruits of creation. Considering the role of self-expression in the creation of copyrighted content, creators may have motivations other than remuneration. Thus, copyright recognizes the creation as being intrinsically the property of the creator. In contrast, as the quote at the start of this chapter suggests, many argue copyright has no place in the modern economy. Instead creations should not be controlled by the creators and should be freely shared.

4.04 Recent technological developments have brought these contrasting views of copyright into conflict. The creative destruction brought about by disruptive technologies in the digital era has wrought havoc on the traditional structure of copyright-dominated industries at the same time as it has spawned new industries, new structures, and economic growth. The turmoil experienced in this transition period has placed existing copyright structures under strain. In these debates, copyright is alternatively framed as an anchor to steady the tilting ships of the creative industries or an albatross around the neck of development and creation. Anchor or albatross, copyright may need reform.

The Creative Industries

4.05 Economic analysis of copyright necessarily includes consideration of the sectors most impacted by copyright. The current term for these sectors is the creative industries although similar terms such as the copyright industries, the cultural industries, and the creative and cultural industries are also common. The creative industries have various definitions but in general include: arts, crafts, design, fashion, film, video, photography, computer games, music, visual and performing arts, publishing, television, and radio. Other sectors that may be included are toys, gastronomy, architecture, antiques, and advertising. Additionally, the definition of these sectors also varies as, for example, defining what constitutes 'design' is a challenge.

4.06 A common theme amongst the creative industries is that of the reliance on copyright as a key means to assert rights over content. In addition, the creative industries have seven key economic attributes (Caves, 2000) which distinguish them from other industries, as noted below.

4.07 Unique attributes of the creative industries are:

1. *Ars longa*—The market duration of some creative content is sufficiently durable that copyright protection may allow for the collection of economic rents.
2. Art for art's sake—Creators may be intrinsically motivated to create instead of being financially motivated (the starving artist).
3. A list/B list—Creative industries are a hits-driven business where the winner takes all. A small differentiation in talent may translate to a large differentiation in rewards.

4. Infinite variety—Creative content is unique and allows for significant differentiation. (This attribute also lends itself to the kind of originality required to achieve copyright status.)
5. Nobody knows principle—Demand for creative content and services is very uncertain and consumer reaction to content cannot be predicted.
6. Motley crew principle—The production of some creative content requires a wide variety of specialist skills.
7. Time flies—In the development of complex content, time can be costly.

Ars longa directly refers to copyright and the appropriation of the returns to innovation. However, other unique attributes of the creative industries are key to the economic analysis of copyright. If art for art's sake dominates the incentives to innovate in the creative industries, then the incentive impact of copyright is questionable. A list/B list, which is discussed in more detail later, suggests that rather than rewarding and thus incentivizing the many, copyright may only reward a few. Infinite variety reinforces the wide scope of copyrightable content in that the potential for unique content is infinite.[2] **4.08**

The unique aspects of the creative industries are reflected in the unique characteristics of copyright. As this chapter will further develop, economic analysis, empirical evidence, licensing practices, limitation, and technological development interact with copyright in unusual ways. **4.09**

Empirical Evidence

Empirical evidence in copyright is notoriously difficult. Unlike registered rights, where official registers collect a wealth of information and thresholds of inventiveness are assessed, copyright instead exists as an unregistered, amorphous right. Economics has traditionally been poorly equipped to address difficult to measure concepts like copyright. While the era of digital capture and big data may change this, significant advancements are required until empirical analysis of copyright matches that of other IPRs. **4.10**

As noted in Chapter 2, the overall economic impact of IP is difficult to measure. Much of the data in copyright industries is privately held, potentially confidential business information such as royalty rates, sales, licensing income, and related data. The wide scope of copyright also makes it difficult to compare rights. While this is true in the case of patents and trade marks, claims and classes delineate these rights. In comparison, the amorphous nature of copyright provides even less guidance to answer the question, 'How big is a copyright?' **4.11**

[2] The remaining three unique attributes of the creative industries are also relevant but less important and are therefore not addressed in detail here.

4.12 This lack of either access to, or unavailability of, data leaves economic analysis with only theoretical arguments to examine important concepts such as incentives to innovate, cumulative innovation, and the role of copyright in development.[3] As a result, much of the debate on the economic role of copyright is supported by anecdotes, case studies, and surveys. However, as noted in Chapter 1, economists view these methods as insufficiently objective to provide robust conclusions.

Examples

4.13 Recent empirical analysis has focused on incomes and Gross Value Added (GVA) of the creative industries. The data found in incomes can be used to analyse the salaries of creators and reflect the A list/B list nature of these industries. The data confirms the reality that the financial rewards stemming from copyright are concentrated in the few while the vast majority of creators earn very little. The following figures highlight the starkly skewed distribution of incomes:

> The top 10% of literary authors earn about 60–70% of total income in the sector.
>
> The top 10% of composers/songwriters earn about 80% of total income in the sector.[4]

4.14 This compares to the total population of employees where top 10% of earners earn about 20% of total income. The results are not surprising. The creative industries are hits-driven and similar distributions are observed in the distribution of estimated trade mark and patent values. However, this distribution of income implies that the economic success of copyright is only realized by a minority. Yet trade marks and patents have other strategic values (cross-licensing, branding) which copyright does not afford. Does copyright provide sufficient incentive to innovate if the rewards are concentrated in the few? It also implies that changes to copyright law are likely to affect the few rather than the many. Changes in the copyright term, as discussed later, affect the top portion of income earners disproportionately. Analysis based on income only does not capture the decision-making process of creators. A complete economic analysis would include better empirical evidence of the incentive role of copyright.

---

[3] Copyright in economic development is a nascent area of research (see Sundara Rajan, M. (2012). 'At the Frontiers of Law-making: Copyright and the Protection of Culture in India' *World Intellectual Property Organisation Journal* 4: 111–20, as an example). Given the global dominance of creative content stemming from developed countries, the economic impact on developing countries is unclear. Again, the A list/B list, hits-driven nature of the creative industries contributes to this dominance.

[4] Figures from Kretschmer, M., Derclaye, E., Favale, M., and Watt, R. (2010). The Relationship Between Copyright and Contract Law: A Review commissioned by the UK Strategic Advisory Board for Intellectual Property Policy (SABIP), 2010. Available at: http://ssrn.com/abstract=2624945.

Another approach to the analysis of copyright is the macroeconomic analysis of GVA. GVA measures the contribution of a sector to the economy. GVA forms part of the estimation of whole economies known as Gross Domestic Product (GDP). One of the challenges of measuring the creative industries is that they do not map well to the traditional measurements supported by Standard Industrial Classification (SIC) system of classifying industries. SIC codes are commonly used to measure the size of parts of the economy; however SIC is ill-equipped to identify and measure industries as diverse as the creative industries. From an industrial perspective, computer games have very little to do with painting. Thus, the creative industries do not have a unique SIC. **4.15**

Work by the UK's National Endowment for Science, Technology and Arts (NESTA) highlights the challenges associated with SIC: **4.16**

> For example, lacking its own SIC code, the value of Fashion Design in the UK is estimated as 0.5% of 'Clothing Manufacture' and 5.8% of 'Specialised Design Activities'. Improving these weights requires detailed modelling for each industry, which has not been undertaken. There are also concerns that the value added generated by very small creative businesses and sole practitioners is under-estimated. For example, the reason given by DCMS for the absence of value added data for Crafts is that the 'majority of businesses (are) too small to be picked up in business surveys'. (Bakhshi et al., 2013)

To address the challenges of measuring[5] the contribution of the creative industries, as detailed in DCMS (2015) a three-step methodology constructs a GVA for the United Kingdom: 'First, a set of occupations are identified as creative. Second, the creative intensity is calculated for all industries in the economy. Third, all industries with a creative intensity above a certain "threshold" are classified as Creative Industries.' This methodology allows for estimates of key figures such as employment and exports. The figures reported in 2015 suggest, 'GVA of the Creative Industries was £76.9bn in 2013 and accounted for 5.0 per cent of the UK Economy.' **4.17**

Readers should be wary of large, headline figures associated with the measurement of the impact of industries (not just the creative industries). This wariness stems primarily from two main concerns: the methodologies themselves and manipulability. For example, UK Music, in conjunction with the Office of National Statistics (ONS), using a wide definition, calculated the GVA of the music industry at £3.5bn for 2012 (UK Music. (2013). 'The Economic Contribution of the Core UK Music **4.18**

[5] It is worth noting that different institutions use different methods for creating these estimates. WIPO, for example, uses a slightly different model as detailed in Gantchev, D. (2004). 'The WIPO Guide on Surveying the Economic Contribution of the Copyright Industries' *Review of Economic Research on Copyright Issues* 1: 5–15.

Industry'); the Arts Council used the same ONS data source (national accounts) but a narrower, SIC-based definition to estimate a value of £0.9bn in 2010 (Arts Council. (2013). 'The Contribution of the Arts and Culture'). The DCMS methodology is well regarded, as is the WIPO methodology, noted in footnote 5. However, given the challenges discussed earlier, these methodologies may suffer in practice. Additionally, figures provided by vested interests can be suspect as methodologies and application can be manipulated and figures massaged. Furthermore, estimates are only as good as the data used. When in doubt, it may be worth asking a friendly economist to critique figures and methodologies.

4.19 This section has discussed methods to empirically analyse sectors dominating the copyright arena. The general conclusion is that data is scarce and measurement methods require further development. In the absence of better data and methods, the analysis relies on surveys and individual case studies. While this data may be subjective, it potentially sheds light on areas otherwise unexamined. However, the question remains whether flawed evidence is better than none.

Licensing: Collecting Societies, Copyright Tribunals, Public Domain, and Territoriality

4.20 The licensing of copyright, and, in fact, any IP, is a common way of generating revenue. It allows for owners of copyrighted content to earn by licensing the content to others. The individual creator may have limited capacity to market, distribute, and sell their content; licensing to others facilitates transactions throughout markets and can widen the market reach.

4.21 Licensing allows for movement of copyrighted goods throughout the supply chain. Vertical integration, in which a firm owns the entire supply chain, from content creation to retail outlets, may not be feasible in the creative industries. The alternative, horizontal integration where the firm acquires inputs along the same point of the supply chain, is a common model. Yet the vertical model of record labels is falling out of fashion as the horizontal model of online distribution platforms such as iTunes gains market share. In both of these structures, the licensing of copyrighted materials allows for their distribution throughout the supply chain.

4.22 Licensing copyrighted content is important for generating value from copyright and encouraging the diffusion of innovation. A single creative work may encompass many copyrights as, for example, a recorded musical performance will encompass performance, recording, mechanical, and other rights all in the domain of copyright. Licensing practices in areas such as music are well-established (see Passman (2009) for details) and the chapters on valuation will cover practices of licensing.

This section focuses on market failures in licensing and the policy solutions of collecting societies and public domain, and the European Single Market as an application of territoriality concerns.

Collecting societies

The number of copyrighted works is very large and the possibilities for new works are seemingly endless (infinite variety). The result is that there are many creators producing many creative works on the supply side. On the demand side, the use of creative works is ubiquitous as images, decorations, and music are consumed *en masse*. This demand is spread across many consumers and uses. **4.23**

It is difficult to imagine how the many consumers of copyrighted goods could contract with the many creators of these goods. It is unlikely that a hairdresser in rural South Wales would find it practical to license a work directly from global pop star Beyoncé. Likewise, it is hard to imagine Beyoncé attempting to enforce her copyrights in said hairdresser's premises. The benefit in both situations is massively outweighed by the costs. The transaction costs are simply too high to make these interactions practical or efficient. This is an example of a market failure. **4.24**

Collecting societies, or copyright collectives, serve as an intermediary to solve the market failure problem in copyright industries. By representing many creators, collecting societies achieve an economy of scale which reduces the per transaction cost sufficiently that the benefits of licensing outweigh the costs. Instead of attempting to license directly with each creator, licensees need only interact with these larger organizations. Creators outsource their licensing, royalty collection, and enforcement to these organizations. Both the supply and demand sides of the market benefit. **4.25**

Internationally, collecting societies have agreements in place that subcontract their activities in other countries. For example, a British collecting society may have an agreement with a West Indies collecting society as it is unlikely to be cost effective for either society to operate independently in both countries. **4.26**

Given the tremendous power of economies of scale in licensing markets for copyrighted goods, collecting societies are considered natural monopolies. As Drexl (2007) finds, some countries have policies which provide legal monopolies for collecting societies and in countries which have not provided this legal protection, natural monopolies have developed. **4.27**

In addition to their licensing-focused duties, collecting societies have a wider remit that includes lobbying. Towse and Handke (2007) argue that the societies also function as 'authors' trade unions, as instruments of cultural policy and as a form of social insurance.' These wider activities, in addition to the social value associated **4.28** with cultural activities and the creative industries, mean that collecting societies wield a strong lobbying power.

4.29 Given the breadth of activities performed by a collecting society, the breadth of their repertoire is also of interest. In countries such as the United Kingdom, each collecting society will represent a particular sector and right. In music, the United Kingdom has both Phonographic Performance Limited (PPL) and PRS for Music as societies. In the visual arts, organizations like the Design and Artists Copyright Society (DACS) represent artists. In other countries, such as Brazil (as discussed in Page and Gandelman, 2010), a supra-collecting society is an umbrella organization for a myriad of collecting societies representing the various creative industries. In smaller countries or countries where collecting societies are relatively new, a single collecting society may represent all the creative industries.

4.30 There are pros and cons to variations of collecting society structures. A single collecting society may benefit from economies of scale; however its diverse members will have differing interests. The representation of multiple sectors of the creative industries presents problems as authors and performers of the same piece will be under the same organization. Additionally, a single society may find itself representing both licensees and licensors if, for example, it represents both music and films licensing said music. However, a structure with multiple societies, akin to a hegemonic structure, means that consumers of copyrighted goods may have to license from multiple societies. Yet the hegemonic structure is probably better suited to the lobbying and union functions of collecting societies as its members are more homogenous.

4.31 The future of collecting societies is unclear. As with nearly all industries, the digital age has dramatically transformed the market conditions in which collecting societies function. Thus far, the impact has predominately focused on the demand side as consumers have shifted away from purchasing physical copies of copyrighted goods and instead are consuming, and not always paying for, digital copies. The market is also undergoing significant business model innovation as content consumption shifts from purchase to renting and streaming (Searle, 2011). The response of the collecting societies and the sectors they represent to these new conditions has been a mix of lobbying to strengthen copyright and enforcement policy, enforcement itself, and technical protection measures. The market does not yet appear to have reached equilibrium.

4.32 Collecting societies may also face a transformation in their function as an intermediary between the supply and demand sides of the market. In general, the internet reduces transaction costs, increases information, and lowers barriers to entry. As Porter (2001) argues, 'The Internet provides a channel for suppliers to reach end users, reducing the leverage of intervening companies.' In the United Kingdom, an initiative called the Copyright Hub[6] seeks to create an online one-stop-shop for identifying rights holders and licensing content. While the Hub and similar initiatives are in their infancy, it is likely that the challenges to success will be dependent on the political, legal, and economic forces as their technical success is theoretically straightforward. Collecting societies, as intermediaries, face a future where their bargaining power changes and their natural monopolies may erode. Continued innovation suggests a future in which these organizations will face disruptive technologies, which could ultimately affect creators.

Copyright tribunals

The monopoly like nature of IPR implies that the price for a copyrighted good is likely to be above the economically efficient price under perfect competition.[7] Therefore, there is a deadweight loss of transactions that would have occurred in perfect competition but do not under the monopoly conditions. The monopoly status of collecting societies suggest that, like all monopolies, collecting societies will set prices to maximize revenue.[8] As such, the societies may not have incentives to negotiate individual licences and this may increase the size of the deadweight loss. **4.33**

To counteract the negative implications of monopoly power and the strong bargaining positions of collecting societies, low-cost tribunals exist in some jurisdictions specifically to address conflicts. Watt (2010) puts it succinctly: 'The ensuing monopoly power [of collective management and blanket licenses] is often seen to be detrimental to social efficiency, and so in exchange for allowing the collective to form and operate, the price at which it grants access to its repertory is regulated.' For example, in the United Kingdom, the Intellectual Property Office (IPO) operates a copyright tribunal to settle disputes with collecting societies. Cases brought before the tribunal typically cover disputes over royalties and the tribunal members determine the terms of the licence. **4.34**

In tribunal cases, parties may provide evidence to further their case. Economic and valuation evidence used in disputes will engage with a variety of techniques (as discussed in Chapters 2 and 11, the economic research and valuation sections of this book). Watt (2010) also argues that it is not simply the valuation, but the equitable sharing of this value to each party. It is important to note that the definition of evidence used in litigious contexts differs from that of the economic definition of evidence. For example, expert testimony would count as **4.35**

---

[6] The Copyright Hub. Available at: http://www.copyrighthub.co.uk.

[7] As discussed in the introduction, the flaw with perfect competition is that it does not exist. Furthermore, the infinite variety of creative works complicates the pricing of works; see Section 4.

[8] To add to this, economies of scale dictate that collecting societies will typically have standard licensing royalty rates, and terms and conditions.

evidence in court but would largely be considered anecdotal in economic analysis. Nonetheless, copyright tribunals must determine the appropriate licensing fee to resolve the dispute.

Limits to Copyright: Public Domain and Exceptions

4.36 Copyright exists to construct property over intangible goods. In essence, copyright carves rights out of what would otherwise be public domain. This is the flip side of copyright—that which is not under copyright. This includes expired copyrights, ideas, and significant parts of cultural heritage.[9] Precise definitions vary as public domain could also be construed to include materials freely available for use, such as those licensed for use under creative commons.

4.37 Under economic theory, IP exists to incentivize innovation. Yet the expiration of IPR and its release into the public domain of IP is an important part of the innovation ecosystem. However, as with other areas of IP, such as expired patents for antibiotics, there exist concerns over custodianship. If copyright does not exist over a particular piece of content, what incentives exist to make it available? What value does this have to the economy? Finally, it is worth considering that copyright must also strike a balance between protecting existing rights holders and providing sufficient flexibility to allow for further innovation.

4.38 The breadth of the public domain is immense. It largely includes works where copyright has expired or works captured by copyright exceptions. Shakespeare, Dante, and, a more recent addition, Sherlock Holmes are key works within the public domain and maintain their tremendous cultural value. Cultural and creative content is seeped with a mix of public domain and copyrighted works.

4.39 Public domain content can generate value in new, creative works building on the public domain. As Lantagne (2014) notes, a recent BBC series re-imagining Sherlock Holmes has re-invigorated the character and increased sales of the copyrighted and public domain original works. She notes, 'After the airing of the AU [Alternate Universe] fanfic *Sherlock*, sales of the original Sherlock Holmes stories increased 180%. Nor did it harm "Elementary" or Robert Downey, Jr.'s Sherlock Holmes movies.... Many of the fans of these works are old Sherlock Holmes devotees, but many others are new to Sherlock Holmes, introduced by these new fanworks that they are enjoying.'[10]

---

[9] Some parts of cultural expressions may be protected under other rights such as Traditional Knowledge or Traditional Cultural Expressions.

[10] Lantange, S. (2015). 'Sherlock Holmes and the Case of the Lucrative Fandom: Recognizing the Economic Power of Fanworks and Reimagining Fair Use in Copyright' *Mich. Telecomm. & Tech. L. Rev.* 21: 263.

4.40 A challenge to calculating the economic relevance of public domain creative goods is that they are subject to the same challenges associated with the valuation of creative and intangible goods. As Caves (2000) argues, the creative industries are characterized by an A list/B list distribution in which the winner takes all. This is further confirmed by the network effect of the consumption of creative goods where the more people consume a good, the more valuable it is. That is, the more people watch a particular television show, the more people can discuss the show and the more utility these viewers enjoy from the show. Essentially, we as consumers collectively select winners who take all. The losers, B lists, also-rans of this world are simply not allocated much value. Thus, those public domain works still in use are the *crème-de-la-crème*. Like works still in copyright, public domain works will consist of a few works of high value and many works of low value.

Copyright expiration

4.41 An additional consideration of public domain content is the removal of content from the public domain. New content is granted copyright on inception. However, old content sometimes returns to copyrighted status. An example of this is the extension of copyright term for recordings in the European Union (EU) in 2008. On one side of the debate, the argument is that the incentive to innovate had served its purpose and should not be revisited. This suggests retroactive copyright extension is a violation of the social contract. On the other, there is the argument that recorded performances should receive the same protection as other forms of copyrighted materials.

4.42 From the social contract perspective, Masnick (2008) notes, 'Copyright was a bargain between the public and content creators: if we grant you a monopoly on this content for a certain number of years, you'll create that content. There is no excuse to go back at a later date and change the terms of the deal. Clearly, it was enough to get the content created at the time. The musicians accepted the deal. To go back later and extend it for another 45 years is simply taking that content out of the hands of the public who made the deal on the other side.'

4.43 On the flip side, the argument that fairness to performers is the primary issue came from Internal Market Commissioner, Charlie McCreevy. He noted (Commission, 2008), 'I strongly believe that copyright protection for Europe's performers represents a moral right to control the use of their work and earn a living from their performances. I have not seen a convincing reason why a composer of music should benefit from a term of copyright which extends to the composer's life and 70 years beyond, while the performer should only enjoy 50 years, often not even covering his lifetime.'

4.44 Alongside copyright is an additional right denoted 'moral rights'. Moral rights in most jurisdictions cannot be licensed or sold (although they can be waived) and may last beyond the term of copyright. Instead of being a property right, moral rights grant creators the right to attribution and some control over the destiny of their creations. For example, moral rights may allow the filmmaker to prevent the colourization of a black and white film, even if the filmmaker no longer owns the copyrights of the film. Moral rights are inherently personal and exist not to provide economic power, but control over reputation. However, moral rights can interact with economic rights when moral rights are used to block the use of other rights, as in the example of the film.

4.45 Evidence-based approaches to copyright policy are poorly equipped to address questions based solely on morality or fairness. While economics can inform these debates and provide evidence to inform solutions, it is not a morality system in itself. As Krugman (2011) notes, '... economics is not a morality play; the social and economic order we have doesn't represent the playing out of some kind of deep moral principles.' Instead, economics is a tool to analyse different options but does not, by itself, provide principles to weigh outcomes.

Licensing, limitations, and exceptions

4.46 A second important consideration of public domain is exceptions and exemptions to copyright.[11] If copyright is carved of our public domain, exceptions are pieces of public domain carved out again of copyright. Exceptions seek to provide sufficient room for innovation without unduly hampering existing right's holder ability to appropriate the returns from their innovation. Limitations and exceptions such as the private right of copying, derivative works,[12] research, quotations, and others provide this flexibility. In the absence of these exceptions, users of copyright would require licences for each instance of these permitted acts.

Private right of copying, format shifting, and time shifting

4.47 The right of individuals to make copies of copyrighted content they have purchased, such as creating a copy of a CD for private use, is commonly seen in law.

[11] As noted by Strowel, A. and Dussolier, S. Workshop on Implementation Issues of the WIPO Copyright Treaty (WCT) and the WIPO Performances and Phonograms Treaty (WPPT): Legal Protection of Technological Systems. WCT-WPPT/IMP/2. Geneva: WIPO, 1999. Available at: http://www. wipo. int/edocs/mdocs/copyright/en/wc t wpptimp/wet wppt imp 2. Doc (accessed 31 March 2010), different legal systems use different terms for limitations and exceptions in copyright. 'The term "exception" is not to be found in all legal systems.... But the same concept has another name in other countries. For example, the word "limit" is used in Germany and Spain, while the similar term "limitations" is used in Sweden, Greece and the United States. Switzerland refers to "restrictions", while the United Kingdom uses "authorized acts" and Portugal "free use".'

[12] 'A derivative work is a work based on or derived from one or more already existing works' (an underlying work). United States Copyright Office (2013). 'Copyright in Derivative Works and Compilations'. Available at http://www.copyright.gov/circ14.pdf. Use of a derivative work may require licensing of rights associated with the underlying work.

In the United States, this practice falls under fair use. The economic justification argues that restricting individuals' right to copy would unduly reward copyright owners and that the price of a copyrighted good implicitly includes this right. These are hotly debated, but generally the domestic consumers of a copyrighted good will, rightly or wrongly, assume that the price includes the ability to make some copies. Landes and Posner (1989) argue that lack of a private copying exception encourages a situation in which firms benefit disproportionately, as they put it, 'the deadweight costs of allowing a firm to appropriate what has become an industry standard [outweigh the] disincentive effects on originators if such appropriation is forbidden'.

Limiting the copying of books, films, and music for private use would require enforcement efforts that are impractical, prohibitively costly, and/or potentially violate principles of privacy. How could copyright owners monitor the use of a copying device such as a domestic scanner in a cost-effective manner that would not invade the privacy of the owner of the scanner? The development of Technical Protection Measures (TPM) or Digital Rights Management (DRM) has made some of this monitoring possible but has proven unpopular with consumers for privacy, security, and flexibility reasons. The private right of copying both addresses the impracticality of enforcing the unenforceable and brings the law in line with practice. **4.48**

Similar exceptions[13] include the right to format shift. This occurs when consumers copy to move from one media format to another; for example, from CD to MP3. In the absence of the legal ability to format shift, consumers would be forced to re-purchase content as technology evolves. This situation would unduly reward copyright owners, as they would be able to charge prices for the new format well above the marginal costs of shifting the content to the new format. In practice, in the music industry, the cost to the consumer of porting from vinyl to CD was relatively high and resulted in reduced quality. However, the shift from CD to MP3 file comes at a minimal cost and stable quality for the consumer. Indeed, the introduction of the CD significantly increased music sales; this increase has not been repeated with the introduction of subsequent digital formats.[14] **4.49**

Time shifting has emerged as a topic of debate as technology develops. The ease with which consumers can record broadcasted content to watch at a later time has improved. The ability to programme a VCR (videocassette recorder) was long a running joke as programming the recording of a particular broadcast was more of an art **4.50**

[13] For developments in UK copyright exceptions, see the Copyright and Rights in Performances (Quotation and Parody) Regulations 2014, SI 2014/2356. This regulation was subject to Judicial Review in 2015 and parts of it have been quashed.

[14] See Degusta, M. (2011). 'The *Real* Death of the Music Industry' *Business Insider*. Available at: http://www.businessinsider.com/these-charts-explain-the-real-death-of-the-music-industry-

than a science.[15] Modern technologies have made this recording much simpler. In time shifting, consumers must create a copy of the content, thus the time shifting exception enables the legal copying of content in these circumstances. However, many concerns about time shifting are outdated; the introduction of catch-up and streaming services[16] (business models in which content is delivered on-demand as opposed to as a scheduled broadcast) has negated consumers' need to time shift.

Derivative works

4.51 The role of copyright in incentivizing innovation also applies to cumulative innovation. Cumulative innovation encapsulates innovations and new works that build on the existing body of works. It can vary from interpreting folklore, sampling portions of music and translation, to the re-use of entire works. The transformativeness, the degree to which a derivative work transforms existing works, maps nicely to the economic concepts of cumulative innovation and the inventive step. The creation of new works that derive content from existing works encompasses a range of innovative steps; however some of this work may fall afoul of copyright laws.

4.52 The classic example of derivative works is Duchamp's L.H.O.O.Q. (1919) painting, which consists of Da Vinci's Mona Lisa painting with the addition of a moustache. A more modern example would be Kristleifur Björnsson's series 'My Girlfriend Natalie' (2002) in which the artist takes photos from the internet of the actress Natalie Portman, prints them on A4-sized paper and assembles them as large prints. The credit of the work is noted as, 'All images used are of Natalie Portman and found on the Internet. Photographers unnamed. Courtesy of the internet.'[17] In both cases, public debate questioned the transformativeness of the works. These works, and the controversy surrounding them, suggest that copyright law may not always be aligned with creative practices.

4.53 Leaving aside any moral rights and consumer confusion concerns, the net economic impact of derivative works consists of the benefits of the new works, both to creators and consumers, weighed against the potential costs to owners of the rights associated with the original works. The benefits to consumers and creators are fairly straightforward: greater variety for consumers and revenue streaming from new

---

2011-2 for an analysis of the relationship between formats and changes in music sales. The author argues that the shift from vinyl to CD increased sales but the ease of copying from CD to digital did not have the same positive effect. He also notes the shift from the purchase of albums to single tracks as a cause of decreasing music revenues.

[15] Your authors remember a number of childhood instances in which small mistakes in programming meant missing final episodes of favourite television shows. Oh the disappointment of never knowing whodunit!

[16] This topic could warrant its own book as the different business models and legal machinations associated with streaming, downloading, and time shifting are seemingly endless.

[17] From the artist's website, at http://www.kristleifur.com/works/my_girlfriend.html (accessed 28 January 2015).

works for creators.[18] The potential costs to the owners of the original works are less straightforward. The new works may have no impact on sales of existing works; equally, the derivative works may serve as substitutes for existing works and cannibalize sales, or complements for existing works and increase sales. Thus, while the benefits of derivative works are relatively clear, the costs are decidedly unclear.

Parodies present an excellent case where the parody, as a derivative work, provides new content for consumers and potential revenue for creators of the parody, but the impact on the original work is unclear. In general, consumer confusion between the parody and the original may be minimal, and the parody itself may not be directed at the original work. The parody exception allows makers of parodies the right to creative these derivative works without obtaining licences from the owners of the original works. **4.54**

An amusing example of parody is that of the 2010 music video, 'Newport (Ymerodraeth State of Mind)' which was a parody of the Jay-Z and Alicia Keys 2009 song, 'Empire State of Mind'. The Newport version used the original song to poke fun at the city of Newport. Due to a lack of copyright exemptions for parody, the Newport version was removed[19] from online platforms at the request of the rights holders of 'Empire State of Mind'. The makers of the Newport version were unsuccessful in obtaining a licence from the owners of the original content. It is unlikely that the Newport version negatively impacted the revenues for the original version, as it would be difficult to describe the two versions as substitutes. The irony is that the main offices of the UK IPO, responsible for copyright policy in the United Kingdom, are located in Newport. The United Kingdom introduced parody exemptions in the Copyright and Rights in Performances (Quotation and Parody) Regulations of 2014. **4.55**

A related concept is that of orphan works. Orphan irks are copyrights with no identifiable or contactable owner. When a work is orphaned, it becomes essentially unusable and therefore its economic benefits are curtailed. An orphan works exception allows for the use of orphan works with provisions for reasonable royalty in the event the rights holder is identified. **4.56**

Research exceptions

Licensing concerns also apply to educational and research activities. Again, the licensing of each copyright for use in education is prohibitively resource-intensive. Likewise, non-commercial research would also struggle to copyright works in the event individual licences were required. In some cases, such as libraries, copyrighted content is sold with rights to photocopy or publicly lend. **4.57**

---

[18] This over-simplifies the benefits to the economy, as it does not consider competition considerations, non-monetary benefits in cultural expressions, the overall impact of innovation, and related concepts.

[19] See Kiss, J. (2010). 'Newport State of Mind: Songwriters Pulled the Video from YouTube' *The Guardian*.

4.58 An emerging concern, spurred by technological advances, is that of data[20] and text mining. The ability to create computer programs that assemble data across many sources has only recently become possible and has great potential. In medicine, the practice of meta-analysis involves the analysis and compilation of multiple sources to gather further insights. For example, examining 200 research projects on diabetes may provide insights not identified in individual projects. In many cases, this data is expressed in journal articles or other copyright-protected materials. Licensing each and every article used in data mining would be prohibitively expensive. A data and text mining exception enables data mining without incurring these licensing costs.

4.59 Ultimately, copyright and public domain co-exist in a duality. They are interconnected and complementary as without one, the other does not exist. Policy debates on public domain typically focus on the boundaries between the two and the exceptions. The copyright discussion outlined here easily extends to patents (Chapter 3), trade marks (Chapter 5) and other rights.

Embracing Digital: Copyright Challenges in the Digital Era

4.60 The advent of the digital era has thrown copyright law and practices, developed in a pre-digital era, into question. The distribution of copyrighted content and the ability to copy have dramatically changed. On the one hand, the digital era introduces technology that transforms means of production, distribution, and business models, and changes bargaining powers; on the other hand, the digital era is incredibly disruptive for industry structures and business models dependent on pre-digital constraints. This section details changes in the market structure and business models of the creative industries affected by the digital era.

4.61 The transition from analogue formats to digital has not been an easy one for most of the creative industries. In many cases the transition has meant increased competition and decreased prices. In sectors such as film, music, and computer games, physical and digital copies are near perfect substitutes and are affecting profits. In other cases, such as crafts, the ability to sell online has both increased the potential market reach of individual firms but also increased competition between firms. An analysis of copyright is incomplete without consideration of the massive, recent changes in copyright-dominated markets. This section analyses the impact of digital on the creative industries using business models and Porter's Five Forces as analytical techniques.

[20] Data mining has many different meanings but in this case is used to indicate the scraping of various sources to assemble data for research purposes. The works are mined but not explicitly reproduced.

Changing business models

A business model 'describes the rationale and infrastructure of how an organization creates, delivers and captures value' (Osterwalder et al., 2009). It is a broad term to describe how a firm structures its business and brings together revenue flows, strategy, and firm organization.[21] The evolution of business models in the creative industries demonstrates the threats and opportunities the digital era brings. **4.62**

Prior to the digital era, the physical restrictions of the creative content provided a key means for firms to control and profit from their goods and services. Vinyl records, for example, were relatively easy to trace from production, distribution, and retailing. In physical, analogue products, such as books, the high fixed costs of producing a book could be recaptured via sales in part because the marginal cost, the cost of printing each additional book, was relatively high. As economics argues price tends towards marginal cost, the total revenue from sales allowed for profit. The business models of the creative industries, based on combinations of production of content, bundling into packages, manufacturing of copies (physical goods), and sales through retail outlets, was based on physical goods. Copyright enforcement was bolstered by the control of these goods and the relatively high costs of copying. **4.63**

Readers may note that the last paragraph was written in the past tense. The digital era has dramatically decreased the marginal cost of production. While the costs of production of the first book, film, or computer game remains essentially the same; the marginal cost of making digital copies of this content is virtually zero. As economic analysis predicts, this new balance is putting a downward pressure on sales. Copyright enforcement in the world where the very essence of the right—the right to prevent copies—is confronted by the incredibly low cost of copying, becomes very difficult. It is, therefore, no surprise that business models based on physical control of content are heavily impacted. **4.64**

The impact of the digital era goes beyond the question of copying. Bundling, the practice of selling multiple goods in a single package, formed a common component of pre-digital business models. Book chapters, music tracks, television episodes, single photographs, and video clips were sold as bundles in books, albums, DVD sets, coffee table books, and complete films, respectively. Consumer demand for the individual chapters, etc. was unmet as the individual components of this content could only be purchased in bundles. For firms, this allowed them to sell less popular content together with more popular content. The cost of selling the single unit was **4.65**

[21] The term 'business model' is relatively new but the fundamental concept is not. See Searle, N. (2011). 'Changing Business Models in the Creative Industries: The Cases of Television, Computer Games and Music' *UK Intellectual Property Office*, available at: https://www.gov.uk/government/publications/changing-business-models-in-the-creative-industries, for further discussion.

relatively high as the cost[22] of, for example, a DVD remained the same for a single television episode as it was for a complete series. However, the price a firm could charge for a single was significantly lower than the bundled version. The unmet consumer demand for singles was finally met when selling singles in digital versions became economical. However, as a consequence, the firm's ability to bundle goods has decreased. Again, the digital era has challenged the reliance of business models in creative industries on physical products. Instead, the production and sale of content must now contend with smaller, individual units of contents.

4.66 As a result of these changes, the creative industry is innovating its business models. For example, subscription services, in which users pay fixed fees (e.g. monthly) to access goods or services, are becoming more popular. This has commonly been found in the newspaper and television (paid-for cable) sectors but has spread to music (e.g. online streaming services) and film (e.g. online streaming or rental services). Profit centres may shift from the sale of goods to the sale of related merchandise or live performances instead. An advantage of the digital era is that it is relatively cheap to develop new business models. The main disadvantage of the digital era is that it can impose the need to develop new models.

4.67 Yet the creative industries have long faced challenges from technological change. Gramophones and radio impacted the market for live music just as films impacted the live theatre industry. Indeed, the creative industries have repeatedly re-invented their business models to keep up with technological changes. This technological change is ongoing and it is likely that the business models of the creative industries will continue to change. With these changes, the role of copyright in incentivizing innovation may also change.

Porter's Five Forces

4.68 Moving from the level of the firm to the overall impact of the digital era, this section applies Porter's Five Forces. Developed in 1980, the five-forces model is based on an industrial organization approach to market structures. Simple but comprehensive, the framework breaks down the market in which a firm operates to five key forces as represented in Figure 4.1.

4.69 The five forces can be applied to the creative industries in the following manner:

1. Industry rivalry: Competition and innovation are the hallmarks of industry rivalry. This encompasses the long-term, strategic behaviour of firms to gain competitive advantages via advertising, research and development, and, as introduced by the digital era, the competition between online and offline environments.

[22] The costs of creating the physical copy, transportation of the copy, the retail space required, and related costs is the same.

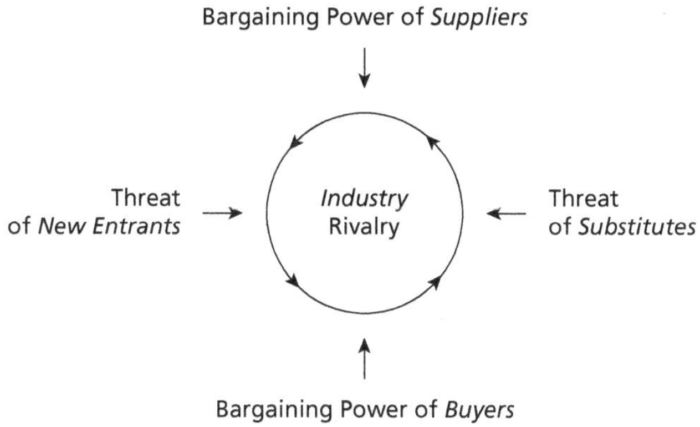

Figure 4-1 Porter's Five Forces[23]

The creative industries have long been characterized by continued innovation and advertising. As the creative industries are hits-driven (Caves, 2000), for every successful work there will be many unsuccessful, loss-making works. For example, only one in ten musicals turn a profit (economist.com, 2013), which is similar to the competitive market of venture capital.

Online retail outlets for creative content, either in e-commerce or digital media formats,[24] have heightened competition between players. Online retailers operate in a lower-cost, more flexible environment than their offline counterparts. These changing costs and new entrants have increased the overall level of competition in the market.

2. The threat of new market entrants: Barriers to new entry define the threat of entrants. If a market is profitable, it will attract new entrants resulting in increased competition. However, barriers to entry (high fixed costs, regulatory restrictions, customer loyalty, and other barriers) may make it difficult for others to enter the market. If these barriers change, then existing players in the market will face new competition.

   The digital era dramatically reduces the costs of creating, distributing, and selling creative content. The ability to distribute and sell online eliminates the need to have significant, up-front capital investment in bricks-and-mortar retail outlets. Digital also impacts existing players to use branding and customer loyalty to fend off new entrants as the digital retail environment changes the

[23] A diagram of Michael Porter's Five Forces based on an image from Porter M. E. (1985). *Competitive Advantage: Creating and Sustaining Superior Performance* (New York: Free Press) 5, image by Denis Fadeev, Wikimedia, available at: http://commons.wikimedia.org/wiki/File:Elements_of_Industry_Structure.svg, accessed 29 January 2015. Licence: CC-BY-SA.

[24] E-commerce denotes the online selling of items and can include physical products such as DVDs; references to digital sales and digital media refer to the sale of digital content (which is intangible).

marketing and advertising environment. For example, rather than browsing a bookstore and viewing the covers, packaging, and placement of many books, customers may either bypass 'storefronts' entirely by searching for a particular book or view the limited selection promoted by the online retail platform.

Perhaps the largest impact is that of dramatically lowering the cost of copying and distributing content. This trend of lowering costs is best illustrated by the evolution of the copying of music. The advent of cassettes allowed consumers and black market sellers to create unlicensed copies relatively cheaply compared to copying vinyl. Compact disks (CD) continued the trend of falling copying costs and MP3s brought the costs of copying to nearly zero. Likewise, while the quality of copied cassettes was markedly inferior to originals, copied CDs approached the quality of originals, and copied MP3s are nearly identical in quality to originals. As economic theory predicts, price equals marginal costs. As the marginal cost of creating a music file approached zero, the music industry suddenly found itself competing with a new entrant: free.

3. Bargaining power of buyers: In any market transaction, buyers and sellers will have various levels of power to influence and dominate terms of the transaction. Successful market transactions, such as the selling and purchase of a movie ticket, depend on a wider negotiation between buyers (consumers) and sellers (producers) as reflected in supply and demand curves. Changes that increase the bargaining power of buyers can exert a downward pressure on prices.

   The internet drastically increases the information available to consumers. Shoppers in bricks-and-mortar stores now have the ability to easily and rapidly check competitors' prices. Online price comparison sites allow consumers to identify the lowest cost provider. This dramatically reduces the information asymmetry, increases the ability for buyers to switch to alternative sellers, and increases the awareness of potential substitute products. Overall, the internet has shifted the balance of power in favour of buyers. For the creative industries, this means downward pressure on costs, decreased brand loyalty, and increased competition between suppliers.

4. The power of suppliers: In business-to-business transactions, the firm buying an input[25] is now a buyer facing the bargaining power of a supplier. The supplier will have strong bargaining power if, for example, there is little competition between suppliers or if the input is unique.

   Many inputs are required for the creative industries; this section focuses on two key inputs: talent (human resources) and Information and Communications Technologies (ICT). Human resources and a diverse array of talents are key inputs into the production of creative content (Caves, 2000). These inputs have changed as the need for programming and other specialist digital skills

[25] In this case, the word 'input' refers to the good being transacted in the business-to-business transaction. As the discussion here focuses on the firm's environment, the goods purchased are used as inputs to produce the outputs of the firm.

have become important. Demand for these specialist skills outside the creative industries has increased, thus increasing the bargaining power of this skilled labour. Additionally, the bargaining power of talent, for example, film stars and singers, has changed as this talent can now communicate more easily to their consumers (fan base) via social media enabled by the digital era. This may decrease the dependency of this talent on marketing by labels and film productions and thus increase the talent's bargaining power. At the time of writing, this does not appear to have had a significant impact on firms operating in the creative industries.

Other debates have ensued over the availability of music on subscription services. Claims that subscription services such as Spotify (a subscription-based, streaming service) and Apple Music (a similar service provided by Apple) provide insufficient remuneration to artists has prompted some high profile withdrawals of music. For example, the musician Taylor Swift removed all her content from Spotify in 2014 and temporarily a specific album from Apple Music in 2015.[26] This has not, however, appeared to impact these services greatly, but it does suggest that the bargaining power of artists and streaming services are in flux.

The ICT infrastructure is a key means of distribution of creative content to buyers. Without the internet, mobile phones, and online platforms, the creative industries would be unable to sell their digital content. However, the creative industries are typically not vertically integrated and do not own the downstream distribution channels. These channels are new entrants in the supply chain for creative industries and in many cases have strong bargaining power. For example, iTunes, owned by the computer company Apple, reportedly owned 74%[27] of the digital music market at the end of 2012. However, streaming services may become more important sales channels for digital content. In 2014, the bargaining power of Internet Service Providers (ISP) became apparent as Comcast, a large American ISP, began charging[28] Netflix, a large video, on-demand streaming service, for access to bandwidth.

Overall, it is difficult to identify the long-term impact of the digital era in terms of suppliers. The introduction of new suppliers will supplant existing suppliers (such as retail stores) but the bargaining power of these new suppliers is still evolving.

5. The threat of substitute products: The threat of new substitutes is related to that of competition and bargaining power of buyers. The more substitute services or

[26] Eamonn, F. (2015). 'Full Stream Ahead: Why Taylor Swift and AC/DC Aren't as Important to Spotify as You'd Think', *The Guardian*, 30 June 2104. Available at: http://www.theguardian.com/music/musicblog/2015/jun/30/taylor-swift-acdc-apple-music-launch-music-streaming.

[27] O'Grady, J. D. (2013). 'Report: iTunes Owns 74 Percent of the Digital Music Market' ZDNet. Available at: http://www.zdnet.com/article/report-itunes-owns-74-percent-of-the-digital-music-market/.

[28] Dignan, L. (2014). 'Netflix: Comcast is Charging Us for Access to Our Subscribers'. Available at: http://www.zdnet.com/article/netflix-comcast-is-charging-us-for-access-to-our-subscribers/.

goods in the market, the less power the firm has. Firms selling a unique product, such as petrol, face reduced competition from substitutes.[29] Firms selling products with lots of substitutes, such as sweets, chocolates, and cakes, instead face a very different market and may need to use strategies such as marketing and product differentiation to counteract this competition.

The internet and digital era has increased the availability of substitutes for creative goods. Consumers devote a budget, constrained by time and money, to creative goods and the internet has changed the availability and cost of these goods. For example, a typical consumer will have a certain entertainment budget in mind, which they will apply to their perceived substitutes. Listening to music, reading a book, playing a computer game, or watching a movie may all be substitutes. As prices for physical products are driven down through e-commerce and competition with digital products, books may become relatively cheaper for consumption. Likewise, movies can now be consumed in more substitute forms: in theatres, streamed online, downloaded online, on DVD, on premium television, and free television. Increased substitutes mean a downward pressure on prices.

Finally, the advent of digital media content has introduced a further, strong substitute: unpaid content. Whether unlicensed (copyright-infringing) content or given away (e.g. blogs), free is a strong substitute. For example, fashion magazines now have blogs and other social media to compete with. These online media are a fast and free substitute to waiting and paying for a print magazine. Free is a forceful substitute and challenges existing business models.

4.70 Porter's Five Forces provides a structured approach to the analysis of a market. This section has provided a very brief overview of the impact of the internet and digital technologies on the creative industries. These technologies are fast evolving and their impact fast changing. It is likely that any analysis becomes out of date from the moment it is written down. However, the trend of the past decades suggests that the internet and digital technologies will continue to impact the structure of the creative industries.

In context: Exceptions and territoriality in the EU digital single market

4.71 To reach the goal of EU economic integration, IP faces a complex path. While the concern for registered rights (trade marks, design rights, and patents) focuses mainly on harmonization and cooperation, debates over the European single market are largely focused on licensing practices in the digital content markets. Unlike analogue copyrighted content, digital copyrighted content does not enjoy the first-sale or exhaustion of rights principle. Instead, the sale of digital content is

[29] In the case of petrol, potential substitutes such as diesel, methane, and electricity have yet to be sufficiently adopted by consumers to be considered true substitutes.

enabled via licensing and is often geographically limited. This leads to a fragmented market marked by territoriality; in stark contrast to the goal of an integrated, single EU market.

Why do economists care about a single market? A single market offers greater capacity for economies of scale, reduced transaction costs, better flow of resources to their most productive use, and increased competition leading to lower prices. In short, for the economy as a whole, single, integrated markets can be more efficient. **4.72**

Yet there is often significant political and cultural resistance to greater integration between nations. National sentiments, and cultural and linguistic differences may lead to protectionist tendencies. A service provider in the United Kingdom may not be pleased with the prospect of the entrance of competitors from other countries. At the time of writing, there is a growing trend of anti-EU, and hence anti-integration, politics. **4.73**

The exploitation of differences in regulations between countries allows business to extract economic rents. The legal profession, for example, may extract rent[30] as the law limits competition between lawyers from different jurisdictions. In digital content, the ability to prevent residents from one state from consuming content from another, for example, a French resident watching digital content from the United Kingdom, is facilitated by legal structures. **4.74**

While economic integration is beneficial for the economy as a whole, the changes necessary to enable integration will inevitably come at the cost to some. Copyright is a particular sticking point. Mazziotti (2013) in his report on the findings of the task force on copyright in the EU digital single market, notes, 'Not surprisingly, the legal treatment of copyright exceptions at EU level was the most controversial subject in the whole work of the Task Force', with the private copying exception and online enforcement also being controversial. The development of the digital single market will require changes to copyright policy. Given the already controversial nature of copyright policy, the policy-making process may be a spectator sport. **4.75**

Conclusion

In the current atmosphere of turmoil in the creative industries, economics can provide some clarity. Like other IP rights, copyright has important incentives to innovation impacts on the creation of new content. Unlike other rights, copyright is very difficult to analyse empirically. However, income and macroeconomic **4.76**

[30] The legal profession may also extract rent from its self-regulation as a profession, as only approved professionals can lawfully charge clients, and from its involvement in lobbying and government.

impacts of industries reliant on copyright, largely the creative industries, reinforces the skewed distribution of the returns to copyright. The generation of revenues from content is facilitated through a complex system of licensing and collective licensing. Outwith copyright and the need to license is the concept of public domain and exceptions. Important to continued innovation, the public domain can spur further innovation and creative content. Policy debates focus on the potential to unlock further value from copyright. All of these debates occur during a time of massive innovation in the digital realm. Disruptive technologies are challenging the traditional business models and copyright-dominated industries struggle to adapt.

5

TRADE MARKS AND DESIGN RIGHTS

This chapter discusses the economics of two key registered intellectual property rights (IPRs): trade marks and designs. In both cases, these rights cover a very broad range of industries and their uses provide a different perspective on IP and innovation. **5.01**

Trade Marks

Trade marks hold an unusual position in the economics of IP in that their relationship with innovation is not obvious. A trade mark instead protects the signs and expressions used to identify products and services. A more complete definition for a European trade mark is: 'A trade mark may consist of any signs capable of being represented graphically, particularly words, including personal names, designs, letters, numerals, the shape of goods or of their packaging, provided that such signs are capable of distinguishing the goods or services of one undertaking from those of other undertakings' (OHIM, 2015).[1] Trade marks are registered rights with potentially infinite duration; although they require renewal every ten years, there is no limit to the number of times they can be renewed. Alongside registered trade marks are also unregistered trade marks, which have weaker protection. **5.02**

This section examines the economics of trade marks. It begins with an examination of their relationship to innovation and proceeds to study the informational and signalling aspects of trade marks. The section then details policy debates, which reflect the use of trade marks by firms and concerns about maintaining trade mark registers. Finally, this section concludes with a discussion on counterfeiting and status goods. **5.03**

[1] In fact the range is considerably broader than this summary may indicate. For example, trade marks can control the use of a specific colour in a particular context and can also protect distinctive 'sound signatures' such as advertising jingles.

Innovation and Trade Marks

5.04 A standard economics approach is to reject trade marks as an incentive to innovate. The argument goes as follows: trade marks give firms property rights over their efforts to differentiate themselves. This differentiation is a means to capture market share. One firm's capturing of market share comes at the loss of another firm's capture. Thus, trade marks provide some protection for monies spent on advertising, marketing, and branding, but in a zero-sum game. Put differently, trade marks incentivize expenditures on branding, not innovation. Under this interpretation, trade mark protection does not fit the social contract theory.

5.05 An emerging school of thought (see, e.g., Corrado and Hao, 2013) puts things differently. This requires a revisiting of the classic definition of innovation. If an innovation is an applied invention, then how does branding fit? There are a couple of potential answers. One is the concept that branding can create new markets or grow existing markets. Another is that the branding itself is innovation. Under this school of thought, branding can incentivize innovation by providing property rights over the results of branding expenditures and protecting brands from copying.

5.06 An important distinction must first be made between trade marks and brands, as the two are often conflated[2] in discussions on trade marks. The trade mark is, as described earlier, the legal protection for distinguishing signs. The brand is the distinguishing sign and includes the market/consumer's perception of the sign.[3] Schwarzkopf (2008) makes a similar distinction and describes brands as, 'a trade mark that has been 'released' to compete in the socio-cultural sphere of the market.'[4] Just as a patent is not the innovation, a trade mark is not the distinguishing sign. Coca-Cola could lose protection for its Coca-Cola mark, but its brand would carry on. However, trade marks, like patents, provide a useful delineation for the intangible asset (branding) and an important right to exclude (prevent) copying.

5.07 A second important distinction is between that of brands and marketing. As defined by the American Marketing Association (AMA) (2015), 'Marketing is the activity, set of institutions, and processes for creating, communicating, delivering, and exchanging offerings that have value for customers, clients, partners, and society at large.' Marketing is about communicating value. The process of marketing can communicate and build brands.[5] Part of marketing is communication

[2] There are a number of other related terms such as brand equity, trade name, goodwill, etc. Somewhat frustratingly, terms used by marketing professionals are not universal.

[3] The market's perception is the psychological side of the brand and goes to ideas such as thoughts and beliefs about the brand.

[4] Schwarzkopf (2008) 2.

[5] Branding and brands are often used interchangeably although some authors describe branding as the activities that support the brand. For simplicity, this text uses them as the same word.

through advertising. As advertising and marketing build brands, collectively advertising, marketing, and branding build product and service differentiation for firms.

The question remains whether trade mark protection for expenditure on branding constitutes an incentive to innovate. If branding to gain or maintain market share is a zero-sum game, then the innovation argument is irrelevant. However, if branding is growing the market, or providing an increased utility for consumers, then branding might not be a zero-sum game. In this case, where the return on branding expenditures is positive, branding could be construed as innovative as research and development (R&D). However, there is little empirical evidence to support these relationships, in part because such relationships are difficult to prove (Johnson, Gibson, and Freeman, 2013). These remain somewhat tenuous arguments as the relationship between branding and innovation is still being debated. As Corrado and Hao note, 'Brands are, then, productive assets in an economy . . . some economists dispute this position (although few in business would!) . . .'.[6] **5.08**

Other arguments regarding trade marks and innovation are better evidenced. Millot (2009) argues that trade marks are linked to the innovative activity of firms, and that, by developing a firm's market, serve to appropriate the returns from the market. A key point she makes is that trade mark applications may be an indicator of marketing innovation or innovative activity of firms. Along these lines, Greenhalgh et al. (2011) find that trade mark ownership is associated with higher productivity, which suggests that trade mark data offers considerable potential for providing a better analysis as a possible indicator of innovation.[7] **5.09**

Another consideration is that trade mark rights can potentially last forever. Assuming the owner pays renewal fees, the trade mark will not expire. This is not part of the social contract, which requires the legal monopoly right (IP) to expire and become part of the public domain. The lack of this public domain benefit is attenuated by renewal fees, in which trade mark owners continue to pay while the benefits to the owner outweigh the costs of renewal. Thus renewal fees can, in theory, serve as a policy lever to bring private benefits in line with public cost. In some jurisdictions, such as in the United States, the owner may be required to provide proof of use (POU) that requires that the trade mark still be in use in order to maintain protection; this can bring unused rights back into the public domain. **5.10**

Furthermore, trade marks are regulated in the examination process. To attenuate the possibility of undue restraint on trade, trade marks are limited to stated classes **5.11**

[6] Corrado and Hao (2013) 3.

[7] The USPTO and UK IPO began publishing more extensive trade mark data in 2013 and 2014, respectively. It is expected to provide a boom in economic studies of trade marks.

and cannot be descriptive. These restrictions serve to balance the granting of the legal monopoly of trade marks with the wider interests of the economy.

5.12 Finally, accompanying the registered rights system are rights for unregistered trade marks. As they are not subject to formal examination, unregistered trade marks introduce a flexible right but enjoy relatively weak protection. Business can create reputation and branding without having to formally register the marks associated with their goods and services. This is particularly useful when confronting with cases of 'passing off' by others (the use of the trade mark to misrepresent goods or services) or in cases of business valuation as discussed in the later chapters of this book.

Economics of Trade Marks: Information and Signalling

5.13 Moving away from innovation arguments and into a wider look at the economics of trade marks, this section examines their function in information, signalling, and firm strategy. Further discussion on branding, counterfeits, and social status signalling is found towards the end of the chapter.

5.14 The role of trade marks in economics begins with the goal of providing property rights over brands. Brands have an important function in information gathering and signalling to consumers. To illustrate the importance of information gathering, imagine a world without brands. In this world, products in supermarkets come in identical packaging. A consumer wishing to purchase cornflakes may be faced with cornflakes from three different firms. The consumer could purchase all three in order to understand the quality differences. However, the next time the consumer needs cornflakes, the process would have to be repeated. Branding, on the other hand, reduces the costs of gathering information about the quality of each brand. Consumers will have specific knowledge about quality and other perceptions of the brand that will inform the purchase. The cost of gathering this information is reduced as the consumer can rely on past knowledge.

5.15 The second element is signalling[8] to customers. In addition to the consumer's direct experience with a product or service, there are other indicators to signal information. For example, food products indicating Scottish origins will evoke certain perceptions for consumers. In the case of oatcakes, the association with Scottish imagery may signal heritage, quality, and authenticity.[9] Thus, the branding (which

[8] Branding is a form of signalling that sends information to each party in a transaction. This reduces the information asymmetry (uneven distribution of information) between producers and consumers.

[9] These are merely examples of particular aspects of a good. In addition, certain symbols that might otherwise be used to imply or communicate a particular heritage or origin can be protected. These are discussed in the section on geographical indications.

is not necessarily the brand name) allows firms to send particular signals about a good or service. At the same time, in order to maintain its brand, the firm is incentivized to maintain certain qualities.

The signalling aspect of branding is very important to its economic justification as promoting efficiency. As Economides (1988) notes, branding may be the most efficient means to signal value or quality to the consumer. Trade marks provide legal protection for the signalling function of branding. Trade marks as a whole can be construed as incentives to create economic efficiency via information signalling, (Landes and Posner, 1987) and the relationship with innovation discussed may simply be a more recent effort to force trade marks into a one-size-fits-all theory[10] of the economics of IP. **5.16**

Further considerations of signalling by firms

In addition to signalling between producers and consumers, there is also a social element in the form of status signalling. The branding of goods and services targets an individual's use of signalling for self-identity. For example, consider which type of cars people prefer. An 'action-based' individual will prefer a sporty car whereas a 'classic' individual may go for a vintage-styled car. The branding of goods contributes to a form of self-branding and status signalling that is discussed later. Again, the information protection by a trade mark has an important role in communication information. **5.17**

Signalling may be particularly important in experience and credence goods. Experience goods are goods or services in which the value or quality cannot be assessed prior to its consumption. A classic example is a movie. The audience will know the price but not how much they will enjoy the movie. Particular actors, producers, and film studios all have brands that will convey the potential value of the movie its audience. Credence goods, in which the consumer is unable to ascertain the benefits of a good even after consumption, are also dependent on signalling. For example, the utility of life coaches and vitamins cannot necessarily be understood even after consumption. However, the most relevant example is legal services. The average consumer of legal services will have insufficient knowledge to ascertain a lawyer's skills and the quality of his or her services. Instead, branding and signalling will most likely communicate this information. **5.18**

Perversely, brands and trade marks may actually serve to 'miss-signal' to consumers. Regulation on this varies by jurisdictions, but firms may seek, through branding, to send signals about quality that are not true. In some cases, such as signals about quality, this may only succeed in the short term. However, in the cases where language and geography may be evoked, such as using the French language or the word **5.19**

[10] The economics of IP is evolving but its current trend seems to be one of developing an overarching, one-size-fits-all theory of IP, which may not be appropriate, as discussed in Chapter 2.

'Tokyo', branding and associated trade marking may actually mislead consumers into thinking that the good or service is French or Japanese, respectively. Likewise, a well-established brand, such as the sports brand Nike or women's apparel brand Victoria's Secret, may rely on its strong American associations to imply its goods are manufactured in the United States when they are often manufactured in other lower-cost countries. Consumer awareness and sophistication, in addition to policy, will determine the extent to which brands are able to mislead.

Free-riding

5.20 Without trade mark protection for brands, other firms could free-ride on the marketing efforts of competitors. Just as copying copyrighted goods or reverse engineering patented innovations is typically cheaper than independent innovation, copying an established trade mark (or creating something with sufficient similarity that it confuses the customer) is a way of capturing the brand owner's branding efforts. Trade mark protection serves as a mechanism to discourage this copying and enforce the original brand, thus preventing its potential dilution from free-riders.

5.21 One difficulty is separating copying from taking inspiration from others. It is economically efficient for consumers and retailers that all whole milks to have the same coloured cap or all lemon-scented washing liquid to be yellow (this is known as a category colour) as discussed in Johnson, Gibson, and Freeman (2013). However, packaging and branding that is nearly identical to an existing brand may lead to consumer confusion and brand dilution. Equally, copying and lookalike packaging may provide consumers with more variety. If trade mark protection is too weak, then brands will be less differentiated and signalling will be reduced. Firms may either reduce their investment in branding because they are less able to protect it, or they may increase their branding efforts to continue their differentiation. If trade mark protection is too strong, then it will be difficult for new brands to develop and competition in the market will be reduced. Like many questions in IP policy, there is a fine balance between protecting existing rights holders and future rights holders.

Economics of Trade Marks: Policy Debates

5.22 Policy debates in trade marks do not seem to have as high a profile as those concerning copyright and patents. It may be that a compelling narrative in trade mark protection does not match the cultural heritage and 'supremacy of science' rhetoric found in copyright and patent debates. The exception is counterfeiting, which governments and rights holders portray[11] as a dangerous activity that supports

[11] A number of authors argue that the use of 'piracy' in copyright infringement is primarily a social construction (Yar, 2005) and one that exhibits increasingly militarized language (Mirghani, 2011). It is possible a similar process is underway in counterfeiting.

terrorism.[12] This lower profile of trade mark policy debates is surprising because marks are generally considered to be one of the most valuable intellectual assets (WIPO, 2013). Forbes (2015) ranks the top 100 brands (not the trade mark itself) which range from USD 6.1 billion to USD 145.3 billion; compared to some of the largest sales of patents totalling only USD 12.5 billion (USD 500k per patent) in 2011 (Babbage, 2011). That said, trade mark policy is subject to a number of key debates, detailed in the following section.

Genericization

Successful brands may be so successful that they lose their distinctiveness and become generic words. For example 'heroin' was once a trade mark owned by a pharmaceutical company (Hiskey, 2012) and 'escalator' was once owned by a company that manufactured lifts (LegalFlip, 2015). The use of words as generics can be economically efficient. Landes and Posner (2003) argue that new generic words are a form of linguistic innovation[13] that results in reduced communication costs (signalling). Trade marking introduces new words and enriches languages. **5.23**

While the economic efficiency of generic words may be beneficial, the loss of trade mark protection through its linguistic popularity seems to counter innovation and investments incentives for firms. In the case of genericization of a trade mark, the success of branding becomes its downfall. However, the addition of genericized trade marks to the public domain, and the potential for genericization in general, increases the expected social benefit from new trade marks incentivized by the legal monopoly. It may serve as a correcting feature such that, when the social benefits outweigh the private benefits of the trade mark protection sufficiently, the social contract rewards society. **5.24**

Grey goods and parallel imports

Another consideration in trade mark policy is that of the parallel importation and sale of grey goods. Grey goods are goods sold outside the distribution network controlled by the producer of the good. Grey goods are not counterfeit goods; they are legitimate goods whose first sale may have occurred (or been intended to occur) in a different country and are subsequently imported (parallel import). Alternately, a retailer within the distribution network may re-sell the goods to other retailers outside the network. In jurisdictions with the exhaustion of rights or first sale doctrines, **5.25**

[12] Two spectacular failures of policy in 2012, the US Stop Online Piracy Act (SOPA, House Bill 3261) and plurilateral Anti-Counterfeiting Trade Agreement, attempted to tackle both online piracy and counterfeiting but were met with widespread popular resistance.

[13] Used in this text not as an impact on the morphology of a language, but the generation of new words and meanings.

the first sale of a good may exhaust the producer's IPRs over that particular item. That is, once a handbag is sold in Switzerland, the producer may not be able to assert trade mark rights over the sale of the same handbag when resold in the United Kingdom.

5.26 Restrictions on grey goods, or policies which extend trade mark protection beyond the first sale of a good, may allow firms to price discriminate. Under price discrimination, firms will charge different prices for the same good in different markets in the hopes of maximizing profits. If firms are then able to restrict the re-selling of a good into a different market, their ability to price discriminate will be strengthened.[14] This situation increases profits for the firm, but comes as a result of the ability to use trade mark protection beyond simply preventing copying, but restricting the flow of goods legitimately using a mark.

5.27 Grey goods and parallel importers can increase competition and lower prices for consumers (Liebeler, 1986). For example, the American-based warehouse club[15] Costco has been engaged in a number of lawsuits with regards to its selling of grey goods such as handbags and watches at prices lower than the authorized prices (McCall, 2013). Grey goods allow firms such as retailers to engage in economic arbitrage where differences in prices in different markets are exploited. The seller of a grey good may be able to sell at a lower price than retailers of non-grey goods in the same market.

5.28 One economic argument for the restriction of parallel imports is that of free-riding by the importer (Liebeler, 1986). Under the free-riding argument, the importer benefits from the advertising and marketing expenditures associated with the authorized distributors. The importer does not incur these costs but reaps the benefits of the promotion of the goods in question. Yet grey goods are not perfect substitutes for authorized goods, as they may not be covered by manufacturer warranties and are sold in different retail environments.[16]

5.29 Another concern is that of the use of public resources for the enforcement of restrictions on grey goods as the line between a counterfeit item and a grey good may be blurred. Goods in transit, for example, may pass through multiple jurisdictions where their trade mark status may differ. Safety concerns may also arise when grey and counterfeit goods are confused. Counterfeit medicines may cause harm, yet

[14] For some copyright discussion on price discrimination, see the section on the European digital single market (DSM).

[15] In this case, a members-only retail store where goods are typically sold in bulk directly to consumers in a fashion normally reserved for selling to businesses.

[16] For example, the purchaser of a status handbag will have a very different retail experience buying the handbag in a high-end boutique versus a warehouse. This may affect the consumer's perception and utility associated with the good.

the confiscation of medical grey goods may prevent legitimate treatment. It is not a clear-cut area; where goods are grey goods and not counterfeit, resources spent on customs controls may be an inefficient expenditure of public resources.

Grey goods highlight one of the challenges of IP systems in the struggle to strike the right balance between the interests of rights owners and consumers. **5.30**

Trade mark registers—cluttering, absolute grounds, proof of use, and squatting

Cluttering

Trade mark registers are the official list of marks in a particular jurisdiction. A potential goal for the offices responsible for the registers is to operate a 'clean' register, which is one that is clear, up-to-date, and accessible to rights holders and users. Cluttering, in which registers are 'cluttered' by trade marks that are either too broad or not in use, raises the search costs for potential applicants as marks that, in theory, should be available, are not. There are a number of potential policy options to maintain clean registers that include debates on relative versus absolute grounds, and POU. **5.31**

Economic analysis of trade mark registers is in its infancy. One challenge with cluttering in particular is that there is little empirical proof it exists. An examination of the European Union Intellectual Property Office (EUIPO) data (von Graevenitz et al., 2012) suggests some cluttering exists, but the findings are described as tentative. Of particular interest is a preliminary indication that trade marks for pharmaceuticals are more likely to involve multiple registrations at once. If cluttering does exist, it means that the linguistic space available for new marks is unnecessarily limited and that applicants may spend more resources on search costs as they identify potentially conflicting marks and their use. **5.32**

Relative and absolute grounds

Another challenge is that of different approaches to examination procedures. While some offices review trade mark applications on relative grounds (e.g. the United States),[17] where the trade mark application is viewed in contrast to existing, third party marks, other offices (e.g. the United Kingdom) use simply absolute grounds, where the application is viewed only based on its intrinsic aspects. Offices using relative grounds spend more resources on the examination process and the process itself is likely to take longer as the likelihood of confusion[18] is considered. **5.33**

---

[17] It is worth noting that the relative grounds examination system includes absolute grounds. Absolute grounds, however, does not include relative grounds.

[18] Likelihood of confusion is a test for examination or to prove infringement of a mark. It asks whether the relevant consumer is likely to be confused by the mark in question. If the answer is

5.34 There are costs associated with notifying the owners of potentially conflicting trade marks of these new applications. Offices adopting an absolute grounds threshold, on the other hand, save on examination costs but may potentially register overlapping marks. The likelihood of confusion is not considered. In this case, the costs of monitoring the register for potential conflict are shifted to existing trade mark owners.

5.35 There are a number of pros and cons to the relative and absolute grounds approaches. For applicants, there does not appear to be a consensus, as evidenced by the fact that the International Trademark Association (INTA) refrains[19] from endorsing either. From an economic standpoint, there is a question as to who should bear the costs of trade mark registries. If the trade mark authority is self-funded, then application and renewal fees fund costs and not the taxpayer. However, the shifting of monitoring costs onto existing owners of marks may disproportionately affect SMEs[20] as larger firms are more likely to have the resources and sophistication to monitor registries.

Proof of use

5.36 Finally, under the POU system, trade mark owners must prove that the mark in question is still in use. In the United States, this happens after the first five years of registration. The advantage of this is, again, a cleaner, less-cluttered register. In registers without POU, unused rights may be identified and invalidated in litigious contexts. Again, there is a question as to who bears the cost of these systems. In jurisdictions with POU, the cost is distributed across all mark owners. In jurisdictions without, the costs are concentrated on those engaged in disputes.

Trade mark squatting

5.37 Trade mark squatting is, 'the practice of registration of brands as trade marks in bad faith prior to the registration by the real trade mark owner in a certain jurisdiction' (Ozeke, 2014). In some cases, the trade mark squatter registers the mark with the intention of holding the legitimate brand owner hostage at the point the brand owner enters the market. This is typically the case with globally known brands that have, based on business strategy, chosen not to enter a market at the time of the registration by the squatter. This becomes a problem if they then enter said market and is globally problematic in the case of trade marks used in domain

yes, then the mark in question may not pass the examination test and/or may be infringing the trade mark.

[19] INTA (2005).

[20] SMEs are small and medium-sized enterprises, often defined as businesses with less than 250 employees or USD 50 million in annual revenues. This definition varies as some countries choose to distinguish by sector.

names. Prominent cases include the registration of Starbucks in Russia in a case in which a squatter sought, but failed to achieve, USD 600k in 2005 (Kramer, 2007), and the USD 3.9 million sought by a Chinese squatter for the Tesla mark (Bloomberg, 2014).

Trade mark squatting has knock-on effects in addition to the vexation they cause legitimate brand owners. Fink, Helmers, and Ponce (2014) examine trade mark squatting in Chile[21] and find that squatters distort the behaviour of the legitimate owners. Squatting causes the brand owner to over-protect their brand by registering more marks in more classes than they otherwise would have. Squatting also increases the cost of doing business by generating legal disputes as squatters exploit IP systems. This over-protection and additional costs are undesirable outcomes of trade mark systems. **5.38**

Trade mark squatting encapsulates the challenges associated with striking the right balance between protecting brands and allowing sufficient room for the development of new brands. For example, protecting brands from squatting runs the risk of over-extending the reach of existing registrations unduly limiting the use of similar brand names. Trade mark squatting is, by definition, in bad faith. Such behaviour can theoretically be prevented by high quality registrations processes or dealt with via existing enforcement mechanisms. However, should disincentives to trade mark squatting be very strong, then a brand with protection will have de facto protection in jurisdictions where formal IP protection has not been sought. To a degree, this already exists as unregistered trade mark protection and brand awareness provide some protection. However, if the threshold for achieving protection via unregistered rights and brand awareness is low, then it may also have the effect of creating extra-jurisdictional protection of trade marks. **5.39**

Additionally, policy and registrations systems set the requirement for the distinctiveness of a mark as in the relative grounds discussion above. If the threshold for distinctiveness is very high, then trade mark registrations made in good faith could be considered squatting. If the threshold for distinctiveness is very low, then registrations that are in bad faith may not be considered squatting. As with many debates in the economics of IP, striking the balance is not easy. **5.40**

Overall, the costs of operating a 'clean' register may make the concept not as desirable as it may appear *prima facie*. While there are pros and cons to each system, there is no consensus as to which system is preferred and it will likely depend on the individual characteristics of a jurisdiction. **5.41**

[21] Very little research has been conducted on squatting. It is possible that Chile, which is unusually stable and prosperous economy for its region, is an outlier.

Domain names and trade marks

5.42 Domain names are unique identifiers for websites. They have entered the trade mark debate because they are key, global assets for brands. Mueller (2004) notes that domain names have two components: the technical unique identifier and the meaningful, symbolic communication. The meaningful component of domain names is highly related to brands and trade marks. Brand owners will clearly seek to have the domain names most highly related to their brands and consumers will associate domain names with certain brands. The value of a domain name lies primarily in its semantic aspects and psychological associations. Mueller argues that demand for domain names stems from a mixture of 'demand for a memorable identifier, the desire to economize on the length of the domain name, concerns about authenticity, and the demand for names that will attract web traffic or aid in search ...'.[22]

5.43 The demand and value of domain names is very similar to that of trade marks. Domain names must be registered and are subject to squatting in what is known as cyber-squatting. While trade marks are protected by national jurisdictions, domain names exist in the virtual realm and are globally accessible. This has caused disputes and has led to the creation of a dispute resolution system run by the World Intellectual Property Organization (WIPO). Registration does not require proof of use. While cyber-squatting is in bad faith, there are good faith business models in which domain name registration is done on a prospecting basis in the hopes that a particular name will become valuable.

5.44 Linguistically, domain names are more limited than trade marks as they must be text-based, are more valuable when shorter, and must include a top-level domain name (e.g. .com or .co.uk), though the range of top-level global names (abbreviated to gTLDs) has recently increased substantially. Additionally, the trade mark class system does not separate domain names. While the 'Polo' trade mark can be registered by three different companies in different classes for different goods (a car, a clothing line, and a mint), the same cannot be said of a single domain name. While trade marks may incentivize the creation of new words, domain names have less room in which to do so.

5.45 What does this mean for the economics of trade marks? In one sense, the limitations on linguistic innovation by domain names may limit similar innovation in branding and trade marking. Firms are less likely to generate branding and registered rights that cannot easily translate into an available domain name. Yet these limitations may increase innovation as brand owners generate new words to fit into the cyber world.

---

22 Mueller (2004) 14.

Counterfeiting and Status Goods

Expanding earlier considerations of signalling by producers to consumers, this section examines how consumers use brands to self-signal. Status[23] signalling is an important form of personal branding and social interaction. For example, consider the perceived status of a lawyer driving a used car, wearing out-of-date suits and generic spectacles compared to the same lawyer driving a luxury car, wearing a tailor-made suit and branded spectacles. While the lawyer is the same in both cases, the perceived status varies significantly. **5.46**

Consumer purchasers of brands are also driven by their desire to be associated with a certain status. This is sometimes referred to as 'conspicuous consumption', which indicates the consumption of goods not for their functional attributes but for their status. Many goods have a combination of functional and status aspects and are referred to as status goods. For example, the status good in the form of a luxury watch has the functional aspect of telling the time and the status aspect of the cost and lifestyle associated with the brand. Brands are able to capture this consumption by focusing on developing the status aspects of their goods and services. **5.47**

Status signalling is particularly important in environments where others have less information about an individual. For example, in cities, where individuals have less background information, status signalling is relatively more important than in small towns, where community members have more information about each others. Another key concept is that of reference groups or the intended audience of status signalling. A doctor will likely engage in different status signalling while amongst other doctors than she would with members of her hiking club. Successful status signalling[24] brings with it many benefits as opportunities and networks will be influenced by status. The important consideration here is that the status associated with brands is important to consumers. **5.48**

Moving from individual perspectives to a social perspective, status signalling does not contribute to social welfare. Given that status is entirely relative, gains in status by one individual come at the loss of another. Status signalling is a zero-sum game. On that basis, conspicuous consumption could be considered a wasteful activity from a social perspective but a productive one at the individual level. **5.49**

[23] It is worth noting that status signalling is important at all levels of socio-economic status. Van Kempen (2007) details the use of pen caps to signal the ownership of the pen and false mobile phones by low-income Bolivian households.

[24] This section provides only a quick overview of status signalling. There is a fascinating array of types of signalling. For example, counter-signalling is when individuals signal a status, typically lower, than that which they are. A good example is the Duchess of Cambridge's consumption of high-street brands associated with the middle class. As a royal, her status is unquestionable and she can 'afford' to engage in lower status signalling. See Veblen, T. (1912). *The Theory of the Leisure Class: An Economic Study of Institutions* (New York, The Macmillan Company) for more.

5.50 Counterfeiting of status goods provides a further IP twist to the story. A key difference[25] between a counterfeit good and the trade marked original is its trade mark. The original good has the legal protection of its trade mark whereas the counterfeit good infringes a trade mark. For the consumer, the counterfeit good is a way of capturing the status of the original good but at a reduced price. This may allow the consumer to successfully send a 'false' higher status signal. However, the success of this false signalling will be how close the counterfeit is to the original, and the knowledge of the reference group.

5.51 Rights holders and firms producing status goods object to the counterfeiting of their goods. This is often done on the grounds of likelihood of confusion or lost sales. This is challenging to prove as counterfeit status goods are often of sufficiently poorer quality than original goods and are sold through different distribution mechanisms, making real consumer confusion unlikely.[26] Just as the sale of a pirated CD does not necessarily equate to a lost sale of the original CD, the consumption of counterfeit goods may not affect sales of the original goods. Gosline (2009) suggests that consumers will 'try out' counterfeit goods before progressing to the original brand. Barnett (2005) argues that counterfeits may increase sales of original goods as they serve as advertising. Qian (2008) finds that an increase in counterfeiting of sports shoes resulted in a short-term decrease in original goods but a long-term increase in quality of originals, as firms use quality to differentiate their products from counterfeits.

5.52 The subject of brands, trade marks, status, and counterfeiting can be examined by economic theory but, with few exceptions, has not been backed up with empirical analysis. The debate over counterfeiting and status has elements in common with that of unlicensed copying of copyrighted goods, where the cultural and creative aspects of copyrighted goods and services provide status signalling for consumers. In both cases, the link between the consumption of unlicensed copies and the loss of sales of the IP protected originals has yet to be established empirically.

Trade Marks Conclusion

5.53 Trade marks emerge from this analysis as something of an economic anomaly, as they do not appear to be a very good fit with the 'incentives to innovate' interpretation of

[25] This is a key difference for the discussion here. However, there will also be quality, cost, and purchasing environment differences.

[26] This is not, however, the case with experience goods as the consumer will not know the quality until after consumption. The same is also the case with credence goods as it depends entirely on the customer's perception.

social contract theory.[27] However, emerging economic thought suggests that trade marks are very important for functioning markets, and that they can fit into an innovation narrative of IP. A consensus has yet to be reached on the role of marks in the wider realm of innovation but there are a lot of interesting possibilities. It may be that trade marks provide a crucial challenge to the traditional understanding of innovation, such as the interaction of innovation with language and signalling. Policy considerations of trade marks highlight some of the distributive challenges they present and hint as to how rights could be adjusted to promote economic efficiency.

Design Rights

Rights for the protection of designs vary significantly at an international level in terms of subject, duration, coverage, and terminology. In Article III of the Design Regulation,[28] the EU defines designs as follows: '"design" means the appearance of the whole or a part of a product resulting from the features of, in particular, the lines, contours, colours, shape, texture and/or materials of the product itself and/or its ornamentation.' WIPO instead defines designs as 'the ornamental or aesthetic aspect of an article. An industrial design may consist of three-dimensional features, such as the shape of an article, or two-dimensional features, such as patterns, lines or color' (WIPO, 2015). Designs might be characterized as falling into a slightly awkward space between copyright, trade marks, and patents where they protect non-functional, aesthetic, or ornamental aspects of goods—that is, where form is important, but does not follow function (as technical functionality is the domain of patenting). This is not the same thing, however, as saying that they cannot influence perceived usefulness, as explained further below. **5.54**

While the terms for rights to protect designs vary (design patent,[29] industrial design, and design rights), the fundamental concept they share is to provide some IP protection for these 'ornamental' aspects. Such aspects may also be covered by copyright or trade mark. This chapter will focus on the UK and EU version of design rights, but the underlying economic principles can be universally applied as, for example, in the US design patent. **5.55**

[27] However, trade marks do fit into a wider interpretation of social contract theory in that the signalling aspects of trade marks address potential market failures as a result of asymmetric information.

[28] Council Regulation (EC) No 6/2002 of 12 December 2001 on Community Designs.

[29] The term 'patent' is misleading. An American design patent is similar to a UK registered design right but with a fourteen-year duration and a narrower definition of eligibility.

Design and industrialization

5.56 This section details the development of design rights, the relationship with design rights law and innovation, and a discussion of the dual system of registered and unregistered rights. It then proceeds to examine the use of design rights and finished with a discussion on the economic measurement and impact of design as a whole.

History and development of designs

5.57 The contrast of design rights with patents and copyrights provides a useful means to frame the history of designs. Initially, many of the aesthetic aspects of goods fell under the realm of copyright. Starting with the development of design law, Carter-Silk and Lewiston (2012) argue that the industrial revolution changed the way design contributed to innovation. As the authors note, 'the Industrial Revolutions of the 19th and 20th Centuries heralded a new era in which designs were applied to utilitarian objects, whose mass production was facilitated by new technologies. This presented a challenge to the legislature and the judiciary; whilst there was a desire to continue to protect creative designs, there was concern about fettering the development of functionality.'[30]

5.58 At the same time, the lines between decorative and functional elements no longer fit the boundaries of copyright and patents; with industrialization, the two are conflated. As Zou (2009) describes it, a work of design is 'not only an article of utility which emphasizes function but is also an artistic article with aesthetic significance'.[31] Design and aesthetics enhance functionality. A classic example is the impact the sleek style of a touch-screen tablet computer has on its functionality. The design can enhance the user-friendliness of goods. Yet the delineation is subtle, which is why purely functional elements lie within the remit of patents and the aesthetic aspects within works of artistic craftsmanship remain the domain of copyright.

5.59 The role of design, and its role in innovation, has changed with technological advancements and industrialization. Similar to competing models of innovation, there are debates as to the impact of design (as a whole) as aesthetic or functional. Zou makes reference to the Bauhaus school of design thought, which places form over function. As design moves into the realm of engineering, it may lack an aesthetic element and not qualify for design rights. The digital age has brought interactive

[30] Carter-Silk, A. and Lewiston, M. (2012). *The Development of Design Law. Past and Future: From History to Policy* (Newport: The Intellectual Property Office) 155.

[31] Zou, X. (2009). 'On Unification of Functionality and Aesthetics of Design Art' *Asian Social Science* 5: 144.

designs by way of graphical user interfaces (GUIs) to improve user functionality. Thus, the role of design in the economy continues to evolve.

Incentives to innovate

Like patents and copyright, design rights are a fairly straightforward fit for the 'incentives to innovate' theory. Designers receive property rights over the innovative designs and can use this to appropriate the returns from their investment in innovation. Consumers (society) accept the potential monopoly situation property rights create in return for sustained design innovation and the eventual contribution to the public domain. The benefits to designers stemming from the design rights act as an incentive to create future designs. **5.60**

Unregistered v registered

Both unregistered and registered design rights protect designs in the UK and EU. This two-track system provides some flexibility instead of a 'one-size-fits-all' regime. **5.61**

Unregistered designs are automatic rights that do not require action on the part of the owner. Registered rights, on the other hand, require the expense and effort of registering the design. The nature of creating designs, the market for designs, and a cost–benefit analysis highlight why this system is logical. **5.62**

The process of creating a new design is often iterative and will generate many intermediate designs that do not make it to market. For example, in the process of pitching a new 'sippy cup'[32] to a children's store, a designer may develop a number of designs, select a few to present to the client, only one of which may ultimately reach the market. Intermediate designs may still benefit from IP protection, but their quantity may make it impractical to register individually. The unregistered design right addresses this issue by granting an automatic right. To compensate for the low hurdle[33] for eligibility, the right is limited to ten or fifteen years[34] (in the United Kingdom). **5.63**

Likewise, of the designs that make it to the market, only a few may have any market staying power. This is particularly the case in markets where trends are dominant, such as fashion and interior design, and the market life of a design may be relatively short. In fact, it can be in the interest of sellers of these designs that old designs fall **5.64**

---

[32] For readers not familiar with the term, a sippy cup is a small cup with handles, a lid, and a small spout often used by toddlers.

[33] Interestingly, copyright does not compensate for its low threshold.

[34] In the United Kingdom, this is the earliest of either ten years after the design was first sold or fifteen years after it was created. For the final five years of protection, a 'licence of right' rule requires that rights holder license their design to any interested party. An EU unregistered design has only three years' protection.

out of fashion and are recognized as being dated. Thus, the majority of these designs will be adequately covered by an unregistered design.

5.65 In the rare cases that designs have market staying power and outlast typical trend cycles, the registered design may be worth the relatively low cost and effort required to obtain it. The registration of designs incurs legal costs and registration fees, but these are modest (though renewals are required more frequently than for trade marks, and in the case of the United Kingdom, increase in price over time, as the policy presumption is that renewal will only occur if economic benefits continue to be delivered by the designs).

5.66 In addition, a registered design right will only protect the precise design in question. Thus, it may be easy for imitators to 'invent around' a design right. Design rights themselves have a very low threshold for eligibility and multiple iterations of a similar design can be protected. Yet designs may have sufficiently strong market power and brand recognition to thwart competition. Designs with market staying power may also be more likely to attract licensing opportunities, which will be easier to define with a registered design right.

5.67 Hence, the two-tiered system of registered and unregistered design rights allows designers flexibility and to choose the appropriate cost/benefit which suits business interests.

Use of design rights

5.68 Despite a relatively flexible, two-tiered *sui generis* system, the evidence suggests that design rights are relatively underused. Moultrie and Livesey (2011) investigated the use of IP and find that design firms use a combination of IP mechanisms. In particular, they found that design firms were sceptical about the costs and enforcement of registered designs. Instead, they focus more on branding. However, they also found that design firms are relatively ignorant of design rights as a whole. Orozco (2009)[35] suggests that this ignorance may be rational as, within an organization, individual or departmental units may place their own interests[36] over that of the firm's interest. In this case, firms are more likely to obtain bundles of other types of IP rights.

5.69 The use of design rights becomes even more challenging when considering the vast array of rights available. In the United Kingdom, firms can choose between unregistered and registered UK design rights, unregistered and registered EU design rights,

[35] Orozco, D. (2009). 'Rational Design Rights Ignorance' *American Business Law Journal* 46(4): 573–605.

[36] For example, the registration of a design right will create more paperwork for the individual whilst the benefit will largely go to the firm.

and, in some cases, copyright. This does not make it easy for firms attempting to navigate the already complex IP system as a whole. Moultrie and Livesey (2011) also find that UK firms are confused by these options.

A further consideration is that the enforcement of designs is key to its effectiveness. The cumulative nature of the design means that new designs will almost certainly borrow from and build on existing designs. Delineating between the end of one design and the start of another is very difficult. Callmann (1940) criticized American design patents nearly eighty years ago, highlighting, 'It is a sorry fact that the legislators of that day failed to realize that the occasion is rare when a purely original design is created, that more usually than not an "original" fashion creation is but a very slight modification of a known idea, and that such a slight modification may be of tremendous commercial value to the creator manufacturer.'[37] It can also be very difficult for a design rights application to accurately reflect the design in question as in the long debate over the use of cross-hatching in design patents dispute in *Apple Inc. v. Samsung Electronics Co.*[38] **5.70**

Additional enforcement can be achieved by way of criminal prosecution of infringement.[39] For designs, this would typically be considered counterfeiting. However, as with criminalization in general, enforcement of criminal law is down to the police and government legal services. For society, the value of dedicating police resources to the prosecution of design infringement is questionable. **5.71**

Measuring design and impact

The economic impact of design and design rights is anything but straightforward. While registered designs offer more by way of potential data for analysis, at the time of writing these data are fairly limited. Unregistered rights, like copyright, are very difficult to measure. Furthermore, design itself is even more difficult to measure. Like innovation, design is a challenge to identify. What qualifies as design is much greater than what qualifies for a design right. Design includes service design, industrial design, decorative arts, fashion design, graphic design, interface design, systems design, database design, landscape design, and urban design: it is difficult to measure something when there is not even a consensus on its definition. **5.72**

The lack of definitions and measurements of designs is a reflection of the science-based focus on economic measurement. This is also a reflection of a fairly narrow, science-based view of innovation. Despite the fact that design potentially plays a **5.73**

[37] Callmann (1940) 1.

[38] *Apple v. Samsung* No. 11-CV-01846 (N.D. Cal.).

[39] Not all jurisdictions criminalize design rights infringement. The United Kingdom criminalized registered design infringement in 2014.

key role in innovation, this is not well-reflected in policy. Haskel (2007)[40] notes that HMRC (the UK tax authority) defines tax breaks for R&D that clearly emphasize science. As economies shift away from manufacturing-based production and towards services, the 'knowledge' economy, based much more on the types of innovations covered by IP, becomes more important. He argues that spending on marketing and design should be considered knowledge investment on the same footing as spending on science-based innovation).

5.74 As discussed elsewhere in this book, data for IP is a challenge. The measurement of a particular industry is key in terms of government strategies, attracting investment, and as a lobbying tool for the industry. Design struggles to fit this, but is nevertheless a key form of innovation. One of the rationales for design rights, detailed at the start of this chapter, is changes in innovation stemming from the industrial revolution and shifting role of design. It is possible that in the more knowledge, service-based economy, design is undergoing a second wave of change.

5.75 Given this potential importance of design and design rights, its measurement is worth exploring. Haskel and Pesole (2011) map the state of UK design using two methods: employment and purchase of design services. They calculate, using National Accounts,[41] that from 2000–10, there were roughly 350,000 design workers. This figure does not include the self-employed. They further estimate that, in 2008, UK firms purchased approximately £26 billion worth of design services and produced in-house an additional £7.5 billion.[42] Yet they find that firms consider registered design rights as being useful for only four years.

5.76 An argument for the use of IP is that IP allows firms to appropriate the rewards from their investment in innovation. This should be reflected by a positive impact (e.g. more profit) on a firm's financial performance. However, this may not be the case. Bascavusoglu-Moreau and Tether (2011)[43] test whether a design right improves a firm's performance and find an ambiguous result, with design rights appearing to neither positively or negatively impact performance. By contrast, a 2015 report by EUIPO[44]

[40] Haskel, J. (2007). 'Measuring Innovation and Productivity in a Knowledge-based Service Economy' *Economic and Labour Market Review* 1(7): 27.

[41] Governments have national statistics offices that are responsible for the collection and analysis of such data. Precise structures, collection methods, and names vary between countries.

[42] These figures are highly dependent on the quality of the data used; this data stems from UK government figures, which are subject to their own challenges.

[43] Bascavusoglu-Moreau, E. and Tether, B.S. (2011). 'Registered Designs & Business Performance—Exploring the Link'. The UK Intellectual Property Office, 2011/6. Available at: https://www.gov.uk/government/uploads/system/uploads/attachment_data/file/310638/ipresearch-designsreport2-201109.pdf.

[44] OHIM. (2015). 'Intellectual Property Rights and Firm Performance in Europe: An Economic Analysis'. The Office for the Harmonisation of the Internal Market, June 2015. Available at: https://oami.europa.eu/tunnel-web/secure/webdav/guest/document_library/observatory/documents/IPContributionStudy/phase2/OHIM_study_report_en.pdf.

argues that firms holding EU-registered design rights on average pay 23% higher wages and generate 15% more revenue per employee than firms without design rights. However, it may be that these measurements are capturing correlation and not causation. Ownership of design rights may be correlated with the level of sophistication of a firm that causes the firm's success.

Assuming these numbers are accurate,[45] then we are left with an economic puzzle. Why does a source of innovation so key to the economy use its *sui generis* right so little? There are plenty of possible explanations. One is that design rights themselves do not provide the protection required or in a manner in which the costs do not outweigh the benefits. There are also questions of firm awareness of design rights. An alternative approach would suggest that, like IP discussed elsewhere in this book, firms may rely on non-IPRs to protect their business interests. As further data on design rights[46] emerge, their role in economics and innovation may become clearer. **5.77**

[45] As discussed extensively, the data associated with IP and other measurements should always be taken with a grain of salt. Quality and methods vary widely and there is a general lack of consensus.

[46] There is a trend in government IP offices towards digitization of design right application processes, which is followed then by more easily accessible data for analysis.

6

TRADE SECRETS AND OTHER RIGHTS

While the attention of economists and lawyers is typically devoted to copyright, trade marks, and patents, there are a slew of other rights with important functions in IP systems. These include trade secrets, geographical indications, plant breeders' rights, and traditional knowledge. This chapter details the economics of these rights. **6.01**

Trade Secrets

Secret by nature, trade secrets present a particularly challenging subject for economic analysis. In addition to being an unregistered right, trade secrets may not be publicly acknowledged. If you cannot measure them or know about them, do trade secrets really have an economic impact? **6.02**

The answer, of course, is yes. Trade secrets have an important role in the economics of IP and innovation. As per Article 39 of the Agreement on Trade-Related Aspects of Intellectual Property Rights (TRIPS), to qualify for trade secret protection, a secret must be not generally known to the public (i.e. secret), confer some economic benefit to its holder (i.e. have value), and be subject to reasonable efforts to protect its secrecy. In law, trade secret protection is typically not found alongside other intellectual property rights (IP rights) but is instead covered by tort, contract, and unfair competition law. This is a source of frustration for some in the legal profession who argue that trade secrets are not IP, or at least IP rights, at all. This frustration, however, does not apply to economists who are generally content to consider trade secrets as they act and look like IP rights and have innovation impacts. **6.03**

For an innovation to qualify as a trade secret, it must meet three important criteria:[1] **6.04**

1. It must be secret.
2. It must derive value from its secrecy.
3. It must be reasonably protected.

[1] Precise definitions vary by jurisdiction.

6.05 Trade secrets cover a wide variety of expressions of knowledge and innovation. Trade secrets can cover recipes, customer lists, bidding information, confidential information, algorithms, processes, formula, software, etc.

Innovation and Importance

6.06 To introduce the relationship between trade secrets and innovation, this section begins with an analysis of the social contract of innovation. As discussed in Chapter 2, the social contract is a bargain between innovators and society. A key principle of the social contract is that of disclosure. Trade secrets, however, do not involve disclosure as they survive indefinitely through their secrecy. On the other hand, trade secrets are a very nice fit for labour desert theory (also discussed in Chapter 2), as they allow innovators some rights over the outputs of their innovation efforts.

6.07 There are a number of arguments that attenuate the lack of trade secrets' compliance with the social contract. As Paine (1991) notes, by acknowledging innovators' right to disclose, IP rights regimes implicitly recognize the right not to disclose. In addition, as the sections in this chapter on patents and other IP rights discuss, trade secrets may actually enable disclosure via other means. Analysing trade secrets independent of their interaction with other rights misses their overall impact on innovation.

6.08 As a relatively flexible IP right, firms can easily deploy trade secrecy. For example, the use of non-disclosure agreements, a form of trade secrecy protection, allows firms to discuss innovations with other firms. Here trade secrets enable a variety of firm interactions such as licensing, the spread of knowledge, and joint research ventures; all of which are considered good for innovation.

6.09 Trade secrets also offer a potentially low cost and flexible means to allow innovators to appropriate the returns to their innovation. As trade secrets do not require registration and apply to a very wide range of intellectual capital, they provide a fairly flexible protection mechanism. Additionally, the protection of trade secrets does not incur the legal and fee costs associated with patents. This discussion on the relatively low cost, flexible protection of trade secrets assumes the reasonable efforts to protect the secrets are low cost. Security for digital content may become more expensive and restrictive as cybercriminals gain skill. Nonetheless, with trade secrets, firms have a relatively flexible, low cost protection for innovation.

6.10 Trade secrets can reduce transaction costs; these reductions allow firms and economies to function more efficiently. Without trade secret protection, firms would have to work around, potentially at great expense, their trade secrets when interacting with other firms. Trade secrecy provides legal structure to these interactions. It does so to a much lesser degree than is found in other IP rights but nonetheless reduces transaction costs. Lower transaction costs theoretically make markets more efficient and can pave the way for innovation and economic growth.

However, the protection of trade secrets differs by jurisdiction and can increase uncertainty. Uncertainty, generally considered bad for markets, refers to unknown risks. A known risk is one where the probabilities are known, whereas with an uncertainty probabilities are unknown. Uncertainty may cause businesses to delay decision-making and, therefore, a reduction in uncertainty improves business confidence. Trade secret protection is less uniform globally than other IP rights. An EU Commission report (Commission, 2013) concludes that uncertainty in the protection of trade secrets negatively impacts business behaviour. The lack of clarity over trade secrets protection, and subsequent increase in uncertainty for business, can harm market activity. Instead, clearer trade secrecy protection should reduce this uncertainty and pave the way for more efficient markets. **6.11**

Coca-Cola's history in India is an example of how the lack of certainty can negatively impact business. Having been in the market since 1958, Coca-Cola left India in 1977 after a dispute with the government over its trade secrets. The government, under the Foreign Exchange Regulation Act (FERA), required foreign companies to reduce their equity share in Indian subsidiaries to 40%, which would include sharing the trade-secret-protected formula (Amine, 2008). Coca-Cola chose to leave rather than share their trade secrets and potentially lose control over their protection. In this case, the uncertainty over the protection of their trade secrets caused a major company to exit a market and may have impacted the decisions of others. **6.12**

Trade secrets appear to be gaining interest in policy, research, and legal arenas.[2] In Almeling (2012), the author cites seven reasons why trade secrets are increasing in importance: digital technology;[3] a mobile workforce;[4] the rising value of IP, of which trade secrets are a part; the widespread adoption of the US Uniform Trade Secrets Act; trade secrets' flexible definition; an increase in international threats;[5] and the shifting calculus between whether to pursue patent or trade secret protection. **6.13**

[2] However, this should be taken with a grain of salt because experts in trade secrets benefit from saying that trade secrets are increasing in importance. The author of this chapter, for example, completed her PhD thesis on the economics of trade secret. Trade secrets are vastly under-researched but this does not mean that the growth in trade secrets research corresponds to a growth in the importance of trade secrecy.

[3] A reference to the increase in cybercrime.

[4] Own employees are often the source of trade secrets theft as per Searle (2012), a mobile workforce places more distance between employers and employees and increases digital content.

[5] This refers to economic espionage. As per the US Economic Espionage Act of 1996, 'economic espionage' is the theft of trade secrets to benefit a foreign agent.

6.14 Work by the OECD and the EU Commission, both bodies renowned for their political influence, suggest that there is policy interest in trade secrets. In 2014, the OECD published a trade policy paper (Lippoldt and Schultz, 2014), which finds that trade secrets are associated with key indicators of innovation and international economic flows. The Commission published an in-depth literature review, legal analysis, and survey (Commission, 2013) which highlights the economic importance of trade secrets, its fragmented protection within the EU, and makes recommendations for government intervention. Indeed, legislative action in both the EU and the US began in 2016. Trade secrets do appear to be enjoying their fifteen minutes of fame.

Trade Secrets and IP Strategies

6.15 Like all IP, trade secrets offer innovators (mostly firms) a strategic tool. What is surprising is that trade secrets may be more important than patents for some firms. A survey by Cohen, Nelson, and Walsh (2000)[6] finds that trade secrets are a popular form of market protection. Other means of market protection include exploitation of being first to market, use of complementary sales and service capabilities, product differentiation, and cost leadership. For the economic study of IP, the concept that trade secrets and market strategies may be relatively more important to innovators than more formal IP has been a disruptive realization. This section considers the interaction of trade secrets with other forms of IP.

Trade secrets and patents

6.16 Discussions on the use and economic impact of trade secrets often begin with patents. This reflects the importance economists place on patents, patent policy, and patent research. It is an important starting point, but perhaps a misguided one as this section will explore. Economic models often place patents as substitutes for trade secrets. The classic assumption is that a firm, upon successful innovation, makes a conscious decision to patent or not to patent. In many cases, the decision not to patent is assumed to be a decision to use trade secrets.

6.17 However, this black-and-white approach is at odds with both the theoretical and empirical evidence. Instead, further examination suggests a more nuanced approach to a firm's decision between patents and trade secrets. Surprisingly, firms may consider trade secrets as relatively more important than patents (Arundel, 2001).

6.18 Economic theory often places patents in opposition to trade secrets and frames trade secrets as a substitute form of IP protection. However, this is not strictly true,

[6] One of the co-authors, John Walsh has noted this is one of his most cited papers. It has never appeared in a peer-reviewed journal but, at the time of writing, has over 2,500 citations.

as while a patent can never become a trade secret, a trade secret could become a patent. Public disclosure, which is required by patents and rejected by trade secrets, influences their interaction. The contents of a patent document are public and, therefore, cannot be considered a trade secret. However, a trade secret might eventually become a patent or could provide the know-how to enable the use of a patent, or could be protected by other IP rights. Post-patenting innovation may also be protected by trade secrets. Thus, patents and trade secrets are not mutually exclusive.

There are other economic interpretations that suggest that the size of the innovation may influence the decision to use trade secrets or patents. For example, Anton and Yao (2004) suggest that firms would patent small innovations and use trade secrets for larger innovations in part because of the duration of protection. It may also be that for medium-sized innovations, firms use a mix of trade secrecy and patent protection. **6.19**

Another consideration of IP is the spread of knowledge. The more knowledge is spread, the more subsequent innovation; yet trade secrets appear to prevent this diffusion. However, firms' use of trade secrets may promote knowledge flows more than patents. Bessen (2005) suggests that firms choose patents when the patent serves to reduce or prevent imitation; therefore trade secrets, as an alternative, may actually serve to increase the diffusion of knowledge. Innovation and knowledge spread more when it is profitable for others to copy the innovation. Patents inhibit this diffusion whereas trade secrets may not. Instead, trade secrets may enable the spread of innovation more than a simple analysis might suggest. **6.20**

Overall, the economic analysis has developed to place trade secrets and patents in a more dynamic relationship in which they can serve as complements and substitutes. **6.21**

Patents, policy, and trade secrets

Policy levers also influence the use of trade secrets. For example, prior use rights—which vary by jurisdiction (Menell and Scotchmer (2005))—are a mechanism to allow the owners of trade secrets the right to continue to use the secret innovation even if it is subsequently patented. To clarify, imagine Firm A chooses to protect an innovation with a trade secret. Firm B later independently creates the same innovation and patents it. In jurisdictions with prior use rights, Firm A can continue to freely use their trade secret. This is likely to reduce Firm A's propensity to patent, but at the same time continues to provide incentives to innovate (Denicolo and Franzoni, 2004). **6.22**

A further consideration of the interaction of trade secrets and patent policy is that of the breadth and inventive step requirement of patents. Breadth defines the line at which other innovations infringe a patent. Inventive step defines what is patentable (Scotchmer, 2006). Narrowly interpreted patents (those with a smaller **6.23** breadth) allow trade secrets more 'room' in the innovation space surrounding the patent. Patents with a wider breadth restrict trade secrets. A higher inventive step increases the probability that any particular innovation is not patentable—thereby also increasing the space in which trade secrets may be an appropriate protection mechanism. A lower inventive step, on the other hand, will increase instances in which a patent may serve as a substitute for trade secrets.

Cost–benefit analysis

6.24 Economics assumes that firms act rationally[7] in deciding their protection strategy. A cost–benefit analysis provides a means to express the decision to patent and/or use trade secrets. There are a host of variables to consider, but a basic analysis includes the following: the length of protection offered, the patentability of the innovation, the enforceability of a patent, and the nature of the innovation itself. Economic analysis assumes that firms choose trade secrets when the benefits outweigh the costs. As in earlier discussions, these are often framed in contrast to patents.

6.25 Accounting for various factors that influence the costs and benefits of a trade secret, according to (Friedman, Landes, and Posner, 1991), firms will choose trade secrets when:

1. The period it will take for competitors to reverse engineer the innovation is either:
   a. concurrent to length of the patent term (for moderately valuable innovations); or
   b. longer than the patent term.
2. The innovation is not patentable but difficult to reverse engineer.
3. The firm wants to avoid disclosure.
4. Patenting is prohibitively costly.
5. The innovation is a process, not product innovation, and consequently patent infringement is difficult to identify.
6. The innovation is not conducive to licensing.
7. The innovation is likely to be an early innovation in a cumulative innovation process.

6.26 Empirical evidence supports these arguments. A 1994 survey (by Cohen, Nelson, and Walsh, 2000) suggests that firms cite the following four reasons as the top motivations for not patenting an innovation:

1. Difficulty in demonstrating the novelty of an invention;
2. Amount of information disclosed in a patent application;

[7] Unfortunately this rationality may not account for the fact that for some, the prestige of having a patent may be more important than the protection it provides.

3. Cost of defending the patent in court; and
4. Ease of legally inventing around a patent.

A number of these factors require sophistication on the part of firms and accurate forecasting, thus the uncertainty associated with relatively less secure trade secrets may be off-putting for firms. However, both the theoretical and empirical evidence suggest that trade secrets are a viable and strategic form of protection for innovations. **6.27**

Trade Secrets, Copyright, and Other Rights

Economics has not deigned to look much beyond the interaction of trade secrets and patent to the interaction with other rights. This section presents some brief analysis, stemming mostly from a legal viewpoint. **6.28**

Trade secrets and copyright

The interaction of trade secrets and copyright is relatively unexamined although they are generally considered to be complementary to each other. Dorvee (1981) argues that, while copyright can be viewed as a 'backup or complement' to trade secrets, it is not an advisable strategy as copyright law will only protect the expression and enforcement of copyright will likely include disclosure, thereby negating the trade secrecy. **6.29**

For firm strategy, an oft-examined sector is that of software, where the protection of source code is challenging. There are relative advantages and disadvantages to trade secrets and copyright for the protection of computer programs (Bender, 1985). Copyright has the advantages of being better suited to a wider proliferation of the software, has a long duration, and relatively effective international protection. However, copyright suffers from a number of points of uncertainty including its scope and enforcement. Trade secrets offer advantages in that they also enjoy a long duration and have a relatively wider subject matter and scope. Yet trade secrets struggle in that they can be difficult to maintain, difficult to enforce internationally, and there is a greater possibility of the loss of protection.[8] **6.30**

Trade secrets, trade marks, and design rights

Very little economic analysis exists on the interaction between trade secrets and other rights such as trade marks and design rights. For trade marks, it is likely that the underlying branding supported by trade marks may be augmented by trade **6.31**

[8] This list is adapted from Bender (1985) who includes a longer list with an in-depth legal analysis.

secrets. Resource-supported marketing and branding, such as customer lists and strategies, may also be protected by trade secrets.

6.32 The trade secret itself may be a key marketing tool. The secret Coca-Cola formula, for example, probably provides the company with a strong marketing proposition.

> ...Coca Cola's secret recipe [is] such a clever marketing technique. Companies have often used secrecy as a marketing tool. The very idea of mystery is one that attracts attention, and is often seen as an element of quality—'if they are doing all these things to protect the recipe, it must be a valuable product', would a typical consumer think. In sum, in the mind of the consumer, secrecy signifies that the recipe must be 'so good' that it needs to be kept secret—which then reinforces the idea of quality (Voyer, 2014).

6.33 Trade secrets may also enable the development of design rights. Prior to the making public or registration of a design right, a particular design may be protected by trade secrecy. Additionally, processes used in the creation of a design may also be trade secrets. Like their interaction with patents, trade secrets may protect innovation surrounding the design otherwise not covered by design rights.

Empirical Analysis and Evidence

6.34 Empirical analyses of trade secrets generally fall into three categories: survey data, evidence from litigation, and research and development (R&D) data.

6.35 As discussed in Chapters 1 and 2, surveys are often indirect measurements of IP and may more adequately capture attitudes. The Cohen, Nelson, and Walsh (2000) survey was a turning point in the economic analysis of trade secrets as it demonstrated their value amongst American firms. Arundel (2001) provides a similar analysis for the EU. These survey analyses can be very useful in understanding how firms view their strategy.

6.36 The use of litigation data brings a whole host of challenges. Litigation data can only measure that which is recorded by the courts and or otherwise publicly disclosed. In practice, only the minority of disputes and litigation activities will be public; data is only the tip of the iceberg. Despite this, when dealing with trade secrets, the iceberg is typically completely submerged and litigation can shed some light. Additionally, legal disputes often represent an end-point that can be useful for backwards induction and framing of analysis.[9]

6.37 While trade secrets themselves are not directly measured, associated measurements such as R&D expenditures, patent registers, and the development of law can be combined to create a better understanding of the environment in which trade

[9] Readers interested in trade secrets and litigation data may wish to consult Searle (2012), Lerner (2006), and Almeling (2012).

secrets operate. This type of analysis is more in line with traditional economic analysis than surveys and litigation data. However, users of such analyses should be cautious that the data and analysis subscribe to robust methodology as impressive, but misleading, results are common.

This more traditional analysis of trade secrets is fairly new.[10] For example, an analysis of American data suggests that increased trade secrets protection may actually reduce patenting which again would suggest that the two are substitutes (Png, 2012). Png's study further suggests that stronger trade secrets law reduce spillover[11] effects of R&D amongst manufacturers and, therefore, reduced R&D expenditures. **6.38**

Further considerations

Two further points in the economics of trade secrets are those of labour mobility and licensing. **6.39**

Labour mobility, the degree to which labour is able to move, is an important means for economic efficiency. Higher labour mobility suggests a freer-flowing labour market where labour is more efficiently employed. However, the labour mobility of employees is restricted by contractual non-compete or non-disclosure causes. These clauses, typically intended to protect trade secrets, limit an employee's ability to work for others. The United States also has the 'inevitable disclosure doctrine', which argues that former employees, when employed by a competitor, will inevitably disclose confidential information in the course of their work duties. When trade secrecy protection is stronger, it may have a negative impact on labour mobility and ultimately economic growth. **6.40**

A second point of consideration is that of licensing. If IP is an incentive to innovate, and the spread of knowledge increases innovation, then the licensing of trade secrets is an important mechanism to promote the spread of knowledge. There are a number of theoretical models examining the role of licensing and trade secrets[12] which provide predictions on how licensing may interact with trade secrets and market competition. Licensing can avoid the duplication of research efforts, increase the diffusion of knowledge, and allow the owners of trade secrets to recoup further value from the efforts of their innovation. **6.41**

---

[10] Interested readers should look at Ivan Png's work (University of Singapore). Comparable to Png's work is an analysis by Morikawa (2014) which uses Japanese data to find that service and manufacturing firms have similar levels of the use of trade secrets.

[11] A knowledge spillover effect is where knowledge generated by one party stimulates knowledge development and innovation in another. Spillover effects are generally considered positive. In this case, free-flowing information can increase the speed of innovation. However, if information is kept secret, these spillover effects are less common.

[12] See Searle (2010) 44–54 for a summary of the relevant literature.

6.42 Trade secrets are an essential complement to IP regimes. Firms rank trade secrets above other forms of IP as important for their market success and strategy. As noted earlier, trade secrets are relatively under-researched as their analysis is particularly challenging. The interaction of trade secrets with another IP right is important as trade secrets may facilitate the development of other IP. The great debate, however, remains whether trade secrets are complements or substitutes for patents. Economic analysis argues that it depends; in some cases, patents and trade secrets will be substitutes as firms choose between the two. In others, they will be complements as both are deployed. Fundamentally, economics supports the idea that trade secrets are an important piece of the innovation puzzle.

Geographical Indications

6.43 Geographical indications, or GIs as they are commonly referred to, are economically different from other rights. A *sui generis*[13] right, GIs are not transferrable and not held privately. Unlike other rights, they confer no freedom to contract or freedom to license, and seek to preserve traditions. In this section, the economic impacts of GIs are discussed from both the supply and demand sides of the market.

Introduction

6.44 A GI is, by the European Commission definition, 'a distinctive sign used to identify a product as originating in the territory of a particular country, region or locality where its quality, reputation or another characteristic is linked to its geographical origin.'[14]

6.45 GIs provide protection and standards for signs that identify a good as being associated with a particular region. This typically is associated with resources unique to the region (e.g. stone or agricultural inputs), skills, local knowledge, processes, and reputation. In this sense, like trade marks, they seek to improve signalling between producers and consumers. Following the line of Bramley and June (2011), GIs are designed to promote consumer and producer welfare, improve market access, contribute to the economic development of rural communities, preserve traditional knowledge, and even preserve biodiversity.

6.46 However, one criticism of GIs is that other rights largely cover their protection. A common argument in favour of GIs is that they protect against unfair

---

[13] *Sui generis* in IP typically means a right other than the traditional copyright, patent, and trade mark rights. It is often a unique right created with a specific sector or community in mind.

[14] 'Geographical-indications' European Commission, Trade. Available at: http://ec.europa.eu/trade/policy/accessing-markets/intellectual-property/geographical-indications/, accessed 24 October 2014.

competition from producers free riding on the goodwill and reputation of the GI. This would entail a producer, not from the region, implying their products were from the region. However, there are a number of other options that would also cover this. For example, trade marks confer similar protection.[15] Bramley and Kirsten (2007) note the differences between trade marks and GIs, 'Trademarks are distinctive signs identifying the relationship between the proprietor of the mark and his goods or services, and thus not limited by any territorial link. In contrast, geography is at the heart of geographical indications (Morran, 1993)—they being distinctive signs identifying goods as originating from a particular geographical area.'[16] There are legal subtleties between these rights, but they all serve the same economic purpose: to allow rights holders to appropriate the returns from their reputation and branding, and to send signals on quality to consumers.

While the protection given by GIs differs from that afforded by trade marks, there are a host of separate but similar rights. Josling (2006)[17] provides a list of these similar rights: designation of origin, indications of source, appellations of origin, indications of geographical origin, traditional specialities guaranteed, certification marks, and protected food names.[18] Legally, these are distinct rights as, for example, Bramley and Kirsten (2007) note, 'All appellations of origin are thus geographical indications, but some geographical indications are not appellations of origin.'[19] From an economics perspective, most of these will provide largely the same economic impact as GIs. However, in the case of privately run certification marks and similar rights, these self-regulating organizations have incentives to exclude others and can be difficult to regulate. GIs avoid some of these problems but present others, as discussed below. **6.47**

Despite a *prima facie* economic rejection of the premise of GIs, GIs do shape their markets. GIs may benefit producers by increasing the premiums associated with particular goods. Consumers benefit from consistency in quality and reduced confusion between products. However, the overall economic impact of GIs is unclear for both the production and consumption sides of these markets. **6.48**

Economic impacts for producers

A GI provides legal structure to the branding and quality of a product associated with a particular geographical region. It is meant to protect producers from **6.49**

[15] This assumes that the marks associated wtih GI would qualify as a trade mark. This may, however, not be the case as they may be considered descriptive, for example, ham from Parma.
[16] Bramley and Kristin (2007) 86.
[17] Josling (2006) 14.
[18] The author has added protected food names to Josling's list.
[19] Bramley and Kristin (2007) 74.

competition from similar goods produced elsewhere that unfairly benefit from a brand premium of the GI. However, the long-term economic benefits conferred on producers and these regions remain unproven. The introduction of a GI may benefit producers through legal protection, economic development, and environmental concerns, but these impacts are unclear. Furthermore, the GI may distort incentives and affect both the quality and quantity of the product.

6.50 For producers of GI products, GIs reduce the potential commoditization of their goods by providing legal differentiation from other, similar goods. For example, bulk olive oil is largely undifferentiated and commoditized.[20] However, niche markets exist in cold-pressed, single estate, regional, etc. olive oils. A GI-protected olive oil has the benefit of the legal protection of its differentiation from bulk olive oil. Thus, GIs can provide legal protection to prevent the further commoditization of a good and its generic use. However, much of the branding required to differentiate a specific oil may be protected by other IP rights.

6.51 Perhaps the most convincing economic argument in favour of GIs is that of economic development of rural areas. Bramley and June (2011) note that research suggests this may be the case although the arguments are largely theoretical. Assuming that producers in rural areas are likely to be smaller entities and not owned by large agri-businesses, GIs may provide a level of protection that smaller producers would not be able to afford. The cost of international registration of trade marks and the resources to maintain the rights may be beyond the mean of small and medium-sized enterprises (SMEs). Enforcement issues, in particular, can be costly and a GI may help to reduce these costs. However, these arguments are weaker if individual producers are owned by larger businesses where profits may not develop the local economy. Indeed, the production of wines and spirits has undergone significant consolidation[21] in past years and, in these markets, the majority of production of GI goods may be owned by large multi-nationals.

6.52 The introduction of a GI affects the value of its inputs. Given the geographical emphasis of GIs, the increase in the value of the land is particularly notable. Gervais (2013) argues, 'GIs, like (all) marks, undeniably can increase the value of a product in the market and exponentially increase the profits in particular if there is not a huge difference in production costs. This, in turn, translates into much higher land

[20] There is a lack of consensus as to whether olive oil is considered a commodity. For the purposes of this discussion, it is sufficient that olive oil be nearly commoditized for GIs to have economic impact.

[21] Emler, R. (13 June 2012). 'Spirits Firms Poised for Further Consolidation' *The Drinks Business*. Available at: http://www.thedrinksbusiness.com/2012/06/spirits-firms-poised-for-further-consolidation, and Morss, E. (14 January 2012). 'The Future of the Global Wine Industry' *Morss Global Finance*. Available at http://www.morssglobalfinance.com/the-future-of-the-global-wine-industry.

value where production under a protected GI or a geographic certification mark is allowed.' Gervais cites the example of the expansion of the Champagne region as an example where arable land qualifying for Champagne GI status has a market value of 350 times that of similar land without GI status.[22] This huge increase in land value and subsequent costs may price smaller producers out of the market and impact the wider real estate market.

An argument in favour of GIs is their environmental impact and long-term sustainability. As Bramley (2011) notes, it is possible that, by mandating producers of GI goods to adhere to traditional practices, producers are less likely to engage in environmentally damaging practices and may help to preserve biodiversity. Given that these practices have sustained the geography of the area long enough to qualify for GI status, they may be more environmentally friendly than modern practices. This long-term sustainability also applies to the branding and reputation of the area that may provide positive externalities for industries such as tourism. In this sense, GIs can serve as custodians for the heritage for the long term. **6.53**

However, the introduction of a GI might actually provide incentives to change the existing quality of the protected good. The structure of the GI and the surrounding policy and institutions will dictate the minimum standards of a GI. For any given producer, the standards may be higher or lower than their existing practice. Thus, the introduction of a GI may in some cases require that they raise standards (and potentially costs). Alternatively, a product may be of higher quality than other products with the same GI standard, which provides an incentive to lower standards. As Agarwal and Barone (2005) note, GIs 'simultaneously reduce the distinction between companies producing competing products in the same geographical area.'[23] This reduction in distinction may result in a change in overall quality. **6.54**

The introduction of a GI may also impact the quantity of a product that is produced in a region. As the ability of an individual producer to differentiate their product is reduced, the good may be exposed to higher production. In economics, this is referred to the 'tragedy of the commons' where shared common resources (in this case the brand) are over-used as the benefits to the individual outweigh the costs. The individual incurs only a fraction of the collective costs and thus the resource is consumed in an unsustainable manner. Thus, the delicate balance between the quality and quantity required to maintain the brand may be disrupted by the introduction of a GI. Agarwal and Barone (2005) note, 'Any producer…is capable of leveraging the brand; the brand is not restricted to a single producer or a group of producers who may have initiated and marketed it. This could lead to an increase **6.55**

[22] Dromard, T. (26 October 2007). 'Le champagne en quete de nouvelles terres' *Le Figaro*. Available at: http://avis-vin.lefigaro.fr/magazine-vin/o8920-le-champagne-en-quete-de-nouvelles-terres.

[23] Agarwal and Barone (2005) 4.

in production in the GI area, reducing the scarcity and hence premiums related to the product.'[24]

6.56 The long-term impact of GIs on producers is unclear. Existing producers may initially benefit from the price premium and reduced competition from products outside the GI protection, but cost inputs and distorted incentives may mean that the economic distribution of these benefits changes over time. Thus, the original goals of the introduction of a GI may not be realized.

Economic impacts for consumers

6.57 Like trade marks, GIs solve problems of information asymmetry in which the consumer will have less information about the quality of good than the supplier. The GI provides a quality signal that a good meets the standards implied by the reputation of the GI. For foodie readers, this means that products labelled Parmesan or Parma ham indeed originate from Parma.[25] Consumers do not have perfect information about the quality of a particular good and attempting to ensure they do is inefficient. Rather than requiring a trip to Italy to check on a particular farm, GIs provide consumers with improved information. However, as noted in the previous section, the quality and quantity impacts of a GI are unclear. It is possible that consumers will face changed quality and higher quantity upon the introduction of a GI.

6.58 The impact on the availability of GI-protected and similar products is also unclear. The variety of products in a particular class may increase if the GI forces products that do not qualify for GI status to innovate. For example, the introduction of the Feta GI in 2006 resulted in similar salted curd cheeses being rebranded as 'salad cheese' or other names. Potentially, this may increase the availability and variety of these cheeses. However, it may also do the opposite in that salad cheeses are unable to compete with Feta and are removed from the market. The price differential between Feta and salad cheeses may widen as Feta commands a brand premium against the newly branded salad cheese. A consumer of salad cheeses may find the price of these cheeses has decreased. Again, the overall picture is indeterminate.

6.59 The retail sellers of GI protected products are also affected by the introduction of a GI. Supermarkets, in particular, are likely to face reduced ability to sell private label brands, and increased costs in purchasing GI goods. GIs may restrict a supermarket's ability to purchase in bulk as GI products may be exported only in packaged form. The GI brand premium may also increase the wholesale price of these goods.

[24] Agarwal and Barone (2005) 4.

[25] Indeed, pre-sliced Parma ham must be sliced and packed in Parma unless cut on the spot such as in a deli. BBC News. (20 May 2003). 'Asda Slams 'Ham-fisted' Parma Ruling'. Available at http://news.bbc.co.uk/1/hi/business/3043283.stm.

Again, all of these impacts are unclear and Bramley (2011) has noted the dearth of empirical analysis to provide evidence of these economic impacts.

Further considerations

If, as this book argues, IP exists to incentivize innovation, GIs struggle to achieve this goal. GIs preserve existing ways of production. These characteristics stem from geography and, therefore, limit the realm in which innovation may occur. Traditional methods will be codified and thus restrict future innovation. With climate change, environmental degradation, changing consumer tastes, and scientific discoveries, it could be that a GI ends up restricting future ability for producers to adapt to changing conditions. Similar restrictions arise from institutions such as charitable trusts[26] where an irrevocable trust is established which may be unable to adapt as needs changes. **6.60**

A case study that highlights the limiting effect of GIs is that of Newcastle Ale. As Evans (2010) notes, when, in 2004, Scottish and Newcastle Brewery moved production of Newcastle Brown Ale from Newcastle to Gateshead, the ale was no longer in compliance with the GI specification. As a result, the GI was cancelled. In this case, efforts to reduce production costs, which could be construed as a process innovation, resulted in the loss of GI status; the GI provided disincentives to innovation. At the same time, the Newcastle Brown Ale trade marks[27] may provide sufficient protection that the loss of the GI may not impact the business. **6.61**

Even when operating within the boundaries of GI compliance, there are concerns. As noted earlier, GIs change the incentives associated with quality and quantity. Debates on compliance bleed into xenophobic debates when the worker base for production shifts from local to those perceived as outsiders. The 'Made in Italy' label, while not a GI, has come under criticism due to the use of undocumented Chinese workers in Italy.[28] Following the scandal surrounding the use of horse meat in 2013, it became apparent that food fraud is a problem[29] and what may look like compliance may not be so. The premium associated with a GI will attract strategic, and sometimes illegal, use of the system. **6.62**

[26] For example, in Islamic structures, a charitable institution called a *waqf* exists which may restrict modernization and redeployment of resources as argued in Jafar-Shaghaghi, K. (2014). 'The Development of the Legal Parameters of the Waqf Institution in Contemporary Iran and Its Socioeconomic Impact'. PhD Thesis (University of St Andrews).

[27] For example, Community trade mark EM500000000192625.

[28] Thomas, D. (23 November 2007). 'Made in China on the Sly' *New York Times*, Op-ed. Available at: http://www.nytimes.com/2007/11/23/opinion/23thomas.html.

[29] Elliot, C. (2014). 'Elliott Review into the Integrity and Assurance of Food Supply Networks—Final Report, A National Food Crime Prevention Framework' *UK Government*. Available at: https://www.gov.uk/government/uploads/system/uploads/attachment_data/file/350726/elliot-review-final-report-july2014.pdf.

6.63 GIs, like all IP, create a legal monopoly. In addition, GIs offer no freedom to contract or license and are non-transferrable. The collective ownership of GIs and the institutions and specifications required to administer them are more akin to a cartel. Economists are not fans of cartels as they typically result in higher prices and reduced competition (see Chapter 7 for further details on competition). Indeed, the last sentence essentially spells out the goals of a GI—to maintain the price premium of a branded product and to prevent others from benefiting from the premium. This presents potential competition problems. While the GIs may benefit producers, it will result in higher prices and reduced competition at the expense of consumers. Overall, the cartel created by GIs will reduce social welfare.

6.64 Other debates in GIs include the expansion of GIs to non-agricultural products. These are typically textiles such as pottery or woollens that still are strongly influenced by the environment in which they are produced. Harris Tweed, for example, is a certification mark that covers textiles, 'handwoven by the islanders at their homes in the Outer Hebrides, finished in the Outer Hebrides, and made from pure virgin wool dyed and spun in the Outer Hebrides.'[30] However, without the benefit of the distinct borders created by an island, defining the region and specification for a non-agricultural GI can be challenging as techniques and materials may be more diffused than agricultural GIs. For example, the area associated with the Persian carpet is ambiguous. As an emerging right, non-agricultural GIs are still developing and further refinement of the right may occur.[31]

6.65 Geographical indications do not sit well with classic economic theory and the incentive to innovate justification for IP. Additionally, the development and social goals of GIs, when viewed through the lens of economics, may not be realized. The unintended consequences on input prices, competitors, and consumers may undermine the overall, positive intentions of GIs. Yet the area is relatively new both to economists and as a policy; the future may further refine GIs to address some of the problems addressed here.

Other Rights

Plant breeders' rights

6.66 Plant breeders' rights (PBR), also known as plant variety rights (PVR), are described by the International Union for the Protection of Plant Varieties (UPOV) as 'a

[30] Anthony, D. (Feburary 2013). 'From the Croft to the Catwalk: The Harris Tweed Certification Mark' *WIPO Magazine*. Available at: http://www.wipo.int/wipo_magazine/en/2013/01/article_0006.html.

[31] Yet to be fully considered by the literature is the use of government resources to protect GIs. The topic raises questions on the appropriateness of government resources to protect these rights not available to the general public.

form of intellectual property right granted to the breeder of a new plant variety. According to this right, certain acts concerning the exploitation of the protected variety require the prior authorization of the breeder.'[32] PBR are a *sui generis* right to protect products that propagate the plant (i.e. seeds and cuttings). PBR are a good fit for the innovation theory of IP in that the rights granted to plant breeders should encourage further innovation.

However, PBR do present some concerns. In the United Kingdom, their protection lasts twenty-five to thirty years. This is longer than a patent but shorter than copyright or trade marks. Like other rights, PBR contain exceptions to create the right balance between existing rights holders and future rights holders. For example, there is a research exemption, which allows for the use of PBR-protected materials in non-commercial research. The incentive impact of research exceptions varies; Moschini and Yerokhin (2007) argue if research costs are high, then exceptions reduce incentives to innovate. However, if research costs are low, the exception may be desirable as it will increase the 'pool' of innovators and potentially result in more innovation. **6.67**

There are humanitarian concerns associated with restricting the use of seeds by farmers in poorer countries. Farmers may struggle to afford protected seeds and PBR law can account for this to a degree by providing exceptions and limitations to PBR. UPOV notes, 'for some crops, there has been a common practice of farmers saving their own seed, i.e. seed is produced on a farm for the purpose of re-sowing on the same farm and not for the purpose of selling the seed. The [UPOV Convention] provision allows each member of the Union to take account of this practice when providing variety protection.' Thus, as in other forms of IP rights, exceptions can attenuate the impact of the limitations imposed by IP rights. **6.68**

Another consideration is the preservation and protection of plant genetic resources. In their analysis of PBR, Swanson and Göschl (2000) argue that PBR provide incentives to preserve genetic resources and biodiversity. However, they find that 'aggregate figures indicate that the incentives to switch toward modern agriculture have overwhelmed the IPR-based incentives to maintain diversity in the developing world over the past few decades.' Hence the short-term incentives to produce crops outweigh the long-term incentives to protect biodiversity, and potentially future innovation based on diverse plant genetic resources. **6.69**

The economic issues surrounding PBR are akin to those surrounding other rights. However, like GIs, these are a relatively new right and may evolve in future years to develop unique economic characteristics. **6.70**

[32] UPOV (2015).

Traditional knowledge

6.71 Traditional Knowledge (TK) is defined by WIPO (2015) as, 'knowledge, know-how, skills and practices that are developed, sustained and passed on from generation to generation within a community, often forming part of its cultural or spiritual identity.' There is not a universally agreed definition of TK and it falls under a larger concept of IP for indigenous peoples.[33] Other types of protection, such as copyright and appellation of origin, have historically been used to protect the intellectual assets of indigenous peoples. The lack of defined boundaries of TK makes it a difficult subject for economic analysis. It also does not conform to traditional incentives to innovate as, like GIs, it protects traditions and not innovations.

6.72 At the moment, economics has done little to analyse TK. This is in part due to the overlapping economic and community identity aspects of TK. WIPO fact finding missions found that, 'Stakeholders consulted considered TK to be a constantly renewed source of wealth, both as an economic asset and as cultural patrimony. In many cases, TK holders did not separate "artistic" from "useful" aspects of their intellectual creations and innovations' (Richards, 2008). While protection for TK does not encourage the generation of further TK, it may encourage product innovation as TK is translated into marketed goods and services. This is a potential source of economic development for indigenous communities.

6.73 A key topic for TK is that of the threat of biopiracy. In biopiracy, an entity (often cast as a foreign pharmaceutical company) that does not form part of the indigenous community uses TK to develop a good or service. This good or service may then be subject to IP such as patents. Theoretically, the existence of TK should form part of the prior art and prevent such a patent. In practice, TK may be insufficiently documented for prior art purposes. Framing such knowledge as TK can account for the undocumented status. However, Dutfield (2011) warns biopiracy scares have been overhyped. He refers to other authors who note that TK may be a key form to preserving information lost with the extinction of indigenous groups.

6.74 Like a number of relatively new rights discussed in this chapter, TK is an area that has not yet been subject to economic scrutiny. It is difficult to fit into innovation theory of IP by itself. Instead, TK has a much more defensive role in that it potentially prevents the expropriation of knowledge and cultural assets, much like GIs. However, the conflation of economically useful knowledge and cultural patrimony

---

[33] The UN describes indigenous peoples as follows: 'It is estimated that there are more than 370 million indigenous people spread across 70 countries worldwide. Practicing unique traditions, they retain social, cultural, economic and political characteristics that are distinct from those of the dominant societies in which they live' (Peoples, 2015).

makes analysis difficult. Emerging sub-disciplines of economics, such as cultural economics, may provide further insight in the future.

Other *sui generis* rights

In addition to the rights discussed earlier,[34] there are a number of other *sui generis* rights. These include database rights, semiconductor rights, ship hull designs, and other permutations. *Sui generis* rights can be a way of addressing challenges associated with a one-size-fits-all regime. By creating specific rights for specific circumstances, the tailored approach of *sui generis* rights can provide more refined incentives to innovation. **6.75**

However, the cases of database (EU) and semiconductor (US) rights suggest that *sui generis* rights may not be a good solution. Both database and semiconductor rights were created in response to technological and market changes. Anecdotal evidence[35] suggests that semiconductor rights have already been made redundant by the speed of technology development. Database rights have also not had the desired effect. Communities (2005) notes that, 'The second problem with the "*sui generis*" right is that its economic impact on database production is unproven. Introduced to stimulate the growth of databases in Europe, the new instrument has had no proven impact on the production of databases.'[36] Communities (2005) adds, '... there has been a considerable growth in database production in the US, whereas, in the EU, the introduction of "*sui generis*" protection appears to have had the opposite effect. With respect to "non-original" databases, the assumption that more and more layers of IP protection means more innovation and growth appears not to hold up.'[37] **6.76**

Given the relative inflexibility of the one-size-fits-all nature of IP, *sui generis* rights are a tempting option. Yet, as database rights, they may not have the desired impact. In fact, the addition of IP rights may actually thwart innovation by making it more complicated for innovators. **6.77**

Conclusion

This chapter has presented an economic understanding of a variety of unusual types of IP rights. In the case of trade secrets, there is still debate as to whether they should be classed as an IP right. The three other rights examined here, GIs, PBR, and TK, are all *sui generis*, relatively new rights. GIs and TK, in particular, present challenges **6.78**

[34] See also the section on Supplementary Protection Certificates (SPCs) in Chapter 3.
[35] Based on anecdotes told to the author and as yet unproven.
[36] (Commission, 2008) 24.
[37] ibid.

to the social contract/incentive to innovate theory of IP. Their compatibility with the intrinsic rights/labour desert theory is more obvious. However, at the heart of all of these rights is an economic interest to protect and preserve knowledge. Economic theory does not require financial, growth-driven goals in its applications. These *sui generis* rights highlight that non-financial interests form a part of individual's preferences and goals and are relevant to IP systems.

7

COMPETITION AND INTELLECTUAL PROPERTY

> 'Monopoly is the purpose of the patent law, and prevention of monopoly is the purpose of the anti-trust laws. How difficult it is to define the respective territory of the patent law and the anti-trust laws, and how numerous and conflicting, even before 1914, were the decisions on this subject. . .'[1] (Montague, 1927)

The interaction of IP with competition has long been of concern to economics, as Montague describes. The creation of monopolies, albeit legal monopolies, is against the economic mantra of the benefits of competition. This pro-competition stance of economics explains in part the general scepticism economics holds towards IP. Despite this, the limitation of competition stemming from IP is economically desirable. This chapter delves further[2] into the economics of competition and the interaction with IP. The first section introductions basic concepts of competition and introduces the analytical framework of structure, conduct, and performance. It proceeds to explain the key market structures of perfect competition, oligopoly, monopolistic competition, and monopoly. The next section, on conduct, details anti-competitive behaviours; the economic consequences are then described in a section examining performance. The final section brings together the concepts throughout the text to synthesize economic aspects of IP and competition. **7.01**

---

[1] Montague, G. H. (1927). 'Anti-Trust Laws and the Federal Trade Commission, 1914–1927' *Columbia Law Review* 27: 650–78, 663.

[2] This chapter expands on the introductory chapter and gives an overview of key concepts in an accessible manner so that the reader can assess common themes in discussions on competition. Readers interested in learning more about the economics of competition and industrial organization may want to consult university textbooks on microeconomics such as Goolsbee, A., Levitt, S. D., and Syverson, C. (2013). *Microeconomics* (New York; Basingstoke, Worth Publishers) and Lipsey, R. G. and Courant, P. N. (1996). *Microeconomics* (New York, Harper Collins College Publishers), referred to in this book.

Economics of Competition

7.02 This section introduces some key terms in the economics of competition and details market structures, behaviours, and market performance to highlight when the lack of competition can be problematic. For IP, the key concept is that the monopoly created by IP can reduce competition.

Benefits of competition

> 'Promoting competition is broadly accepted as the best available tool for promoting consumer well-being. . . . Competition's virtues are so ingrained within the antitrust community that competition often takes a religious quality.' (Stucke, 2013)

7.03 In general, economists consider competition to be a good thing.[3] Firms seeking to gain market share will improve the quality they offer, attempt to lower prices, and innovate in order to provide new products. This is to the benefit of consumers in higher quality, lower prices, greater variety, and innovation. In addition, it promotes a better allocation of resources,[4] improved efficiency, and higher productivity.

7.04 One of the attractions of competition, and, in particular, perfect competition as described below, is that the market regulates itself. This is Adam Smith's (Smith, 1759) 'invisible hand of the market'. As power is dispersed evenly through consumers and producers, no single entity has sufficient market power to affect the market. The more power is dispersed, the more competitive the market. The market self-governs and creates an efficient allocation of resources without government intervention. At its extreme, the theory is a tidy, utopian picture of markets. This utopian vision does not diminish the theory's usefulness for economic analysis, but is a reminder that it is unlikely to be observed in practice.

7.05 Competition can also encourage governments to increase quality. Mankiw (2012) notes that competition encourages good governance and prevents governments from exerting monopoly power over residents. For example, in Europe, competition between national IP offices and the European Patent Office (EPO) may serve as an incentive to maintain high standards of examination and policy. Providing rights holders with options not only provides firms with flexibility but also encourages

[3] This section builds on the discussion of competition found in the 'Introduction to Economics' section of the book.

[4] The allocation of resources is of interest because resources are limited, but consumer wants are unlimited. Allocation of resources is a term that describes the proportion of productive resources in their use across the economy, that is, what is being used where. Better resource allocation means that consumer wants are better addressed. It contributes to efficiency, discussed later in this section.

high quality IP services. Otherwise, as Mankiw reminds us, consumers will 'vote with their feet' and seek services elsewhere.

However, as the Stucke quotation that opened this section hints at, economists' obsession with competition may not be entirely warranted. There are exceptions in which reduced competition may be beneficial. Arguments for a pro-innovation IP system are based on this presumption. With free competition, innovators will compete with those who copy their innovations. The innovators may be unable to recoup their investments in innovation, will not have funds to invest in future innovation, and innovation as a whole will suffer. Another concern is that the arguments in favour of competition are based on the economy as a whole and the benefits may not be evenly distributed. Smaller firms may struggle to grow when competition is high and, given that smaller firms are often cast as key sources of employment and productivity growth, this could limit economic growth. 7.06

Structure, Conduct, and Performance

One useful way to frame and analyse markets, devised by Bain (1959), is that of structure, conduct, and performance. Structure refers to the market structure, which is the composition of the market as defined by the number and size of firms. Conduct is the behaviour of firms within the market. Performance is how well the industry does in terms of a number of factors such as efficiency, overall welfare, and output. Structure, conduct, and performance provide a straightforward structure for explaining the conditions, behaviours, and impact of reduced competition. 7.07

An underlying goal is that of efficiency. Efficiency is a very broad term. In general, it refers to, 'getting the most out of the resources used' (*Economist*, 2015). In economically efficient situations, resources are used optimally at the same time waste is minimized. A more specific type of allocative efficiency,[5] known as Pareto efficiency, is an efficiency in which no person can be made better off without making another worse off.[6] It is not a given that competition leads to efficiency, but this 7.08

[5] Allocative efficiency describes an efficient market where all goods and services are produced up to the point where their marginal cost equals their marginal benefit. For example, if the economy is a family at Sunday brunch, allocative efficiency would imply that the number of pancakes produced is 'efficient' when the last pancake is enjoyed as much as the effort and ingredients it cost to produce. One pancake more, and the cost of the pancake exceeds its benefit. One pancake less, and there is a missed opportunity for an efficiently enjoyed pancake.

[6] The concept of Pareto efficiency says that a market is inefficient if a change can make one person better off without harming others. Returning to the pancake example, assume that there are two blueberry pancakes and two currant pancakes. Two family members each have one pancake of each kind, but one family member really dislikes blueberry and the other really dislikes currants. If these two family members trade their pancakes for their preferred flavours, then they are both better off. In this case, Pareto efficiency is achieved because, after the pancake swap, no family member can be made better off without another being made worse off. However, Pareto efficiency does nothing to provide a moral assessment of whether inefficiency is good or bad.

chapter will largely refer to the broader concept of efficiency as the economics of competition focuses on firms, resources, and outputs. The following three sections examine structure, conduct, and performance.

Structure

7.09 Markets are an abstract place where buyers and sellers of goods and services transact. Markets often refer to specific goods and services, such as 'the market for used books' in which sellers of used books transact with buyers. Transactions are typically exchanges of goods and services for money. The market structure looks at the number, size, and power[7] of firms in a market. There are four main market structures[8] developed in this section: perfect competition, monopolistic competition, oligopoly, and monopoly.[9]

Barriers to entry

7.10 Before delving into market structure, the concept of barriers to entry merits further explanation. Barriers to entry are 'a cost of producing which must be borne by a firm which seeks to enter an industry but is not borne by firms already in the industry' (Stigler, 1993). There are a whole host of possible barriers to entry. Some are structural barriers that are the consequences of the nature of a market. For example, consumer demand, economies of scale,[10] government regulations, or geographical location may create barriers for new firms to enter a market. However, other barriers will be strategic and are a consequence of the behaviour of firms already in the market. These strategic barriers may be as a result of advertising and market loyalty, lobbying, or due to the anti-competitive behaviours detailed in the section on conduct. The more barriers to entry there are in a market, the harder it is for new firms to enter the market and the more market power existing firms will enjoy.

Perfect competition

7.11 Perfect competition describes a market in which firms can enter and exist easily; there are a large number of firms, a large number of consumers, and perfect information.

---

[7] There are ways of measuring market structures and the level of competition. A common measure of the concentration of a market (roughly the relative market share of each firm) is the Herfindahl-Hirschman Index (HHI).

[8] Other market structures include: duopoly, monopsony, and oligopsony. While these are important market structures, they are less relevant to discussions on IP.

[9] These four structures are not necessarily mutually exclusive as markets may exhibit elements of multiple structures, particularly over time.

[10] Economies of scale, as discussed elsewhere, are when per unit costs decrease as quantities increase. For example, baking a batch of sixteen scones is, per scone, cheaper than baking a batch of ten scones. The extra six scones will require more ingredients but not much more labour, thus the per unit costs decreases. If this happens across the market, it can be prohibitively costly for new firms, who may initially produce smaller quantities, to compete.

The ability of firms to enter and exit a market easily is described as 'no barriers to entry'. For example, consider the child entrepreneur and the classic lemonade stand. There are no regulations and very low costs for set-up (capital). Theoretically, any child could open a lemonade stand and sell the same lemonade. Assuming every child in a neighbourhood sets one up and everyone in the neighbourhood wants lemonade, then there will a larger number of producers and consumers. Everyone has all the information needed (perfect information). Lemonade stand owners know each other's costs and production methods and consumers know exactly what they are buying. No lemonade stand will be able to charge more than the others and the price of lemonade will be driven down.

Perfect competition provides the baseline for comparison for other types of market **7.12** structure. Under perfect competition, competition drives prices down. Producers make just enough money to stay in business and consumers get the best price. It is the most efficient, generic market structure. It is also highly theoretical as in practice its conditions are not observed.

Oligopoly

Oligopoly, on the other hand, is a step away from perfect competition. In an oli- **7.13** gopolistic situation, there are few firms. It is a fairly common market structure in which firms are in competition, but there may be barriers to entry or other conditions, which keep the number of firms low. Under oligopoly, firms can observe their competitors' actions and, as a result, engage in strategies to maximize their profits. Unlike perfect competition, where, as noted above, prices are driven down to a minimum, in oligopoly, firms may have the power to influence or set prices.

Imagine that some government regulations require certain hygiene levels of the lem- **7.14** onade stand. This creates a barrier to entry. Not all lemonade producers will be able to meet these standards and there may only be a few lemonade stands in the area. In this case, an oligopoly emerges and there is less competition. Lemonade stands will still be in competition, but may be able to charge higher prices, as there is a reduced threat of entry because of the hygiene regulations. In fact, the lemonade producers may meet up and decide to set a higher price for lemonade.

Monopolistic competition

While oligopolies have few firms in a market for the same (identical) goods,[11] in **7.15** monopolistic competition, firms are competing based on similar goods or services. Like in the case of perfect competition, in monopolistic competition there are many

[11] This is not strictly true as there is also a market structure called a differentiated oligopoly in which there are a few firms but they are able to differentiate their goods and services. Interested readers may want to read more on this in the suggestions mentioned in n 2.

firms. However, under both monopolistic competition and oligopolies, firms have some power over the market. Under monopolistic competition, many firms will sell differentiated goods which they set apart from competing goods through branding, additional services, new features, etc. In very simple terms, each firm has a monopoly on the very specific good or service they are selling, but there are similar goods and services with which the firm must compete. Thus, the monopoly over the specific product is in competition with similar products.

7.16 Under monopolistic competition, there are few barriers to entry and firms have limited impact on the market price. The goods on the market are similar but are not perfect substitutes. An example is that of coffee. Hot coffee can be made at home, at the office, as an instant powder, purchased in a petrol station, bought as takeaway at a fast food joint, consumed in a coffee shop, or in a restaurant after a meal. There are many firms selling coffee, but the hot coffee they offer will be slightly different from other coffees available. Consumers will not view the coffees available as perfect substitutes. Firms will have some control over the market price. For example, the price of Starbucks' cappuccino is likely to influence the price of competitors' cappuccinos, and the brand strength of Starbucks may allow them to charge higher prices. In contrast, raw coffee beans are homogenous and traded as a commodity.

7.17 The challenge of the monopolistic competition is that it introduces a number of inefficiencies. Firms' expenditure on differentiation, through advertising or similar efforts, does not necessarily contribute to social welfare (see Chapter 5 on trade marks for further discussion). Firms do not operate at full capacity and are inefficient; instead, the firm seeks to maximize its profits by setting its quantity at lower than what would be found in an efficient market.[12] As firms have some market power and can set this suboptimal quantity, there are too many firms in the market. However, monopolistic competition is a very common market structure and can be more efficient than an oligopoly or monopoly market structure.

Monopoly

7.18 Finally, imagine a situation where there is only one firm, known as a monopoly. In this case, the firm has a lot of power and can maximize profits by setting its price. There will be a number of barriers to entry in the shape of high start-up costs, legal monopolies (patents), and a host of other possibilities that will create the market conditions leading to a monopoly. In general, this means high prices and lower quantities. Firms maximize their profit and consumers do not get the best deal. In general, monopolies are considered a bad thing.

[12] Specifically, under monopolistic competition, firms set their quantity to where marginal revenue equals marginal cost.

There are exceptions in which monopolies can be beneficial. For example, there are the natural monopolies as discussed in Chapter 1, the Introduction to Economics. The London metropolitan transport system is a good example. More than one tube system would be illogical. Instead, a single, monopolistic tube is the natural market structure for subterranean transport. The social contract theory of IP makes an argument for the monopolies created by IP. **7.19**

To sum up in a very simplistic manner, the four main market structures: **7.20**

- Perfect competition—lots of firms, prices lowest, most competition
- Oligopoly—few firms, prices higher, some competition
- Monopolistic competition—many firms, prices higher, some competition
- Monopoly—one firm, prices highest, no competition

Conduct

Conduct focuses on the behaviour of firms within a market. This includes firm strategies, choices, and how choices are made. Anti-competitive practices are key to this discussion. If firms engage in conduct that is anti-competitive, markets can be manipulated, with a negative impact on consumers and other producers (performance). This section clarifies key terms and then discusses significant anti-competitive practices, following Lipsey and Courant's (1996) list: collusive agreements, contractual agreements, mergers, predatory behaviour, and monopolistic behaviours. **7.21**

Terms: Unfair competition, anti-trust, anti-competitive practice, and competition

Before delving into conduct, there are a number of terms surrounding competition that can be confusing. These include unfair competition, anti-trust, anti-competitive practices, and the more general competition. **7.22**

'Competition' is used for a wide variety of concepts. The use of the word varies from the mundane description of a contest between parties to a very specific use in economics. To make it even more challenging, economic texts may use 'competition' in its colloquial sense.[13] **7.23**

'Anti-competitive practices' is the common term in economics for firm[14] behaviours that reduce competition. As discussed later, these behaviours include: dumping, **7.24**

[13] It can be useful to think about competition as the general concept and Competition as the economic concept, although this is not a convention. A similar distinction can be made between politics (as in playing games, office politics, debates) and Politics (states and electoral systems).

[14] Anti-competitive practices need not be restricted to businesses only, as, for example, governments may also engage in such behaviour. However, for the purposes of this text it is more useful to focus on the business side.

cartels, price fixing, etc. It is important to remember that this is a very specific economics[15] term.

7.25 Anti-trust is often used synonymously with anti-competitive. In reality, there is a line, albeit a fine one, between the two. Anti-trust is specific to the concentration of market power into a few firms (oligopolies, see later) or one firm in trusts or monopolies (Institute, 2015a). The use of 'trust' dates from the nineteenth century when the word was used in the United States to refer to large businesses and, as noted by Hovenkamp (1984), 'historians tended to view the giant "trusts" as products of predation against smaller rivals'. Anti-trust, therefore, refers to efforts and laws to prevent the abuse of power by trusts and even the formation of the trusts. Trusts or monopolies are not a necessary condition for anti-competitive practices (e.g. the anti-competitive practices of cartels, which involve multiple firms). However, 'anti-trust' has largely been subsumed into 'anti-competitive', which is the more commonly used term internationally.

7.26 Unfair competition, which is often discussed with regards to trade marks, is a more diffuse concept. Unfair competition is much more linked to tort law and IP than strictly economic constructs. Institute (2015c) note that, 'Unfair competition does not refer to the economic harms involving monopolies and antitrust legislation. What constitutes an "unfair" act varies with the context of the business, the action being examined, and the facts of the individual case.'

Agreements: Collusive and contractual

7.27 To turn now to specific anti-competitive behaviours, consider collusive agreements. Collusive agreements, as the term implies, are a way that firms collude for their own benefit. These include practices that limit output, fix prices, divide territories, boycott specific firms, or otherwise agree not to compete with each other. Cartels also fall under this category. An interesting element of collusive agreements is that they need not be explicit but can be implicit. Firms observing competitors' behaviours may be able to engage in tacit collusion[16] in which firms in the market engage in strategies which are mutually beneficial but without explicitly agreeing to do so.

7.28 The cartel, which is a formal arrangement, exhibits a number of collusive behaviours. A cartel allows an oligopolistic market to act like a monopoly. Cartels are 'a group of independent corporations or other entities that join together to fix prices, control distribution, or reduce competition' (Nolo, 2015). All of these activities reduce competition. In more competitive markets, firms will not be able to artificially

[15] Again, outside economics other terms may be used. As Lipsey and Courant (1996) note, courts in the United States have used additional terms such as 'restraint of trade', 'monopolize', and 'substantially lessen competition'. The authors point out that these concepts are still evolving.

[16] Tacit collusion is sometimes referred to as tacit cooperation.

maintain higher prices. However, if firms collude, they may all be able to agree to sell a certain good or service at a specified price. If all of the lemonade stands choose to sell lemonade at £3 a glass instead of the competitive price of £2, they will make higher profits. To do so, they may also sell fewer glasses and may agree on quantity. To further reduce competition, they may elect to only have one lemonade stand per block. All of these behaviours can potentially increase profits as the price of goods and services can be artificially inflated.

Another example is that of drug trafficking gangs, which often resemble corporations and operate as cartels (Lacey, 2010). Gangs may divide up territories to minimize conflict and competition, and manipulate prices and quantities to further limit competition. This is not limited to illicit drugs. In Mexico, pharmaceutical companies were accused of similar behaviour when six firms, in the period from 2003–06, consistently bid for government health service contracts with prices within 1.5% of their competitors' bids. Over this period, the six firms won one contract each, and were able to charge higher prices because of the limited competition (*Economist*, 2010). **7.29**

Economic theory suggests that cartels are only sustainable for a limited period as the incentives to cheat are too high. If an individual firm knows the expected strategy of its competitors, eventually it may succumb to the temptation to increase prices, quantities, or encroach on other's territories in order to increase its profits. If a single lemonade stand starts selling at £2 a glass when the collusion price is £3, they will undercut their competitors and sell more lemonade to their own benefit. This may cause the cartel to be dismantled or attempts may be made to force the offending lemonade stand into compliance. In situations involving illicit drugs, cartels may be enforced through violence. In legal markets, however, cartels are often contra competition law, and therefore enforcement by other members of the cartel may be more difficult. **7.30**

As noted, collusive agreements need not be as blatant as a cartel. Over time, competitors can observe each other's behaviour and adapt their strategies as best suits them. For example, Lee (1999) describes tacit collusion in the milk contracts for the Dallas-Fort Worth school districts. There, he finds that the average milk price is 18% higher than the benchmark. His analysis suggests that competing firms engage in complementary bidding where a 'firm tends to submit relatively high bids in districts in which rival firms win repeatedly, hoping that rival firms would submit relatively high bids in his incumbent districts'.[17] In this case, the firms are able to charge the extra 18% based on their anti-competitive behaviour even though they have not explicitly agreed to do so. **7.31**

[17] Lee, I. K. (1999). 'Non-cooperative Tacit Collusion, Complementary Bidding and Incumbency Premium *Review of Industrial Organization* 15: 115–34, 133.

7.32 Collusion involves behaviours between multiple firms (in oligopolies), but there are other forms of anti-competitive agreements.

Contractual agreements

7.33 There are a myriad of ways in which firms can limit competition through contractual agreements which 'limit buyers in their choice of sellers'.[18] These include exclusive dealing contracts, in which a buyer, typically a retailer, is tied to purchasing from a single supplier. The classic example is that of a franchise where the franchisee must purchase supplies from the franchisor. In this case, the franchisor may be contractually forging itself as a monopoly supplier for the franchisee. For example, the franchisor of a coffee shop may require that all coffee sold in a franchised shop is from the franchisor. There is a fine line between what is permitted under exclusive dealing and what is not. It is the performance, addressed in the next section, which assists in assessing whether such behaviour is anti-competitive.

7.34 Another concern is that of resale price maintenance where a supplier contractually obliges its customers (e.g. wholesalers and retailers) to maintain certain prices. This reduces competition between wholesalers and retailers. An interesting example is the case of Nine West, a shoe company. In 2000, the company, which was the largest supplier of women's shoes in the United States, was fined USD 34 million for threatening to withhold supply if retailers discounted certain shoes. The retailer was banned from threatening or penalizing its customers for twenty years (Feeley, 2000). However, in 2008 this ban was relaxed as Nine West successfully argued that the resale price maintenance would not harm consumers in part because the firm had only a 'modest market share' at the time (FTC, 2008). This again suggests that the performance of anti-competitive behaviours may not result in consumer harm.

7.35 Tying is another source of anti-competitive behaviour in which distinct goods must be sold together. The classic example is the battle that Microsoft faced when they were accused of tying a web-browser, Internet Explorer, in with their operating system, Microsoft Windows. In tying-in contracts, consumers are forced to pay for unrelated goods when purchasing the good they wish to buy. This increases sales for the producer at the cost of the consumer.

Mergers and acquisitions

7.36 As the saying goes, 'If you can't beat them, buy them'. Or become them. Mergers, where two firms become one, or acquisitions, where one firm buys another, are another potential source of anti-competitive behaviour. While not all mergers and acquisitions (M&As) are problematic, those that reduce competition or

---

18 Lipsey and Courant (n 2) 273.

form undesirable monopoly conditions can be. Many small start-up companies are created with the goal of being acquired by a larger company. However, in an oligopoly, if the larger firm(s) begin(s) buying up smaller firm(s) then potentially competition will be reduced to the point where prices and quantities are adversely affected.

There is no hard and fast rule as to what constitutes an anti-competitive M&A. **7.37**
Again, as the next section on performance will explain, it is the impact of these anti-competitive behaviours which matters rather than simply the behaviour itself. In technology, there has been a lot of M&A in past years. Google, for example, has a history of buying start-ups. The increase in M&A could be interpreted as corporations moving into a model more like venture capitalists where portfolios of start ups are purchased in the hopes that a few will be successful (*Economist*, 2014).

Predatory behaviour

Predatory behaviour, which can occur under most[19] market structures, is the use of **7.38**
strategies to drive out competitors, force competitors into cooperative behaviours or mergers (Lipsey and Courant, 1996), or create barriers to entry. Undercutting, or predatory pricing, is one such behaviour where a firm deliberately sets a very low price to either undercut competitors or discourage firms from entering a market. However, there is no consensus amongst economists on the prevalence of predatory pricing (OECD, 1989). Non-price predation, in which firms behave in manners that raise competitors' costs, can also be anti-competitive.

Dumping is a specific type of predatory pricing in which firms export a product to **7.39**
another country at a price below the price of production. This may be done to kill off existing competitors and gain market share. Dumping can often be difficult to prove and is controversial as it also touches on domestic trade policies and protectionism. A recent example is that of French solar glass manufacturers accusing Chinese competitors of engaging in dumping. Chaffin (2013) notes the French manufacturers were seeking import tariffs (taxes) of over 100%. Proving dumping, or any anti-competitive behaviour, is a long process that requires investigation, amassing evidence, and negotiations.

Monopolistic behaviours

As discussed earlier, monopolies have a lot of market power and can influence both **7.40**
price and quantity. The market structure of monopolies enables this behaviour. Again, however, it is the impact this behaviour, the performance addressed in the next section, that determines where this behaviour is harmful.

[19] It cannot occur in perfect competition.

Performance

7.41 Performance essentially looks at the impact that market structure and behaviour have on the market and the economy as a whole. This includes considering prices, quality, and efficiency. The fundamental question to ask is whether firms are enhancing economic welfare. Governments, as the institutions in charge of welfare and economic policy, are responsible for monitoring the performance of industries and considering the impact of anti-competitive behaviours.

7.42 There is no hard and fast rule for determining whether firm behaviour enhances economic welfare. Government economists typically perform the assessment of market performance and anti-competitive behaviour. For example, a competition authority will assess a market by: measurement of market share, consideration of anti-competitive behaviours, analysis of barriers to entry, and assessing how this impacts the economy as a whole. Depending on the jurisdiction and political priorities, this may result in actions taken against firms engaging in anti-competitive behaviours.

7.43 In the case of the Mexican pharmaceutical cartel, it is estimated that the collusive bidding practices cost the taxpayer an additional USD 46 million in inflated prices (*Economist*, 2010). Clearly the anti-competitive behaviour, in this case, did not benefit the economy as a whole. Potential solutions include fining the firms involved, banning them from certain commercial activities, blacklisting, changing government procurement methods, regulating the sector further, and other similar methods.

7.44 The main question for governments in assessing the performance of a market is to determine whether government intervention is warranted. There are significant costs, such as legal fees and human resources, associated with pursuing firms engaging in anti-competitive behaviours that may outweigh the benefits. Political pressure will shape which sectors, firms, and countries are targeted. In some cases, it may be that a one-off fine will resolve problems. However, in other cases, it may be that the sector merits further regulation in order to maintain economically efficient markets.

Firms granted monopolies

7.45 Even when monopolies exist and anti-competitive behaviour is observed, it is possible that the monopoly situation may not have a negative impact on performance. There is the case where firms are granted monopolies or, as Lipsey and Courant (1996) put it, have monopolies thrust upon them. In some cases, this will be due market conditions that lead to a natural monopoly. In other cases, this may be due to government regulations or IP.

7.46 As discussed earlier, natural monopolies may be beneficial for societies. Rather than wasting resources on duplicating transport and communication systems, allowing these to function as natural monopolies may be efficient. Interesting questions arise in social networks as, for example, the social networking site Facebook could be considered a natural monopoly. In the case of Facebook, the network effect—where the more people use a service, the more valuable the service becomes—could generate a natural monopoly. The alternative, a lot of Facebooks, would be less efficient.

IP can create monopolies. This is discussed at length in Chapters 2–7. Yet the impact of IP on competition may or may not be negative–it depends. **7.47**

Analysis of structure, behaviour, and performance gives a complete picture of the functioning of the market. Breaking down these three elements helps to assess whether or not market realities are harmful. The government decision to subsequently intervene or not is where the policy debate begins. The next section will look further at IP and competition. **7.48**

Specific Competition Issues Related to IP

IP is an economically justified reduction of competition. As the previous sections have explained, economists are generally not supportive of monopolies. Instead, IP is a rational solution to the challenges of encouraging long-term innovation. However, the monopoly granted by IP can lead to anti-competitive behaviours. This section details these behaviours and the potential policy implications. It uses the market–behaviour–performance analysis outlined earlier. **7.49**

Market

IP is about the market for innovation. On an economy-wide basis, IP creates incentives for innovation. However, in each market, IP may create a monopoly. For example, in the market for watches, a patent on a crucial timekeeping mechanism may grant the patent holder a significant monopoly. This will depend on how much demand there is for that mechanism. In contrast, a patent for a very specific watchband may confer no monopoly power as there may be no demand for the watchband. Therefore, it is important to remember that the legal monopoly of IP does not necessarily translate into a market monopoly. **7.50**

Monopolistic competition is a common structure for markets involving IP rights. While, by definition, innovations and creations protected by IP rights are unique, products and services incorporating IP rights are likely to compete with similar goods and services. The IP right grants a very specific monopoly, but competition with substitute goods means that the IP right does not equate to a legal monopoly. Instead, the IP right's specific monopoly serves to bolster a firm's differentiation. **7.51**

When IP does create a market monopoly, it reduces competition. Like a lot of issues in IP policy, there is a balance to be struck between the creation of these monopolies **7.52** and the potential for anti-competitive behaviours. Simply enforcing IP rights is not, by itself, anti-competitive behaviour. There is no hard and fast rule as to where this balance lies, and it is the behaviour of firms and performance of the market that determines whether these monopolies are problematic.

Behaviour

7.53 There are a number of behaviours related to IP that border on the anti-competitive. These are largely categorized as concerns about licensing, and oligopolies and cross licensing.

Licensing

7.54 The practices of IP licences do not, in principle, differ from licensing in other non-IP related licences. However, as IP rights may limit competition between potential licensors, it may make licensing markets more vulnerable to anti-competitive behaviours.

7.55 Scotchmer (2006) details nine specific anti-competitive patent licensing practices, paraphrased below:[20]

1. Royalties not related to the patented products;
2. Tie-outs (restraints outside the scope of the patent);
3. Tie-ins (requiring licensee to purchase supplies unrelated to the patent);
4. Mandatory packaging licensing;
5. Exclusive grant backs (exclusive licensing to the licensor of further innovation by the licensee);
6. Veto power by licensee over further licences;
7. 'Restraints on sales of unpatented products made with the licensed process';
8. Restraints on resale violating first sale doctrine; and
9. Retail price maintenance.

7.56 This list is similar to that found in non-IP licensing practices, but the presence of patents provides an additional layer of enforcement. Similar principles will apply to other types of IP rights.

Pools and collective rights

7.57 Economic discussions on licensing typically focus on patents as they are used in relatively more dynamic[21] ways than other rights. In particular, patent pools

---

[20] Scotchmer, S. (2006). *Innovation and Incentives* (Cambridge, Mass., MIT Press) 171.

[21] The word 'dynamic' here suggests that patent licensing may be used to generate further innovation. In comparison, trade marks and design rights are less likely, *prima facie*, to be used in subsequent innovation. Copyright is still ambiguous as it can be licensed for derivative works but this is a relatively unexplored area from a competition perspective.

are of interest. Patent pools are a collection of patents owned by different rights holders that can be licensed via a single licence. These are useful when a particular technology requires multiple innovations that are covered by patents with different owners. This can be efficient and pro-competitive as it reduces the costs of negotiating multiple licences. However, patent pools can also leave room for anti-competitive behaviours.

The primary advantage of patent pools is the reduction in transaction costs. **7.58**
Firms are not faced with the costs of negotiating multiple licences and the process is streamlined. It also reduces the possibility of one firm securing most of the required licenses, but being unable to obtain one or more of the remaining licences associated with the technology. In this case, the firm would be unable to use the technology. Patent pools provide an efficient mechanism to assure that a technology can be licensed.

Patent pools are not without their disadvantages. Patent pools can be anti- **7.59**
competitive if they include competing patents (e.g. two different patents for a similar innovation) that would otherwise be in competition outside the pool. The inclusion of unnecessary patents in a pool is also an anti-competitive practice. Patent pools also require significant bargaining between the owners of the patents in the pool. This leaves room for disagreements on royalties and for owners of patents to hold up the bargaining process. Much like a cartel, there will be incentives for patent owners to 'cheat'.

Another concern is that of collective rights management (CRM) organizations **7.60**
which function as the copyright equivalent of a patent pool. As discussed in Chapter 4, CRM serves to solve a greater problem of the high transaction costs associated with licensing music individually. However, CRM organizations have a significant monopoly power, which may disadvantage smaller licensees who have limited bargaining power. This can be addressed through arbitration (see the section on copyright tribunals in Chapter 4).

Standardization

Standardization is beneficial for economic efficiency. Travellers facing incompatible **7.61**
electrical outlets and voltage will understand how a lack of standards can be inefficient. In many technologies, industry organizations will develop standards in order to promote this efficiency. Standards may include patented technology. Standard essential patents (SEPs) are 'patents that must be licensed in order to implement a given technical standard'.[22]

[22] ITU. (2014). 'Understanding Patents, Competition & Standardization in an Interconnected World' (WIPO) 47.

7.62 When a patent becomes a SEP, its market power increases significantly. To account for this, SEPs are usually bound to use (fair), reasonable, and non-discriminatory ((F)RAND) licensing practices. However, this still leaves standards and SEPs open to anti-competitive practices. Bad faith bargaining, when those in standards negotiations either do or do not disclose patents or subsequently create a SEP, creates an opportunity for firms to gain market share unfairly. Again, the balance between the economic advantages of standardization and the potential abuse by owners of SEPs is key.

Oligopolies, licensing, and joint ventures

7.63 The potential for anti-competitive behaviour is, as Barton (2003) notes, probably most prevalent in oligopolies and cross-licensing. In particular, this can be seen in the rise of defensive patenting, non-practising entities (NPEs), and strategic patenting. In an oligopoly, firms are in competition with each other. Holding patents that competitors may be infringing is a useful bargaining chip. However, the situation may be mutual as a firm may also be infringing competitors' patents. In which case, there is an incentive for neither firm to sue as litigation may be costly. Despite this, high profile litigation between competitors continues.

7.64 A similar détente can be seen in other sectors, such as copyright. The fashion sector, for example, operates in an environment where copying is rife. However, this copying is beneficial for the sector. If you assume the high-end brands innovate and this slowly trickles down as lower-end brands copy, then the higher-end brands are better able to establish themselves as trendsetters. In addition, the faster trends go out of fashion, the more demand there will be for new trends.

7.65 Yet, in both cases, the avoidance of litigation because of mutual benefits may create a barrier to entry. Firms new to a market are less likely to have the arsenal of defensive patents and may be a target for lawsuits. That is, established firms in the market may have relatively strong IP rights arsenals to engage in litigation. This constitutes a barrier to entry as new firms will face costs not incurred by existing firms. In fashion, there is concern that when larger brands copy smaller brands, the culture of copying disadvantages smaller firms. Again, this potentially constitutes a barrier to entry.

7.66 In recent years, research has suggested that this analysis is incomplete. The rise of NPEs implies that IP alone can be a useful resource for generating revenue. By definition, these NPEs are not competing for market share of the sale of products and services, but merely for a market share of patents. In addition, as Scott Morton, and Shapiro (2013) argue, there has been an increase in the number of strategic patent acquisitions. Instead of acquiring patents as a means to prevent assured mutual destruction, they are instead being acquired for both defensive and offensive strategies.

In addition, there is the suggestion that practising entities, or those firms that are actively selling in the market, may also be engaged in NPE-like behaviour by acquiring patents for the sole purpose of litigation. Scott, Morton, and Shapiro (2013) develop a similar concept of a 'hybrid-NPE', which they argue can operate anti-competitively by using the threats from the NPE to unreasonably raise rivals' costs. This strategic behaviour raises concerns as it may unduly harm consumer welfare by raising costs, delaying innovation, or indirectly encouraging the adoption of lesser technologies. **7.67**

Joint ventures (JV) are agreements where two or more firms agree to work together for a defined amount of time. More specifically, 'A joint venture is a legal organization that takes the form of a short-term partnership in which the persons jointly undertake a transaction for mutual profit. Generally each person contributes assets and shares risks.'[23] The analysis associated with JV can apply to more general co-operation between firms. **7.68**

JV are often created when complementarities exist between firms. JV may also be strategically useful for firms wanting to enter new markets. The challenge is, however, that JV can serve to reduce competition. As Scotchmer (2006) notes, JV can reduce competition between innovations and, therefore, slow down progress, and limit the development of substitute innovations. In both cases, the JV contributes to reducing competition. However, JV are not inherently anti-competitive, it depends entirely on their impact on the market. **7.69**

IP can contribute to anti-competitive behaviours, as this section has detailed. However, the proof is in the pudding. As in the discussion on anti-competitive behaviours not related to IP, it is the impact on market performance that determines whether these behaviours are problematic. **7.70**

Performance

Assessment of the performance of markets, in light of suspected anti-competitive behaviours, may determine whether government intervention and regulation are warranted. Market dominance stemming from IP, and the potential for abuse of a dominant position,[24] is not a given. **7.71**

Intervention in the form of fines and restrictions on specific firms is a punishment for specific instances of damaging anti-competitive behaviours. There is no specific test that determines whether intervention is warranted. Given that each IP is, by definition, unique, defining the relevant market and measuring the impact of **7.72**

[23] "Joint Venture" *Wex Legal Dictionary*, Legal Information Institute, n.d. Web, 12 December 2015.
[24] Abuse of dominant position is the term used in law and policy to anti-competitive behaviour by a firm with a dominant market share.

reduced competition is the challenge. Assuming that economic analysis suggests the damage that is occurring, the decision to prosecute a firm will depend on a host of strategic and political factors.

7.73 A further question is that of government regulation. Most of the themes discussed in this chapter are related to IP but more precisely fall under the realm of contract and competition law. This subtlety raises questions as whether a policy response under the guise of IP is appropriate. It may be that regulation is required to introduce restrictions under contract and competition law. In particular, suggestions that policy should limit the behaviours of NPEs using IP law are problematic. It is difficult to restrict regulation of IP owned by NPEs without also impacting IP owned by practicing entities. Defining an NPE in legal terms is already challenging and restricting their behaviour is likely to be further challenging. Furthermore, increasing government intervention typically increases the cost of doing business and may otherwise negatively impact the market.

7.74 As the market for IP rights itself evolves, the impacts of anti-competitive behaviour will be better understood and policy options may present themselves.

Conclusion

7.75 The interaction of IP and competition is based on the fundamental fact that IP rights are rights to exclude. This exclusion creates the potential to exclude others and reduce competition. However, the legal monopoly of IP rights does not necessarily translate to a market monopoly. Thus the monopoly associated with IP rights does not necessarily cause competition concerns. This is where legal approaches and economic approaches may diverge, as economics is less concerned about the legal details and more concerned about the overall economic impact.

7.76 As this chapter has discussed, the economics of competition and IP can be problematic for the performance of markets. This chapter has also highlighted that there are emerging issues in competition and IP such as its extension to IP rights other than patents, and the strategies used by NPEs. For both general anti-competitive behaviours and those associated with IP rights, the principles of structure, conduct, and performance remain the same. As firms' use of IP changes, so may the impact of competition.

Part III

HOW, WHY, AND WHEN INTELLECTUAL PROPERTY DELIVERS VALUE

Summary

If IP is generally regarded as being a specialist and complex subject, the same is even more true of the approaches taken to attach a value to it. Suspicion regarding the merits of IP valuation is widespread, with criticisms generally falling into two camps: it is either viewed as being more (black) art than science, and therefore of dubious integrity as a process, or it is regarded as being pointless because the volatility of IP value, combined with the absence of transparent markets for it, mean that even an 'accurate' valuation may not give useful insights into realizable worth. **PIII.01**

There is no doubt that IP valuation does require skill and care. In order to provide a robust account of IP value, some degree of due diligence[1] is necessary, owing to the fact that no one person's IP is identical to another's (if it is, it has almost certainly been stolen). For the same reason, it is seldom possible to draw any reliable inference from the IP sales that occasionally hit the headlines, such as the prices paid for Nortel and Motorola Mobility patents. These say more about the competitive climate in industries such as mobile communications than they do about the intrinsic merits of the assets that have changed hands, and like other assets that are acquired, **PIII.02**

---

[1] 'Due diligence' is a widely used term which suggests a legal or quasi-legal duty. It is typically used in the context of expressing the need for a company's directors or officers to act prudently and give proper consideration to risks posed by prospective transactions. In the case of IP, particular areas requiring a degree of due diligence would include verifying the existence of registered rights, confirming their ownership, and investigating the presence of existing or prospective litigation, to name but three.

the price paid for such assets is not necessarily consistent with the long-term valuation applied to the assets, even by the acquirers themselves.

PIII.03 In practice, IP valuation is eminently do-able and worthwhile, and it is economically important to understand IP's real value as a business driver, especially given the high percentage of contemporary firms that depend wholly, highly, or even partially on their IP to make money. The primary reason why valuation of IP is not embedded in the consciousness of more business managers is simply this: expenditure on intangible assets, being mostly internal, does not have the same visibility within the company's accounts as the other types of costs that also represent investments in a firm's future.

PIII.04 The problem of ignoring IP value is well illustrated by the maxim that, 'if you can't measure it, you can't manage it'. If IP's contribution cannot be quantified in some reasonable manner, it is unlikely that shareholders and markets will take its importance properly into account when judging and rewarding management. This, in turn, brings to mind another frequently used business consulting maxim: the things that are measured have a tendency to be the things that get prioritized.

PIII.05 There are other complicating factors with IP and intangibles, and two are worth acknowledging at the outset of any discussion on value. The first is that this subject is not really dealing with a single type of asset. As will be evident from earlier chapters, each member of the IP rights 'family' has a substantially different set of 'rules' (a combination of law and practice) associated with it. These rules become even broader when other important assets within the wider category of intangibles are taken into consideration, such as trade secrets.

PIII.06 This is not just a question of quantity. While it is generally true that a single isolated patent offers less utility and protection, and therefore less value, than a family of related patents, the more important point is that *different* asset types add value to each other, often in a 'non-linear' way. Hence, in most cases, a patented product that is also associated with a strong and widely recognized brand name is likely to hold increased value, and this will probably be evident from the superior cash flows such a combination of rights generates (even if subsequent analysis of how much value each one contributes to the whole may become rather subjective). Therefore, to extract maximum value, IP needs to be *understood* at the level of the individual component assets, but (for most purposes) *valued* and traded as a 'bundle'.

PIII.07 The second point is that when their role in the value creation process is analysed, IP and intangible assets appear to do different things at different times. A patent, for example, may well arise initially as an *outcome* of a process of study at a company or a research institution; there may have been no specific intention to create a patentable invention, but events transpire in such a way that something genuinely novel is discovered, which the organization decides is worth protecting. In some contexts, patent filings have come to be used as a 'proxy indicator'[2] of underlying innovative competence or productivity, in part because their inventiveness and novelty gets tested via external examination. However, as the preceding chapter on patents has demonstrated, this view lacks sophistication.

Once the patent exists, it is no longer an outcome or a result. If it relates to a production process or a novel material, it may fulfil the function of an *input* and the value of the asset will lie in *how* it enables a business or organization to produce goods. However it may equally well permit goods to be produced that are themselves patent protected, in which case the patent is better understood as part of an *output*. **PIII.08**

Whichever characterization—input, output, or outcome—seems more appropriate in any given context; when it comes to valuing the IP in question, it will be important to consider how much all the other factors typically present in a production environment are contributing to the overall benefit being derived by a company. Otherwise, there is a risk of conflating IP value and business value. **PIII.09**

Given that the subject of IP valuation is complex (though not as mysterious or arcane as it is often made out to be), it is important to 'deconstruct' it, for the benefit of those fresh to the subject, or who may have come across it as a professional adviser or company director. Therefore, whilst Chapter 11 does go into valuation methodologies in some detail in order to examine their advantages and disadvantages, it does not purport to provide a 'ready reckoner' for any particular set of assets. **PIII.10**

This choice has been made for three reasons. First, because there are other existing guides on valuation technicalities;[3] secondly, because it is seldom a good idea to try to calculate a value without some degree of external involvement or scrutiny, as noted earlier; and thirdly, from an economic perspective, there are issues surrounding valuation that are more important to address than the 'mechanical' aspects. **PIII.11**

Accordingly, this Part first sets out to address how business value arises in IP and intangible assets at the micro-economic, individual firm level, by looking at the financially beneficial effects that the ownership of IP may produce. It then moves on to the question of how much value may be accumulated at the macro-economic level, putting IP value into a wider context by referencing both investment levels **PIII.12**

[2] A 'proxy' or indirect indicator can be defined as a measure or sign that approximates or represents a phenomenon in the absence of any direct measure or sign. Because 'innovation' is such a broad concept it tends to be studied in terms of its inputs (investment) or outcomes (registered rights) simply because these are measurable, but neither in isolation is a good indicator of productivity or quality.

[3] As one example of many: Sykes, J. and King, K. (2003). *Valuation and Exploitation of Intellectual Property and Intangible Assets* (London, Tarquin).

and the market value attributed to identifiable assets in the context of merger and acquisition activity.

PIII.13 The discussion then moves on to consider the contexts in which the question of IP and intangibles value is most likely to be raised, such as sales (of the IP in isolation, and the business that owns it), fundraising, licensing, litigation and damages, company administration, and liquidation and tax planning/tax reliefs. The main aspects of an IP portfolio most likely to enhance or reduce its value are then considered prior to an investigation of valuation methodologies, the extent to which standard approaches apply to valuation, and the differences between valuing IP and valuing a business as a whole.

PIII.14 Finally, staying at the micro-economic level, consideration is given to the ways in which this value is normally accounted for (or remains unaccounted for) within corporate financial statements, beginning with the question of why balance sheets seldom if ever represent it. Current reporting standards are examined as well as new accounting and accountancy-related practices that are seeking to address this issue.

8

HOW INTELLECTUAL PROPERTY DELIVERS VALUE

Why IP Value Matters

Before commencing these more detailed discussions, it is first necessary to address a further question, which is perhaps the most interesting one of all. Why should IP be valued at all, when economies seem to have managed without doing much about it for decades, even centuries? The answer is that the fundamental way in which value is created within commercial activity has been transformed, and is being continually modified, through the powerful twin operators of globalization and technological advancement. This change is well illustrated by the difference in monetization options between physical and intangible assets, a subject worth briefly examining here, because of its profound implications for business investment and growth. **8.01**

The old industrial paradigm of generating wealth through the multiplication of physical production capability is inexorably giving way to the need to multiply non-physical methods of creating value, that is, knowledge. However, as organizations such as the US-based Athena Alliance have argued for some time,[4] the methods of financing needed to perpetuate this trend are not keeping pace with it. **8.02**

Consideration of the United Kingdom's manufacturing heritage seems to confirm this observation. The industrial revolution was facilitated by machinery that enabled the outputs a single person was able to produce unassisted to be multiplied many times over. Since much of this machinery was comparatively expensive, or at least beyond what growing companies could finance purely from retained profits, it was made available using finance provided by manufacturers, banks, and specialist lenders. This was based on two judgements: first, that even if a particular venture failed or could not meet its debts, the equipment in question would still be of value **8.03**

[4] See, for example, Jarboe, K. and Furrow, R. (2008). *Intangible Asset Monetization: The Promise and the Reality* Athena Alliance, available at: http://www.athenaalliance.org/pdf/IntangibleAssetMonetization.pdf.

to a different business;[5] and secondly, that because this equipment was directly related to the way in which a firm generates cash, an investment of this kind should (provided it relates to a business-critical activity) be more than capable of paying for itself.

8.04 Thus asset-backed finance was born, creating a new category of 'thing'—known as 'personalty'[6]—against which lending could take place. It took root, enabling companies to buy what they needed and to pay for it in instalments as it delivered value to them. Over time, these financing instruments became more sophisticated and also enabled businesses to unlock value in machinery they *already* owned, freeing up capital for new investment.

8.05 Methods such as hire purchase and leasing continue to be relevant for the tangible fixed assets companies need to acquire today. However, while these 'hard' physical assets still represent tradable commodities (and therefore have an identifiable and relatively reliable collateral value, as explored in more detail later), they are much less central to business than they once were. In functional, economic terms, one car or computer brand is largely interchangeable with another. This in turn means that the motivation to repay is, arguably, not what it once was.

8.06 More importantly for financiers and for businesses, few Western nations (with the possible exception of Germany) have anything approaching the manufacturing 'clout' they once had; for example, it is estimated by the World Bank[7] that 79% of output in the United Kingdom is now accounted for by service industries. The companies that drive modern European economies generally rely on the multiplication of know-how, not production capacity. Even within the manufacturing base that remains, the most profitable companies are those with a strong emphasis on research and development (R&D) (and therefore a high dependency on IP and intangibles), and they typically outsource the production of their physical goods (in whole or in part) to lower-cost economies in other world markets.

8.07 Financing models that can support the investments knowledge-based companies need to make are clearly far less developed at this point of the ongoing technological revolution than those which emerged rapidly in the industrial age. In many areas of

[5] An example of this is to be found in the history of Isaac Singer and the Singer Sowing Machine Company. Singer developed a new design of sewing machine and made it available to companies and individuals on instalment terms, leading to the establishment of a separate finance house. In doing so, he is also thought to have been involved in the first ever 'patent pool', where companies decided to license their patents to each other rather than litigate for infringement. A biography of Singer can be found at http://www.rootsweb.ancestry.com/~nyrensse/bio206.htm.

[6] This can be defined as 'moveable assets (things, including animals) which are not real property, money or investments'. See http://legal-dictionary.thefreedictionary.com/personalty.

[7] Quoted by the Office for National Statistics: see http://www.ons.gov.uk/ons/dcp171766_360847.pdf.

Europe, governments have recognized the risks inherent in growing R&D intensity and modified their taxation policies to compensate for them, a point discussed in greater detail in Chapter 9. More recently, in view of the reluctance of banking institutions to engage positively with new asset classes, a few governments[8] have concluded that this 'disconnection' needs to be tackled by state-backed intervention to identify and underwrite value within the assets that high potential enterprises create. The principle is that these need to be leveraged in order to pay for the acquisition and development of more assets, and therefore growth.

Since, as explained in more detail in Chapter 12, a company's accounts will seldom (if ever) accurately reflect the value contribution made by its intangible assets, generating some notion of IP value is necessary in the course of negotiating any transaction based on it. It should perhaps be stressed at this point, however, that an indication of this nature does not always have to be precise in order to have the desired effect; in fact, it may only become precise once the anticipated transaction has happened. **8.08**

How Does IP Value Arise?

Given the off-balance sheet status of most intangible assets, it is important to demonstrate that this 'invisible' quality does not prevent them from contributing business value in the long term, in just the same way as other, more obvious 'conventional' forms of investment. Beyond the direct connection that IP often has with revenue generation (i.e. producing IP that is sold, as in the case of many creative works), there is a diverse range of ways—at least ten distinct ones—in which intangibles contribute directly to turnover and profitability. Whilst not all are relevant to all businesses, and some benefits only arise after a period of trading, there will be few firms that cannot and do not benefit from one or more of them. **8.09**

In this section, these value-generative attributes are identified and expanded at a micro-economic (individual firm) level, followed by a macro-economic discussion on how much value some of the key attributes are capable of adding to economies in general. Whilst the discussion is brief, it should be sufficient to illustrate the fact that IP is a multi-dimensional asset as well as a highly mobile one. **8.10**

Direct income

The most obvious connection between IP and value creation arises when goods that are themselves a form of IP are bought and sold. In the creative industries, **8.11**

[8] Governments providing collateral guarantee schemes in recent years include China, South Korea, Malaysia, and Singapore.

this is generally how things work. A piece of music, composed and/or recorded; a set of photographs submitted to a publisher; a painting, produced to order or created speculatively; a magazine article or book; all of these are instances where one or more people, or businesses, create artefacts whose value lies in the fact that they are copyright works and therefore legally protected from imitation or duplication.

8.12 Since first being introduced under the statute of Queen Anne in 1710,[9] the term associated with copyright protection has increased substantially from its original twenty-one years (for works already published) and fourteen years (for works yet to be published). As explained previously, the economic rights associated with many copyright works now last for the life of the author plus seventy years. Also, because copyright offers relatively broad protection, rights holders can turn individual works into lucrative sequels and spin-offs. As one example, consider the *Harry Potter* book series, which has spawned a remarkable array of copyright materials including films, games and many other types of merchandise which are protected by other rights, most notably the Harry Potter brand.

8.13 Copyright is not the only IP right that operates in this way. Goods featuring a distinctive design also owe their ability to generate value to the underlying IP rights, because the design *is* the product. While design protection (registered or unregistered) is in some respects weaker than copyright (being shorter-lived; also, it can prove harder to prove infringement in the case of fairly close copies of physical goods than literary or artistic ones), the combination of original design and a strong brand association can support long-term sales. Without these aspects, it is too easy for imitators to steal value.

8.14 There is also often a direct connection between patents and income generation. Patents can sometimes make it possible for companies to market goods with unique properties and make sales that would not previously have been possible, as is apparent in the case of pharmaceutical companies like GlaxoSmithKline, discussed in Chapter 3. More often, the superior performance characteristics of the patented technology create sufficient differentiation to generate sales that would otherwise be lost to competitors, with a notable example being Dyson in the vacuum cleaner industry. There are also markets in which patents are necessary to carve out freedom to operate.

8.15 Interestingly, even where some 'base' elements of IP are made freely available, other parts can be kept back and made chargeable items. This is the 'freemium' business model used by many software 'apps' and social games, and it can be a highly

[9] The date is often quoted as being 1709, but the facsimile of the Act itself indicates that the law is introduced from 10 April 1710. See http://www.copyrighthistory.com/anne.html.

effective one: whilst referencing any names may be apt to make any book date more quickly than it should, *Angry Birds* and *Farmville* provide examples.

These models have arguably served to reinforce an expectation across many consumer offerings that digital goods should offer some basic level of feature or function that can be accessed free of charge. Commercial micro-economic considerations aside, the wider, more worrying macro-economic implication is that contemporary consumers simply do not see the same value in digital goods as their predecessors used to associate with their analogue counterparts. **8.16**

Indirect income

The more extreme example of this business model is where IP content is made available for no charge at all. In such cases, the usual motivation is to attract the maximum possible number of users, so that the IP can be monetized in a different, less direct way. Arguably this risks reinforcing the value perceptions alluded to in the previous section. **8.17**

Leaving aside TV licensing, the commercial television model has long been dependent on attracting advertisers and (latterly) programme sponsors in order to turn viewer attention into income. This continues to be an important source of revenue, notwithstanding the fact that there is now a great deal more competition for these established terrestrial TV models from satellite and internet channels, which are also seeking advertising spend as well as subscriptions (in some cases). **8.18**

In the early days of online marketing, the most usual route for generating indirect income was similar, involving the placement of advertising next to popular content. This would often be done using 'banner ads' to provide a click-through link to a different site, enabling the advertiser to benefit from someone else's web traffic. In recent years, the use of these banners has become considerably more sophisticated, and it is now common to encounter sites where all the advertisements that appear are tailored to the user, based on their previous online behaviour. **8.19**

The underlying trend is that data is becoming the main driver of indirect IP revenue generation. This is nowhere more apparent than in the success of Google, the primary actor in monetizing consumer online behaviour. Google's operating models have been the subject of much adverse comment, and it is interesting to reflect that initially, the company had very little formal IP of its own—it made money from simplifying access to other people's IP (though the increasingly sophisticated processes which it uses to do this have become the subject of strong, patented IP since). **8.20**

Examples of intelligent data use to boost incomes are not, of course, limited to online pioneers. As the number of ways to access content proliferates and the costs of obtaining it continue to fall, it is increasingly difficult for companies manufacturing fast-moving consumer goods to make conventional advertising work for them. **8.21**

Their way of compensating for this is to use data gathered from online interactions (including social media) to tailor content more directly to perceived customer requirements.

Trading value (sharing and swapping)

8.22 Whilst IP may often be referred to as the 'currency of the knowledge economy', as currencies go, it is a fairly illiquid one, at least in terms of the difficulty in buying or selling it on transparent marketplaces, a subject dealt with in more detail in Chapters 9 and 11. However, there are many occasions in which one form of IP is exchanged for another, particularly among businesses at an early stage of development.

8.23 It is very common for organizations to assist each other by swapping their knowledge or capabilities for mutual benefit. Sometimes this may take the form of activities that directly substitute a cost which would otherwise be incurred by one or both parties. As an example, a start-up business founder who has expertise in coding websites might well provide a free service to a graphic designer in exchange for benefiting from their skills in producing a logo, which will lead to copyright material changing hands. While less common, it is also the case that more mature companies may choose to share IP for no direct financial consideration, potentially by way of licence, as an investment in building up a product or service that can generate income in future.

Sales value

8.24 Notwithstanding the obstacles that exist, IP is sometimes sold (as opposed to being reproduced for profit, as is the case with music, publications, software, and so forth). Whilst the language of sale may vary (e.g. a trade mark or a patent will be deemed to have been 'assigned' rather than sold), IP is nevertheless a form of property that in most respects can be disposed of in the same ways as any other type of goods. The main exception to this rule concerns the moral rights associated with copyright works, which cannot be assigned, but can be waived.

8.25 When IP is sold, however, the value achieved may not necessarily be an accurate reflection of the intrinsic value of the IP itself. Price, always a factor of supply and demand, will be further affected by the financial status of the seller and buyer, most acutely where the seller is in liquidation, administration or some other degree of distress. These issues are discussed in more detail below.

Increased profitability

8.26 It is important to bear in mind when discussing profitability that IP rights are essentially negative in nature—that is, they provide a company with the ability to stop a competitor from doing something that infringes these rights. Contrary to the expectations of many inventors, there is no particular profit entitlement that arises from being an IP owner *per se*. Subject to this important caveat, improved profit performance is a key characteristic of companies that exploit their IP effectively. It arises from several sources.

Most obviously, customers are often prepared to pay extra for the inherent qualities and associated reputation of products and services that are underpinned by strong IP. A brief inspection of a supermarket's shelves will confirm that these differences in price can be striking. The added margin that a higher selling price provides may be offset to some degree by the investment in marketing necessary to maintain it, and this relationship between marketing investment and shelf price quite often changes over time, as products which initially have been positioned as being premium items achieve scale and market penetration. **8.27**

This is a benefit that can be quantified. Assessing the premium that branded and proprietary products are able to command over their generic competition is one established method for determining IP value. At the same time, it can also be volatile, particularly if a product quality issue arises (as was famously the case with Perrier water in 1989).[10] **8.28**

This price premium may not of course be limited to an individual sale. One of the main purposes of promoting brands is to generate loyalty in the long term, and if this is successfully done, profitability is further enhanced. In other contexts, particularly in business-to-business sales, IP may well provide an enduring 'lock-in', for example when a component becomes an integral part of a larger product offering. **8.29**

Sometimes, the IP used to create a product or service can enable it to be delivered at a significant cost saving, but this may not be passed on to the buyer. This is a different way of achieving a margin improvement. It may also be the case that products can be bundled together, introducing further cost savings. **8.30**

The relationship between IP and the profit motive can also be controversial. One particular example of this is in the tax efficiencies companies can sometimes realize based on where they choose their IP to be domiciled (discussed in more detail in Chapter 9). A yet more problematic area relates to the pricing policies adopted by multinational corporations in developing world markets, particularly in respect of pharmaceutical products, as has been explored in Chapter 7 on the economics of patenting. In India, a location where many drugs are manufactured, the problem of **8.31**

[10] In 1990, county officials in North Carolina (who had been using Perrier as a purity standard to test other mineral water products) discovered traces of benzene in batches produced during 1989. It withdrew 160 million bottles of water from the market. In 1992, Perrier was acquired by Nestlé.

desirable treatments becoming unaffordable has led to IP rights applications being rejected, overridden, or subjected to compulsory licensing.[11]

Tax efficiency

8.32 There are a number of ways in which tax efficiencies can be generated from IP. These are discussed in detail in Chapter 9, but two aspects worth touching on at this point are 'off-shoring' and tax reliefs.

8.33 Off-shoring refers to the practice of moving part or all of a company's IP into a more advantageous tax jurisdiction. This is commonly used by large multinational corporations, where the consistent use of technologies, designs, brands, and copyright materials internationally makes it sensible to hold these assets centrally (where they can be controlled and monitored) and to license these into individual territories as required. Sometimes, the entity owning the IP will be a specialist vehicle created for the purpose.

8.34 Since the general rates of corporation tax vary extensively between countries, and some countries have particularly advantageous treatment available for IP assets, it has become common to find IP-owning companies located in Ireland and Luxembourg. This has become a source of contention for European governments, who believe that this perfectly legal practice is being used to avoid payment of taxes that would otherwise be due.

8.35 At the same time, however, most European governments (and some in other parts of the world such as the United States and China) offer policies designed to encourage the creation of IP that include voluntary tax benefits. In April 2013, the UK government adopted a 'patent box' regime which enables companies to reduce their tax liability on sales of patented products and technologies to as little as 10%[12]. Separately, R&D tax credits provide generous incentives to small and large companies to innovate.

Licensing and franchising

8.36 IP licensing is not, of course, limited to circumstances where the primary motivation is to reduce tax liabilities. The primary purpose of licensing is simply to realize an economic benefit by agreeing a set of terms on which another party can use the IP assets. Licensing is becoming an increasingly attractive export strategy for both physical and non-physical goods; partnering with a company based overseas with

[11] For example, Bayer, Pfizer, Roche, and Novartis have all had cancer or hepatitis C patent applications revoked, refused, or overridden, according to the *Financial Times* (see Kazmin, A. (15 May 2013). 'India: Patents and Precedents').

[12] The UK Patent Box scheme is due to be revised. See Chapter 9.

existing distribution channels, then licensing them the rights to produce and/or sell products, often provides a quicker route to market at less cost and reduced risk than would be incurred in establishing multiple subsidiary undertakings.

Licensing can take many forms, and IP licensing agreements are very flexible instruments. For example, licensing rights can be exclusive (limited to one party), sole (limited to one licence but retaining all the licensor's rights) or non-exclusive (permitting similar agreements to be entered into with many different people). They can be divided up according to the particular purpose for which a brand, technology or another asset can be used, the territories where it can be used, the markets to which it can be offered and the time period for which permission is granted. Also, whilst it is normal for licensing agreements to cover a 'bundle' of IP rights, it is perfectly possible to offer different rights to different parties. For example, an organization may decide not to license its brand name, but to permit other parties to make similar products under their own names. **8.37**

Licensing is value-additive not only because it generates income, but also because it proves that there is demand for the assets and that they are separable from the business that originally devised them. Taken to its logical conclusion, licensing becomes franchising when an entire concept is offered to the market for others to use. Franchising has become a popular method of business expansion across a very wide range of industries, from fast food outlets to lawn care services; typically, it provides a sales-related income stream back to the franchisor while giving the franchisee an opportunity to build their own business with the backing of an established network. Industry statistics indicate that franchising has grown rapidly in popularity in recent years.[13] **8.38**

Franchising always requires strong IP to be in place in order to be successful. The most obvious component is a recognizable brand, which the franchisor is generally responsible for promoting and protecting (using income generated by the franchisee network). However, the franchise often includes the benefit of advantageous supply contracts, sharing of specialist and technical know-how, proven marketing materials (which are themselves subject to copyright), and sometimes patented technologies. **8.39**

Blocking value

'Blocking' is a concept particular to patents. Companies may make discoveries regarding potential improvements to their products or services which they do not **8.40**

[13] According to statistics from a NatWest/British Franchise Association survey in 2013, franchising now generates £13.7 billion annually—up from around £5 billion in 2003. See https://www.thebfa.org/about-franchising/franchising-key-facts.

wish to bring to market, but which could prove damaging to their sales were a competitor to introduce them. The motivation for keeping such a development back from the market may simply be that the costs of introducing it are too high, or that other considerations mitigate against any change to the status quo. To prevent the loss of a competitive advantage, such companies may apply for patents.

8.41 This strategy is not without risk. Unless the patent is granted in a sufficient range of territories, it will simply 'show the company's hand'. Whilst a single patent is sufficient to destroy novelty in any subsequent application that might be made by a competitor, it would not prevent that party from using the patent in unprotected countries. However, the granted patent does provide the negative rights necessary to prevent any licensing, sale, or importation in the territories that are protected.

8.42 Assessing the value of a blocking patent is not straightforward because, by definition, there are no income streams directly associated with it. However, it can generally be established that other income streams are being protected by its existence.

8.43 It should also be noted that blocking tactics can also be used without necessarily needing to register new patents. For example, publishing findings in a recognized journal is a well-established way of ensuring that a rival organization will not be able to file a patent of its own (though this also prevents the author from doing so, if they have not already made an application).

Influence and reputational enhancement

8.44 Whilst not easy to quantify in the absence of an acquisition or merger, organizations owning strong IP that are successful in marketing it clearly derive value benefits which go beyond the sums directly attributable to the IP (in terms of directly related turnover and profit). This is sometimes colloquially described as 'goodwill' accruing to the business, although goodwill can only be present in an accounting sense when a business has been acquired.[14] Accordingly, to avoid confusion, it is more helpful to think of it as being an uplift that may be crystallized when and if the company is in fact sold.

8.45 The IP that a company owns can make it more influential in the market than would otherwise be the case. There are many examples, but one that stands out is the growth of Apple as a corporation. Its recent expansion was kick-started by the introduction of the original iPod music player in 2001 but received a decisive

[14] In the accounting context, specifically in international standards for post-acquisition accounting described below, goodwill has a particular meaning. It is the premium paid for the business over and above the value that is attributed to the tangible assets, the identifiable intangibles, and the liabilities. See Chapter 12.

additional boost when the App Store was added as an update to iTunes in 2008. This service provides a shop window enabling users to select and download apps developed using the software development kit (SDK) created by Apple for the iPhone. It made the population of new Apple devices available to external developers (a change in strategy from that originally pursued by Apple for its Macintosh computers, which were associated with a closed, proprietary operating system). The move has had huge financial benefits both for Apple and the community as a whole, but beyond the immediate returns, it has given Apple a highly influential position in the independent developer community (not least because it can dictate which content reaches the App Store and benefit from part of the income generated by app sales).

Reputational enhancement is a slightly different benefit. When a company comes to be seen as a trendsetter by virtue of its innovative business model, product or services, its growth and development is facilitated by more than just the income it generates. Specifically, it becomes a company with which other organizations (including large and influential corporations) wish to be associated, often leading to an acquisition. However, reputation can be rather a fragile commodity and it is particularly susceptible to damage if product quality or performance issues arise (as evident from the Perrier example given earlier) or if the company's fortunes change materially. **8.46**

Security value

One of the challenges faced by IP-rich companies is that quite often, their ways of creating value are heavily dependent on intangible assets rather than tangible ones. For software and service companies, it is no longer necessary to own substantial 'hard' assets in order to operate profitably, and even for some manufacturing businesses, the opportunity to outsource aspects of production has reduced dependency on plant and machinery, and even premises. **8.47**

Traditionally, for the reasons explored in more detail in Chapter 9 and in other recent works,[15] it has not been possible for companies to offer intangibles as security for borrowing. However, increasing lender recognition of IP as a driver of business value is leading to gradual change. Already, venture debt and growth finance providers are incorporating IP within their 'security nets', and while a specific value is not necessarily being attached to the IP in isolation, there is clearly an expectation that the IP will form an important part of any strategy for business recovery if needed. Also, specialist finance variants are starting to attribute value directly to intangible assets. **8.48**

[15] Brassell, M. and King, K. (2013). 'Banking on IP? The Role of Intellectual Property and Intangible Assets in Facilitating Business Finance' (IPO).

8.49 In addition to other, enterprise-related methods intended to compensate for the absence of traditional collateral in knowledge-based businesses, some governments (including those in China, South Korea, Malaysia, and Singapore) have introduced state-backed guarantees to underwrite the collateral value of certain types of IP, subject to conditions (offering as much as 80% 'cover' in the case of Singapore). Whilst interventions of this nature are generally justified by the need to 'pump-prime' markets and are therefore usually time-limited, insurers are gradually warming to the idea of backing a minimum IP value, and specialist underwriters (such as M-CAM in the United States) have developed methods of identifying a 'floor' value with sufficient confidence for reputable re-insurers to issue cover. This has the additional benefit that, being a rated instrument, the insurance policy can be used as collateral even if the IP itself cannot.

Seed funding

8.50 Of course, finding adequate security for borrowing is only an issue for businesses that are already generating sufficient cash flows to be able to service debt at all. Start-up companies are seldom in this position, and for many, the only realistic prospect of obtaining funding to grow (apart from attracting paying customers) is to pitch the business idea to crowd-funders or private investors (usually referred to as 'business angels').

8.51 At an early stage of development, very few companies have anything material by way of tangible assets to underpin a valuation of the business, which is needed in order to determine a share price. Their IP will therefore be critical in giving an investor confidence that their plan is achievable in terms of delivering barriers to entry (to prevent direct copying from better resourced competitors) and freedom to operate (to lend confidence that the business will not be sued by anyone else).

8.52 While it would be stretching a point to suggest that private investors, particularly those operating on crowd-funding platforms, are necessarily sophisticated in their understanding of IP, it is normal for questions to be asked at investment network meetings to determine whether the company seeking funding has a strategy in this area. In the case of software businesses, the scrutiny may be less, as the assumption will be (in the United Kingdom at least) that this is unlikely to be patentable and that the company will have to rely on copyright and/or brand protection. Conversely, in the case of specialist sectors such as biosciences, consumer electronics, and environmental technologies, questions about patents will invariably be asked. While it is not necessary for such a company's patent applications to have been granted prior to fundraising, it should at least have taken steps to ensure that it is not infringing anyone else's IP and that it still has an opportunity to obtain rights as and when required.

Business valuation outside the acquisition context

In the ordinary course of trading, the amount of value that IP is contributing to a business is seldom obvious. Even where intangible assets are featured on a firm's balance sheet, these will only indicate what they have cost, for the reasons explained in Chapter 12 on accounting rules. **8.53**

Sometimes, a business may have a need to understand this hidden value element even when it is not contemplating a transaction involving the IP itself. As one example, if a private company requires an interim valuation in order to introduce a share option scheme, and a substantial period of time has passed since shares were last issued, it will need to find a way to quantify any uplift in value it has experienced in order not to set the option price at an artificially low level. Whilst the trading performance of the business will provide one indicator of value, a valuable additional way of doing this is to obtain a valuation of the IP so that the company's advisors can use it to quantify and support this level of uplift. **8.54**

Exit value enhancement on business sale

Many growth companies are founded—and funded—based on an assumption that they will at some point be floated on a stock exchange or sold, typically to a trade purchaser. A flotation (e.g. on the Alternative Investment Market (AIM)) always requires a company to compile an intellectual capital statement as part of its prospectus, explaining what its assets are and how they are deployed. **8.55**

As in other contexts, the law of supply and demand is a powerful factor in company sales negotiations, so if the business is working towards a trade sale, introducing a degree of competition into the sales process is usually necessary in order to obtain the best possible price. In the case of strategic acquisitions, the main consideration for the buyer is likely to revolve around the potential for the target business to contribute meaningfully to future incomes and profits by enabling the purchaser to expand its capabilities, reduce its costs, or enter new markets. IP is a key contributor to these desirable characteristics. **8.56**

Traditional methods of private company valuation rely on discounting future projected cash flows back to their estimated net present value, or applying multiples to current earnings. Such multiples are often derived from stock market information, with appropriate adjustments made for the size of the business being acquired and the comparative illiquidity of its stock. Recently, it has become popular to consider turnover multiples rather than profit multiples (though cynics have observed this may be due to the fact that many companies offered for sale are yet to make substantial profits). **8.57**

However, it has also become apparent that companies with very strong IP and intangible assets can command prices that are well in excess of current earnings, **8.58** particularly if they have powerful networks of users and can demonstrate market traction on which a buyer may be able to capitalize further. One example of this was the purchase of Instagram by Facebook in 2012, in which the buyer offered USD 1 billion to acquire a two-year-old web start-up company with no revenue and thirteen full-time employees—because it had the asset of 30 million users on iPhone alone. Within a year of acquisition, this number had risen to 100 million (though according to industry commentators, the revenue conundrum had still not been solved).

8.59 In summary, it is fair to observe that whenever a company manages to achieve an exceptional price that is not underpinned by an earnings or revenue multiple, it is a reflection of the fact that its IP (in the broadest sense) is seen to have a very significant amount of potential future value. It follows, therefore, that a lack of attention to IP can also have a negative impact on negotiations: buyers generally look for reasons to pay less than the asking price for any business, and if problems are discovered in the IP portfolio (or it becomes apparent that there is no IP portfolio to speak of), this is highly likely to have an adverse impact on the purchase price, and may stop the deal from happening at all.

How Much Value Arises?

8.60 The question of how the IP of individual businesses is valued will be considered in chapter 11. However, each of the three methods that underpin nearly all approaches to IP valuation—considering market comparisons, the likely cost of re-creation, and the IP's effects on income—can also be used to obtain a good indication of the extent to which IP now influences the value of businesses at a macro-economic level.

Market values

8.61 When seeking to understand the contribution that intangible assets make to company values, it is easiest to begin with the large firms whose share price is publicly quoted and to examine their associated balance sheets in order to understand their asset make-up. Early and influential work was done on this subject in the United States by the Brookings Institution, looking at the change over time in the basis for market valuations of S&P 500[16] companies, and this has subsequently been taken up and built upon by Ocean Tomo, a US company concerned with a number of aspects of IP exploitation.

[16] The Standard & Poor's 500, as its name suggests, is an index of 500 companies which are quoted on the New York Stock Exchange (NYSE) or NASDAQ. It dates back to 1957 in its current form, and is developed and maintained by S&P Dow Jones Indices.

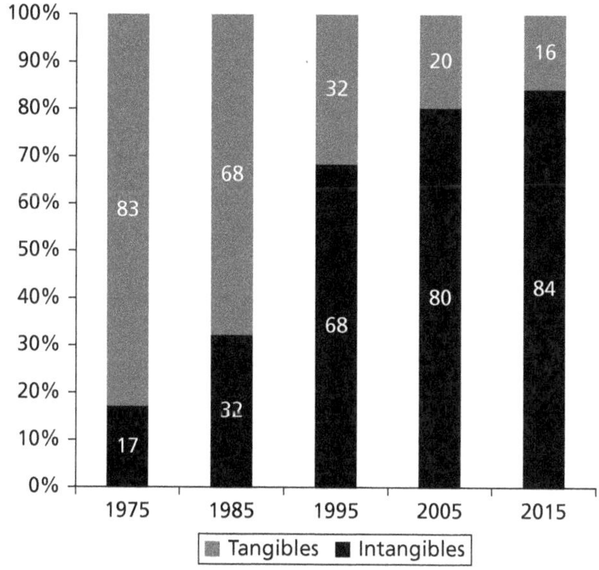

Figure 8.1 Movement in implied intangible asset value as a percentage of overall company value, 1975–2015 (source: Ocean Tomo)

The research shows that a very significant change has occurred in terms of the asset base of companies listed on the S&P 500 over the last forty years.[17] In 1975, 83% of the value attributed by stock markets to these companies was underpinned by tangible assets which were present on their balance sheets. Since that time, as Figure 8.1 shows, there has been a complete reversal; now, only 16% of the value attributed by the market to these stocks can be traced back to tangible fixed assets. By implication, according to Ocean Tomo's analysis, the remainder must be attributable to intangible assets. **8.62**

For the reasons explained in Chapter 11, it is not easy to obtain detailed insights into the value associated with individual IP transactions. However, there are other ways of making market-based comparisons that show the amount of value now being attributed to intangible assets in business sales transactions. The first is to take the example of transactions that have occurred in recent years where the price paid is clearly predicated on the IP and intangible assets that are being acquired, as indicated by the Instagram example given earlier, and returned to in more detail later. **8.63**

The second is to examine acquisitions made by large corporates who have then had to account for these transactions on their balance sheets using available accounting standards. These standards, recently extended to small and medium-sized enterprises, require a distinction to be made between tangible assets, identifiable **8.64**

[17] Naturally, the composition of the index has changed very substantially too over this period, so this study does not attempt to track the changes in share prices of a static set of corporations.

Table 8.1 Percentage of purchase price allocated to identifiable IA

Deloitte sector *(KPMG sector)*	Price % allocated to identifiable IA (Deloitte)	*Price % allocated to identifiable IA (KPMG)*
(Automotive)	–	*34%*
Chemicals & industrials *(Chemicals: Industrial products)*	38%	*48%: 36%*
(Computer & semiconductors)	–	*45%*
Financial institutions *(Financial services)*	42% (banks 32%)	*34%*
Food & beverages: Household goods *((Consumer products & services)*	39%: 29%	*55%*
(Internet & e-commerce) (Software)	–	*33%: 28%*
(Life science & healthcare)	–	*45%*
Media *(Entertainment & media)*	34% (range 20%–50%)	*43%*
Retailers	25% (general), 5% (food/drug)	–
Support & construction	27%	–
Telecommunications *(Telecommunications)*	33%	*34%*
(Transportation & logistics)	–	*34%*

intangible assets, and goodwill (which is the price premium paid, as explained earlier). Research published by major accounting firms Deloitte in 2007 and KPMG in 2010 demonstrates that when this exercise is conducted and a fair value assessment needs to be made, the amount of value attributed to identifiable intangible assets can be substantial: as Table 8.1 shows, over one-third of the total purchase price is typically found here, and figures of over 40% are not unusual.[18]

Cost calculations

8.65 The changing relationship between the role of tangible and intangible assets in company value attribution is also reflected in their investment behaviours. Over the last two decades, the expenditure profile of UK businesses on hard physical assets compared with intangibles has changed substantially, to the point where the latter has overtaken the former.

8.66 This transition is aptly demonstrated by research funded by Nesta and the Intellectual Property Office (IPO) and conducted at Imperial College.[19] This uses

[18] Original reports: Deloitte and Touche LLP. (2007). 'Grasping the Intangible' and KPMG AG Wirtschaftsprüfungsgesellschaft. (2010). 'Intangible Assets and Goodwill in the Context of Business Combinations'. The results are re-baselined to create a direct comparison between identifiable intangible asset values.

[19] Goodridge, P., Haskel, J., and Wallis, G. (2014). 'Estimating UK Investment in Intangible Assets and Intellectual Property Rights' (IPO). This is based on data from several Office of National

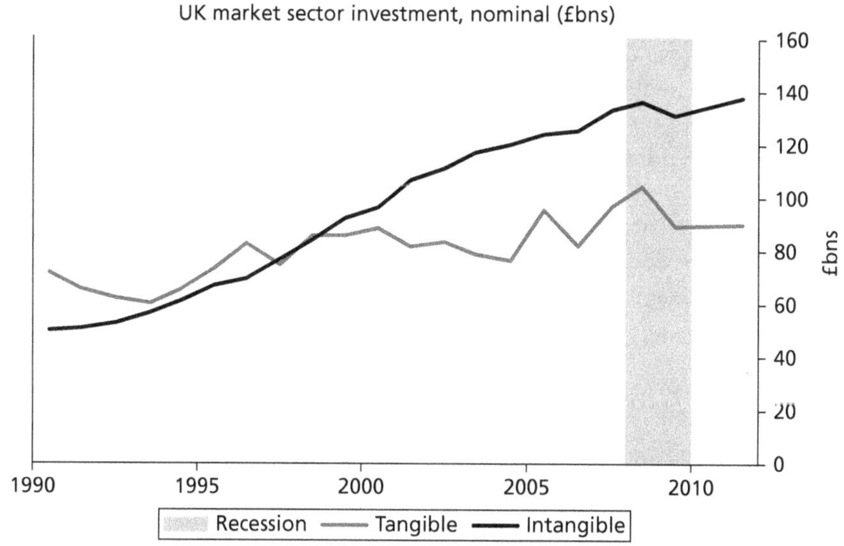

Figure 8.2 Estimate of UK company investment in tangible and intangible assets (source: UK IPO)

the framework developed by Corrado, Hulten, and Sichel[20] in the United States to identify expenditure on knowledge or intangible assets, and then apportions elements of the knowledge investment using principles established in prior work by the same UK authors.[21]

The most recent 2014 report summarised in Figure 8.2, using data recorded up to 2011, found that UK business investment in intangible assets had reached £137.5 billion, compared with £89.8 billion in tangible assets, and that 48% of this total intangible investment was protected (or protectable) by IP rights, principally (given the importance of software) copyright. More telling than the absolute numbers is the trend, which clearly shows that having overtaken tangible asset investment in 1999, intangibles have continued to grow strongly and have recovered since the 2007–09 recession in a way that tangible assets have not. **8.67**

Estimates produced on a comparable basis for the United States paint a similar picture and suggest that the annual investment by companies there is in the order of USD 800 billion–USD 1 trillion, with the 'stock' of intangibles present in the **8.68**

Statistics (ONS) sources including the Annual Survey of Hours and Earnings (ASHE), National Employers Skills Survey (NESS), and the UK Innovation Survey (UKIS).

[20] Corrado, C., Hulten, C., and Sichel, D. (2005). *Measuring Capital and Technology: An Expanded Framework* (Washington D.C., University of Chicago Press).

[21] Goodridge, P., Haskel, J., and Wallis, G. (2012). 'UK Innovation Index: Productivity and Growth in UK Industries'. Nesta Working Paper 12/09.

United States being as high as USD 5 trillion.[22] Also, this investment emphasis is by no means unique to the United Kingdom and the United States: the Organisation for Economic Co-operation and Development (OECD) commenced a two-year project to investigate the role of knowledge-based capital (KBC), in 2011, and the synthesis[23] of its primary findings references increases in investments in a range of countries including China, India, Brazil, Thailand, and Singapore. Overall, the OECD's findings are very consistent with the IPO/Nesta research, noting that as tangible asset expenditure has progressively fallen over the past ten or more years, spending on intangible assets has increased and appears to have held up significantly better during the 2008–10 period of recession.

Income

8.69 Without scrutinizing a company's financial performance, it can be difficult to ascertain with accuracy what proportion of its income is directly attributable to its IP and other intangibles. However, it is possible to derive some indications of the magnitude and importance of IP by looking at specific organizations that are clearly IP-centric. It is also possible to understand, in overall terms, how much value is being generated by 'pure' IP transactions by studying licensing income flows (though given the contentious nature of some of these licensing flows, 'pure' is perhaps a poor choice of descriptor).

8.70 Returning to the example used earlier, there can be few globally recognized companies that are more dependent on IP for their incomes than Apple. Not only are the physical devices that it produces protected by a combination of patent and design rights, and carefully branded using the firm's trade marks, but it also owns a powerful copyright asset in controlling the iOS operating system format. The combination of style and functionality has proven to be extremely popular on a global level and is an engine of massive revenue growth. Public records indicate that turnover in the year ending 2010 was USD 65 billion; by year end 2014 this had risen to nearly USD 183 billion, with a gross margin reduced by less than one percentage point.

8.71 Interestingly, Apple's balance sheets are not as devoid of tangible assets as one might expect, with machinery, equipment, and software investments all being very significant. Whilst the company is perceived as not owning its own factories, it certainly appears to be making some substantial investments in ensuring it has appropriate controls over its supply chain.

[22] OECD 'New Sources of Growth: Intangible Assets' (2011).

[23] OECD, 'New Sources of Growth: Knowledge-Based Capital—Key Analyses and Policy Conclusions' (2013).

Table 8.2 Top 10 global licensors by income

Rank	Name	Licensing incomes	Key 2014 brands
1	Disney Corporation	$45.2 billion	Star Wars, Marvel Avengers, Frozen
2	PVH Corporation	$18 billion	Calvin Klein, Tommy Hilfiger
3	Meredith	$17.7 billion	Better Homes and Gardens
4	Iconix Brand Group	$13 billion	Peanuts, Umbro, Lee Cooper, Strawberry Shortcake, Pony
5	Mattel	$9 billion	Barbie, Thomas and Friends, Monster High, Fisher-Price
6	Sanrio Inc	$6.5 billion	Hello Kitty
7	Warner Bros Consumer Products	$6 billion	DC Comics (Batman, Superman), Harry Potter, The Hobbit
8	Major League Baseball	$5.5 billion	New York Yankees
9	Nickelodeon	$5.5 billion	SpongeBob SquarePants, Teenage Mutant Ninja Turtles
10	Hasbro	$5.06 billion	My Little Pony, Transformers, Monopoly

Whilst it is tempting to think of IP licensing as being a comparatively new phenomenon, Thomas Edison was using it as a means of monetizing large parts of his portfolio of more than 1,000 patents in the early part of the twentieth century, licensing these to other companies to manufacture goods and provide services. However, there is no doubt that licensing is now very big business, particularly when it comes to brands. Analysis of the current top ten international licensors (Table 8-2), as compiled by Global License,[24] reveals the extent of the value being created by IP. **8.72**

Conclusion

As has been demonstrated, then, IP can be used to create economic value in many ways, and can be seen to have done so on a massive global scale. The following chapter moves beyond the general question of IP being an important value contributor and considers in more detail how this value gets realized in individual cases. **8.73**

[24] Data sourced from http://www.licensemag.com.

9

WHEN INTELLECTUAL PROPERTY ADDS VALUE

The previous chapter has set out in general terms the principal ways in which IP adds value to the organizations that create and own it. Before going into the detail of how that value is calculated, it will be helpful first to delve a little further into the circumstances in which conversations are likely to focus on the worth of a given 'bundle' of IP rights and intangible assets. **9.01**

The most obvious context, though not the one most frequently encountered, relates to sale and purchase transactions of IP. More commonly, IP changes hands as part of a company acquisition, though this does not mean it is any less important a consideration; IP and intangibles will often be the main motivator for an acquirer to buy another entity. **9.02**

Other contexts examined in this chapter are fundraising, licensing, litigation, company administration and liquidation, and tax benefits. Fundraising and licensing are 'positive' uses of IP value that are used to bring capital or revenue into a business and which are growing in importance. Whilst litigation arises from using the 'negative' rights associated with IP (i.e. their power to prevent other people from doing certain things) it is interesting to reflect that this too has developed into a revenue-generative strategy for some organizations, though a proper analysis of 'patent trolls' would be (and has been) the subject of a separate work. **9.03**

The area of tax is particularly relevant when considering the macro-economics of IP rights, and is therefore examined in greater detail at the end of this chapter, in terms of its policy background and economic outcomes. It is considered from three perspectives: first, specific tax reliefs available for IP, generally called 'patent boxes'; second, more general tax treatments available to IP-intensive companies, generally referred to as research & development tax credits; and last, the steps taken by some **9.04** multinational companies to reduce their overall effective rate of tax by structuring IP ownership advantageously.

9.05 Not all of the following scenarios will necessarily require an IP valuation to be conducted using methodologies set out in Chapter 11, though wherever there is a commercial agreement to be negotiated, knowledge of a reasonable and independent 'arm's length' view of fair value is likely to be helpful in reaching a mutually beneficial outcome.

Buying and Selling IP vs. Buying and Selling a Company

9.06 As a form of property, IP is a highly flexible asset that can be bought, sold, exchanged, or given away in much the same way as any class of tangible goods. Sometimes, IP sales hit the headlines and seem to confirm the impression that these assets have been the real source of value in companies all along: two cases in point are the patent portfolios of Nortel and Motorola Mobility, both of which have been widely documented elsewhere.

9.07 It certainly suits the IP enthusiast, or IP practitioner, to argue that IP is fundamental to value creation. However, it is very debatable whether those IP sales that are publicized actually provide usable insights into underlying IP value. The fact that they attract headlines may support the view that these are simply symptomatic of a 'feeding frenzy' at a particular point in time, prompted in part by anxiety over the activities of 'patent trolls' referenced in Chapter 3 and examined in a little more detail here.

9.08 To be more confident about the relationship between IP sales and underlying IP value, it is necessary to have access to a wider and more representative body of data. This can, in theory, be achieved by offering IP for sale on a marketplace, and there are various operators who purport to do just that, most of whom are based in the United States. One of the longest-standing is Yet2.com (http://www.yet2.com), which places a particular emphasis on linking technology requirements expressed by multinationals with the specialist capabilities offered by smaller businesses; another is Tynax (http://www.tynax.com), which sets out to be a global patent and technology exchange.

9.09 There are also organizations, most notably Innocentive, who act as intermediaries between those seeking IP-based solutions and those capable of providing IP-based answers by running 'challenges' which have prize funds associated with them. The size of the prizes offered by Innocentive's 'seekers' to successful 'solvers' are not necessarily a good proxy for value, however, because while they are generally attractive, they are set at a level which recognizes that even a very successful outcome is likely to be not much more than an idea or approach which will require substantial investment before it can deliver business benefit.

At the time of writing, it would be hard to argue that any of the current actors has succeeded in creating a dominant national or international platform for trading IP, and it is very clear that not all of the attempts to create marketplaces have worked. One of the problems of using IP as a tradable commodity is its uniqueness (see later), and efforts (particularly by Intellectual Property Exchange International, known as IPXI) to turn this into more standardized 'units' ultimately proved unsuccessful, in part due to the continuing appetite amongst rights holders for litigation rather than sale or licensing as a route to IP monetization. 9.10

Whilst recent legal developments in the United States suggest that the honeymoon period for 'patent trolls' is now over, it is worth reflecting that many IP owners have benefitted substantially from selling their assets to 'offensive' patent aggregators, such as Intellectual Ventures. These organizations have driven the market in IP sale and purchase over recent years, with large organizations having to arm themselves against this threat by acquiring portfolios for defensive purposes also discussed in 3.26. There is no one technological area that is most likely to appeal to such buyers, but IP that sells best is likely to be of a type where infringement is relatively easy to detect and prove (e.g. patents over materials are likely to be easier to enforce than those over processes—simply because in the latter case it is harder to prove that infringement has taken place). 9.11

The complication with drawing inference of value from any IP sale is that IP itself is supposed to be unique, while most other items that are frequently traded are to some extent commodities (in the sense that they are readily comparable with other, similar examples). This absence of commodification, more than the frequently cited absence of readily accessible marketplaces, is arguably the more fundamental challenge in realizing IP value, though it would be fair to observe that the need to understand IP at an individual asset level but assess its value as a 'bundle' is an important additional complication. 9.12

As explored in more detail in chapter 12, the concept of transferability (and more fundamentally, separability) is an important one in attributing value to IP. Undoubtedly there are instances where IP rights and trade secrets are highly separable and portable (e.g. where a company has developed a superior chemical formulation that addresses an existing need and offers clear performance advantages). However, in many cases, the IP that exists is simply built into the way in which a company delivers value to its customers and cannot be sold without detracting from its market and/or its competitive advantage. Under such circumstances a purchaser is much more likely to seek to buy the whole business. 9.13

There are a couple of further reasons why company acquisition emerges as a preferred strategy. The first is that acquisitions satisfy other strategic objectives for company growth (and are easier for markets and commentators to understand). This is particularly the case for large organizations that operate in well-developed markets. 9.14

9.15 However, a second and important pragmatic consideration is also at work: when seeking to obtain access to IP that can add value to another business, it is often important to ensure continuity, particularly during the initial period when the IP and intangible assets that have been acquired are being assimilated. This may prove difficult to do effectively if the know-how that underpinned these assets' original creation is not directly accessible.

Fundraising—Equity, Debt, and Grant

9.16 As has been demonstrated in the previous chapter, IP is now a major contributor to most companies' market value, the focus for the majority of their expenditure, and a key factor in ultimate value realization at exit. It would be logical to assume, then, that IP would be closely scrutinized by financiers. However, this is not always the case, particularly when it comes to lending.

9.17 In reality, companies find it challenging to get their IP value properly taken into consideration when raising funding, to the point where it represents a significant constraint on firm growth. This section seeks to summarize the role IP currently plays in each of the three main types of business finance: equity, debt, and grant.

Equity

9.18 The first, equity, involves the purchase of share capital in a company for cash (or other shares). Where the firm is listed on a stock market, investment strategies may appear to be directed towards relatively short-term gains (and there are all manner of complex investment vehicles used to benefit from value appreciation of share capital that are outside the scope of this work). By contrast, the comparatively illiquid nature of private company shares mean that equity investments generally involve a longer-term commitment. It is this type of investment that is more relevant for the economics of IP.

9.19 IP will generally be a consideration in any equity deal. As interviews conducted for the 'Banking on IP' report[1] found, investigation of IP can get 'pigeonholed' under either legal or technology-related due diligence, either of which risks missing the question of how far intangible assets are in fact an integral part of the business model. Nevertheless, such processes are an acknowledgement that IP is an important part of establishing barriers to entry and freedom to operate, without which a company risks having its market share eroded and being tied up in disruptive and expensive litigation (which it may not win).

[1] Brassell, M. and King, K. (2013). 'Banking on IP' (IPO).

While equity investment in more established businesses may be done with the expectation of receiving dividends based on the company's profitability (dividends being only payable out of profits), the type of investment conducted by private investors such as 'business angels' is more commonly done in expectation of an upside via a future exit—the sale or refinancing of the company at a higher value. In principle, it pays to invest when a company's value is comparatively modest (at an early stage of development), so that there is an opportunity to benefit from future value appreciation. This, however, is a high risk activity, with industry norms (backed by research)[2] indicating that only one or two in ten angel investments typically achieve the desired rate of 10x return. Of the remainder, around half will fail, and the others will achieve modest success but may prove difficult to exit. 9.20

Given these risks, the primary consideration for most investors is the quality of the management team; but thereafter, having a defensible competitive advantage comes very high on the shopping list. Also, showing that valuable intangibles are present is an important 'antidote' to the generally insubstantial balance sheets typically found in knowledge and technology businesses seeking investment, to the point where technologies and products which are not supported by an IP strategy (probably involving patenting) may struggle to obtain funding. In that most if not all of the assets present are likely to be intangible, the valuation of the business is effectively an assessment of its IP plus any evidence of early traction. 9.21

Debt

Whilst equity investment is always associated with share purchase (or options to buy shares in future), debt can be attached to a number of different types of asset owned by the business or its founders. Conventionally, banks will provide, and companies will use, overdraft facilities to cover short-term working capital requirements, and term loans to obtain funding for investments that are expected to pay suitable returns over a longer period (thus contributing to the serviceability of the debt). In both cases the default position for banks, being the usual source of such funding, is to seek to obtain a charge over suitable collateral that could be used to repay the debt if the business defaults on its obligations; if no such collateral is available (and often, even when it is), the bank will also seek reassurance in the form of personal guarantees. 9.22

The potential role of IP (and the reason for considering its value) in lending is the fact that it may be capable of being used as security for a sum to be borrowed. However, to be of interest as 'collateral', any asset must meet several tests. 9.23

[2] Wiltbank, R. (2009). *Siding with the Angels*, Nesta, available at: https://www.nesta.org.uk/sites/default/files/siding_with_the_angels.pdf.

9.24 The key one is that it must be capable of being sold at a predictable price, regardless of whether or not the business that owns it still exists. Here, the absence of marketplaces in which IP is bought and sold is one of the factors that make it a problematic asset class. Moreover, international agreements (most recently Basel III)[3] dictate the types of asset to which a bank is allowed to attribute value for the purposes of determining its own capital adequacy, a particularly important point following the Global Financial Crisis. Where a loan is underpinned by collateral that is used as security, it reduces the cost of borrowing for all parties. IP's role in business recovery activities does not seem to feature.

9.25 Despite this fundamental difficulty with IP in what might be termed 'mainstream' lending, there is increasing recognition that intangible assets do have a value that can be leveraged in more specialist ways. For some years, it has been possible for firms with little collateral but strong backing from recognized venture capital companies to bring in debt finance alongside their share capital in order to support more rapid growth without equity dilution. This 'venture debt' has been operated successfully for several decades by specialist funds and is one of the principal funding mechanisms utilized by Silicon Valley Bank; it is underpinned by the view that if the company gets into difficulty, its shareholders provide an alternative exit route for the lender. In such arrangements, it is standard practice to obtain a first charge over the business's IP, in order to ensure that the lender's priority will be understood and respected.

9.26 Regardless of whether formal security is taken over IP, an understanding of the direct income streams it generates or supports can assist a lender in assessing whether a proposed debt is likely to be serviceable. In the case of copyright assets, for example, knowing that a certain literary or artistic work has a repeatable royalty income stream associated with it does enable a lender (especially one with specialist experience in the area, such as Coutts & Co) to obtain more 'comfort' than could be justified by analysis of the balance sheet. Sometimes these assets may be directly securitized and used by businesses to generate income streams.

9.27 Asset finance, which lends against the value inherent in tangible assets such as vehicles, plant, and machinery, has also been turning its attention to IP in recent years. For some time, it has been possible to finance certain intangibles (chiefly invoices) using asset finance approaches; now, some lenders have successfully harnessed business-critical software, initially after realizing that much of the technology already being used for asset finance cannot be operated without software (and that the pace of change in technology and massive price deflation has led to very steep depreciation for computer hardware). In 2014, for example, Lombard Technology

[3] Basel III is a set of reform measures addressing the regulation, supervision, and risk management of the banking sector.

Services introduced a Software Licensing Solution product secured against the underlying copyright in business-critical software (valuing the asset using a combination of cost and income methods, explained in Chapter 11).

Other creative strategies to harness IP value in lending include its use by pension funds. In some cases, the IP is simply used as security for a loan; in others, the pension fund acquires the IP and then makes it available to the company that needs to use it via an exclusive licensing arrangement. The hidden value of a company's IP has been used by large companies as part of their strategy to address pension deficits, and by smaller companies to free up capital from company or personal pension reserves and lend it to the business. Under certain circumstances, a pension fund can simply lend to a business and take the IP as security based on an IP valuation. **9.28**

Grant

The third area of business funding is grant funding, namely the provision of finance which does not have to be repaid, provided that performance- or output-related metrics are met. The relevance of IP in this instance is that, owing to state aid rules, there are a limited number of purposes for which grants can be made available, one of which is for the performance of research and development (R&D) activity (because of the risks inherent in this process). **9.29**

Grant funding is a complex area, made more so by the fact that many of the funding sources providing grants prefer to award them for collaborative projects (which typically involve higher education establishments and companies working together and sometimes require this to be done on a cross-border basis). Participants in such projects need to have a clear understanding at the outset of who owns the IP that already exists ('background IP') and who will own and have rights to use the new IP that will be developed as a result of the grant-funded collaboration ('foreground IP'). This has proven to be such a thorny area in the past that the UK government has intervened by sponsoring the development of standardized agreements to assist universities and companies to navigate the IP position.[4] **9.30**

When such awards are made, there are up to three separate areas of IP scrutiny. These may include an assessment of the innovation track record of applicants (which is often judged with reference to their historical propensity to create and register IP rights); a study of the extent to which a proposal for grant-funded activity is likely to lead to any novel outcomes (because grant funding is seldom available for 'me-too' projects); and/or a requirement that the project, if successful, should lead to **9.31**

[4] The resulting templates are now generally known as Lambert agreements, after the author of the report that recommended their creation.

protectable IP (most often in the form of patentable material), or at least not infringe IP already owned by others.

9.32 IP, then, is closely connected with this area of economic policy intervention, though it is unlikely that a specific value will need to be fixed upon for the purposes of grant application.

Licensing

9.33 As previously indicated, providing other organizations with permission to use a company's IP via a licensing agreement can be highly lucrative. A licence is a very flexible instrument that can be employed for a wide range of purposes: whilst normally used to formalize arm's length commercial arrangements, it can also facilitate tax treatments that significantly enhance profitability when used between companies within a group (as explained below). Typical licences involve a charge linked to the turnover a licensee derives from the use of IP by way of a royalty, which may in turn be subject to minimum and/or up-front payments.

9.34 Since the form of such agreements is not pre-determined, a licensor is free to consider which IP assets it wishes to license, to whom, for how long, at what rate, where, and for which purposes. All of these variables will have an impact on the amount it can charge, with one of the most important considerations being the degree of exclusivity that is provided in each of these categories.

9.35 The attraction of agreeing a royalty between two independent parties is that it provides a means to ensure a fair distribution of proceeds, set at a sufficiently modest level that it encourages the licensee from making and selling as many licensed goods as possible. It is therefore of fundamental importance to have clarity over the unit price on which the royalty is payable. This can range from being fairly straightforward (in the case of a single product produced in the likeness of a film character which has been licensed) to highly complex (such as when licensing a technical component for use in a sophisticated mobile device). It is also important to understand the 'materiality' of the sales any given agreement is likely to be capable of generating, in order to avoid giving away rights too cheaply (the unit price may be very attractive; the number of units sold may not be).

9.36 The flexibility which licensing provides can also have drawbacks. One of the key issues for a licensor is to ensure that the sales of the goods its licence facilitates are properly accounted for. For this reason, many licensing agreements include a right of audit. Another is the risk that the licensee negotiates exclusive rights and proceeds to 'sit' on them and/or put greater effort into promoting rival products. Minimum royalty payments and break clauses for non-performance are common methods used to address this risk.

Traditionally, licensing has also been used as a mechanism for dispute resolution. Cross-licensing in particular often provides a means of settling infringement cases, with both parties entering into an agreement enabling them to continue to use their own IP, as well as the overlapping elements of the other party's IP. In some circumstances, courts may instruct warring parties to agree a licence; more often, an arrangement is entered into before a case reaches that point. However, the arrival of non-practising entities (NPEs), most famously Intellectual Ventures, has caused difficulties for those seeking to use licensing as a counter-weapon; since the NPE does not need to trade, it is not motivated to settle on anything less than its preferred terms. **9.37**

Increasingly, licensing is used as an export strategy. It is much less expensive to agree a basis for the use of intangible assets than it is to set up operations in another country. It is also a powerful tool to facilitate dissemination, even when no money changes hands. A good example of this is provided by the various licence derivatives available under Creative Commons; these provide a framework for waiving elements of copyright protection which would otherwise apply to literary or artistic works (including software) in order to actively encourage replication. **9.38**

Litigation and Damages

The use of IP rights in litigation and damages is properly a subject for another work, but a few points not already made above are worth making here in respect of its economic impact. **9.39**

The potential for litigation arises from infringement; it is the opportunity to enforce the negative right that patents, trade marks, designs, and copyright confer. The legal remedies available vary in each case—for example, in the United Kingdom, infringement of a patent is a civil rather than a criminal matter, while copyright infringement may give rise to criminal proceedings. However, the precondition for there being a case to answer is that some form of infringement or unauthorized use has in fact occurred. **9.40**

As explored in Chapter 10, the fact that there is often overlap between patent claims, the assertion of 'confusing similarity' between different trade marks, the variable quality of design drawings, and the resemblance of one piece of music to another, all have considerable potential to make legal advisors richer and companies poorer. Leaving this point to one side, there is also the question of whether alleged infringement is deliberate or unintentional. **9.41**

Deliberate infringement implies that conscious copying or imitation has taken place. This may happen for a number of reasons, though one of the motivations will almost certainly be the desire to benefit from an income stream associated with the IP rights **9.42** that are being infringed. Subjectivity apart (how closely does one set of product packaging have to resemble another before it constitutes an infringement?), a company may take a calculated risk that it will either be able to argue that no infringement has taken place, or that no actual harm has occurred as a consequence (which may or may not be a valid argument, depending on the rights involved). It may also judge that the risk of detection is so low that it is worth taking—for example in the case of a patented manufacturing-related process where inspection of a production facility would be necessary in order to prove infringement, as it cannot be detected merely by examining the finished goods. Finally, it may consider that even if infringement is established and proven, the scale of the opportunity compared with the likely costs of being successfully prosecuted is so great that the risk is worth taking.

9.43 Returning to cost: whilst the rise of NPEs referred to above may make litigation appear a viable IP monetization route, deep pockets are necessary in order to take on IP infringement cases, and the outcome of such actions is rarely certain. For this reason, the threat of litigation (provided there are grounds for thinking that it might be successful) is often enough to bring the two disputing parties to the table to see if a compromise can be reached. One way in which this is often done is through the agreement of cross-licensing where permission is granted for each patent owner to use the other's IP, with or without an appropriate financial adjustment depending on the facts of the case (and the strength of the relative bargaining positions).

9.44 Even if the two parties decide to pursue the matter through the courts, a licence is often the ultimate outcome, the difference being that the level of royalty payable on future sales is likely to be determined by a court based on market precedents. This has a positive economic dimension; the process adds to the body of knowledge on royalty rates and helps to give confidence in them, and while most of the data which is available comes from the United States owing to its particular filing regimes, the settlements reported are often international in scope.

9.45 As well as a loss of sales or profit, IP infringement can also lead to a loss of reputation, which may be another motivation for taking robust enforcement action. This is particularly evident in the case of reputation-related assets such as trade marks.

Company Administration and Liquidation

9.46 The prospect of a company's closure brings all the concerns that get raised over IP value into sharp focus, and is a primary factor in lenders' reluctance to engage with intangibles as an asset class. Here, the concern goes beyond the practical difficulties associated with IP sales (such as how and where to advertise asset availability) because it relates to a fundamental question: if a business's IP is really unique, will anyone else want it at all, at any price?

This concern is not without foundation, because there are certain types of IP that appear to be so inextricably linked with a particular business that they would not be separable in the event of failure. Brands are a case in point; there have been a number of examples in recent years in high street retailing, disrupted by online competition, where even large and long-established companies such as Woolworths and HMV have found it impossible to compete effectively and have had to cease trading (though HMV has since returned to the high street). **9.47**

IP can be an important tool when companies go into administration, provided it relates to activities that are business-critical. Administrators looking to sell companies on a going concern basis need to keep the company and its IP together; if that is not possible, there can be significant value in some of the intangible assets, particularly customer-related ones—provided their value has not been impaired by neglect or theft, two points that require a little more explanation. **9.48**

When companies get into difficulties, bad things can start to happen with their IP that affects its value, leaving aside any reputational damage that may result directly from these trading problems. The most obvious problem is that deadlines for search, examination, or renewal may be missed owing to financial constraints, many of which cannot be rectified retrospectively. As one example, if the one-year deadline to claim priority on a UK patent application under the Patent Co-Operation Treaty or European Patent Convention is missed, an inventor will lose the opportunity to extend protection beyond their home market, because any subsequent, separate application will have to be substantially different in order not to be 'caught' by the original patent's prior art. **9.49**

As another example; notwithstanding the likelihood that a company's intangible assets are often subject to a floating charge from its bank, there is often a strong temptation for business proprietors and company directors to divert assets when they know that their future trading prospects are looking bleak. Some inventors make a point of not assigning the ownership of patents, designs, and other IP to their companies, even where they own all the shares, because they are concerned about losing access to the inventions if the company performs badly. Their intention is usually to start up some kind of 'phoenix' operation. This is, of course, not good news for creditors who might reasonably expect the assets a business requires in order to trade to be owned by that business; customer-related assets such as lists, specifications, designs, and ordering behaviours are amongst those that are typically taken, not least because they can be duplicated without initially being detected. **9.50**

Despite these potential difficulties, IP value can endure, and the earlier Woolworths example turns out to provide evidence of this. Whilst the Woolworths name may have gone from UK high streets, it continues as an online retailer. The Ladybird children's brand is still well-known and loved, and its clothes are now sold through a number of outlets owned by Shop Direct, which bought both Woolworths and **9.51**

Ladybird from the administrators for an estimated price of between £5 million and £10 million.[5] The Chad Valley toy range, also owned by Woolworths, was bought by the Home Retail Group (owners at the time of writing of the Argos and Homebase store chains) for £5 million.[6] In fact, the brands turned out to be some of the most valuable assets left.

9.52 Since the average life of a UK small or medium-sized enterprise is fairly short, many companies cease trading before they have had an opportunity to build up value in their brand loyalty. In addition, the argument is sometimes made that the demise of a business with particular IP indicates that this IP was no longer effective. Certainly, there are plenty of examples of companies formed to exploit technologies which ultimately have not proved to be viable; however, this is clearly not always the case. Apart from the Nortel example referenced earlier, which provides one of the most striking counter-arguments, there are countless instances of businesses with great IP but poor management.

9.53 There is one other noteworthy consequence that arises from business failure, which particularly affects copyright assets; 'orphan works' get created. Even if it is still possible to identify the original author or creator, it may prove difficult or impossible to find all the rights owners (especially with compound assets such as films) making the asset not legally exploitable. Here too, however, if the rights are transferred, copyright works can prove particularly resilient to the demise of their authors, as the value associated with many music catalogues attests.

Tax Benefits

9.54 At the macro-economic level, governments recognize that innovation involves risk, and that investments in knowledge and skills for the longer term are necessary for companies to be successful (as a consequence of which, they create high value employment which benefits the public). In addition to making grants available for R&D activity, two types of tax incentive have been developed and are increasingly widely adopted—one relating specifically to IP, the other more generally to activities likely to create it. These are examined below.

9.55 It is also the case that governments internationally use tax as a competitive weapon. As well as specific incentives linked to IP and R&D, general rates of corporation tax vary, as do tax treatments of income streams that are derived from licensing activity. As a result, an interesting downward trend is evident in corporation tax rates generally, which have come down from nearly 50% in the early 1980s to less than 35%,

[5] Reported in *The Times* on 3 February 2009.

[6] Reported in the *Wall Street Journal* on 20 January 2009.

driven by international competition,[7] and a focus on the influence tax policies have on foreign direct investment.

Against this background it is not surprising that multinational corporations, which are themselves mobile, have become increasingly adept at moving their IP assets into countries offering beneficial rates of tax in order to increase profits. **9.56**

Both sets of trends are discussed below. Whilst not all strategies aimed at increasing tax efficiency necessarily require IP to be formally valued, the increasing sophistication of IP-related tax planning shows how the mobility of intangible assets adds to their worth. A further, particularly helpful, characteristic of IP is that unlike most categories of fixed assets, its returns can increase its value over time. **9.57**

Patent box

'Patent box', 'IP box', and 'innovation box' are terms used to refer to incentives that now exist in China and a number of European countries (including the United Kingdom, where the current scheme was introduced in April 2013; this is due to be updated in June 2016). The term 'box' simply refers to the fact that there is a specific box to tick on the tax form. **9.58**

The idea of a patent box was first introduced in Ireland, which established a scheme as long ago as 1973, but removed its exemption of royalty income in 2010. However, the idea has found favour in other countries since 2000 and now includes France, Hungary, the Netherlands, Belgium, Luxembourg, Spain, Malta, Liechtenstein, the Swiss Canton of Nidwalden, Cyprus, and the United Kingdom.[8] **9.59**

Patent boxes differ from other types of tax incentive for innovation in that they target the outputs that are produced rather than the amount expended (as is the case with R&D tax credits, addressed separately below). They operate by providing a lower rate of tax on qualifying profits. This means that the incentive is not simply to conduct research, but to commercialize it also, the argument being that it is the commercial exploitation of IP that provides the desired driver of growth. **9.60**

There are two main economic arguments for patent boxes. First, they reduce the financial risks of innovation, arising from market failures and dilution of benefits caused by 'spillover' to other companies which have not made equivalent investments (one research project some years ago by Tewkesbury et al. studied twenty **9.61**

[7] Atkinson, R. (2009). 'Effective Corporate Tax Reform in the Global Innovation Economy' (Technical report, ITIF, Washington DC). Available at: http://www.itif.org/files/090723_CorpTax.pdf.

[8] Evers,L., Miller, H., and Spengel, C. (2013). 'Intellectual Property Box Regimes: Effective Tax Rates and Tax Policy Considerations' (Centre for European Economic Research, Discussion Paper 13-070).

prominent innovations and found that the median private rate of return was 27%, but the median social rate of return was 99%).[9] These risks are exacerbated in some sectors (notably pharmaceuticals) because the length of time taken to bring a new product from discovery to market can be decades.

9.62 It has been suggested that many of the inventions that produce the greatest societal benefit require substantial amounts of costly basic research, and that the risks associated with this provide one explanation of why venture capital appetite for early stage investments has declined.[10] Tax incentives can align the rewards companies earn with wider societal benefits, which include the creation of more knowledge-intensive (and therefore better paid) jobs. This is especially important for Western countries unable to compete effectively with emerging economies on the costs of production.

9.63 The second argument is that by lowering the effective corporation tax rate of knowledge-based enterprises, patent box measures improve companies' (and countries') international competitiveness. The mobility of R&D activity has become a significant concern for national governments, given that the innovation process has become much more globalized, particularly in sectors such as life sciences, aerospace and defence, and electronics.

9.64 In all countries operating such schemes, patents qualify for this tax benefit. In some cases (such as Ireland, Luxembourg, and Spain), income from designs, copyrights, and trade marks is also allowable. Perhaps the broadest scope of allowances of all is currently to be found in China, where proceeds from exploiting commercial know-how such as process innovation are also eligible, and the calculation simply applies to firms that spend between at least 3 and 6% of gross revenue on R&D, depending on their size.[11] The Netherlands also allows firms that are in the process of applying for protection to claim a proportion of the total tax benefits, despite not yet having a granted patent.[12]

9.65 Most, but not all, current schemes have additional qualifying conditions. While patents that a company has acquired or licensed-in are generally allowable, this is not the case in the United Kingdom, Belgium, the Netherlands, or Spain, where acquired IP is not included. Also, in Belgium for example, where a company carries out contract research on behalf of another organization, it does not benefit from

---

[9] Tewkesbury, J., Crandall, M., and Crane, W. (1980). 'Measuring the Societal Benefits of Innovation' *Science* 09/1980: 658–62.

[10] Atkinson, R. and Andes, S. (2011). *Patent Boxes: Innovation in Tax Policy and Tax Policy for Innovation* (The Information Technology & Innovation Foundation).

[11] Stender, N., Stark, J., and Ye, F. (2010). 'China Income Tax Preferences for High/New-Tech Enterprises (HTNE)' (Technical report, Orrick, Herrington & Sutcliffe LLP, Wheeling, WV). Available at: http:www.orrick.com/fileupload/2420.pdf.

[12] Atkinson and Andes (n 10).

patent box reliefs because it is not the owner, rights holder, or licensee of the resulting patents.

It may seem a little counter-intuitive to focus tax benefits on an IP right that is intended to provide its owner with a state-backed monopoly, as is the case with a patent (it looks rather like 'double-dipping'). However, there are counter-arguments. First, successful products tend naturally to encourage the production of 'copycats' that are intentionally engineered around the patent protection (e.g. the plethora of tablet devices that followed Apple's iPad), illustrating how difficult it can be to reap maximum returns from innovation investment. Secondly, increasing the benefits associated with success makes such investment more attractive (in a different way from reducing the costs of R&D, but with a potentially bigger upside, because by definition a company would usually hope to reap significantly more than its costs on any successful R&D). Thirdly, patent box incentives recognize that many good R&D outcomes will never make it to market and that commercialization rather than R&D is the real driver of economic growth (as noted above). **9.66**

One feature that has been notable by its absence is that while there are rules governing the territories eligible patents must cover, there is no specific requirement for the underlying R&D work leading to the patent to have been conducted within the territory offering the benefit. Originally, local development was a requirement in Ireland, but a European Commission ruling in 2007 determined that such a condition violated the freedom of establishment and free movement of services clauses in Article 226 of the EC Treaty.[13] However, increasing concerns over the effect of incentives have caused this view to be modified, and it is understood that the new UK scheme will only allow tax benefits to be claimed for the proportion of global R&D actually conducted in-country.[14] **9.67**

Considering that much larger market distortions appear to exist between different countries' corporation tax rates and R&D tax credit allowances, it seems odd to prevent patent box reliefs from having national limitations in this way. The absence of restrictions on R&D location may also have the unintended effect of making it easier for firms to move IP within Europe simply to benefit from tax treatments (and also seems to ignore the fact that companies are not restricted to European locations when reviewing their tax options). **9.68**

The tax incentives provided certainly vary widely, with some of the most generous countries being Malta at 0% tax (provided R&D costs have not previously been deducted) and Cyprus at 2%. France appears the least generous at 15.5%, though this is still less than half the standard rate of corporation tax which would otherwise **9.69**

[13] European Union. New release, 23 March 2007. 'Direct Taxation: Commission Requests Ireland to End Discriminatory Rules on Tax Treatment of Patent Royalties'.

[14] http://www.pwc.co.uk/services/tax/insights/patent-box.html.

be payable. In other cases, the calculation is performed by exempting a certain percentage of qualifying (gross) income from tax altogether, meaning that the 80% allowance in Belgium provides a maximum effective rate of 6.8% (being 20% of the statutory rate of 34%). Some countries also have caps limiting the maximum amount of tax benefit that can be claimed, though not all. In the United Kingdom, the rate of 10% is calculated after certain deductions relating to associated expenses rather than the gross income generated; royalty income and income that is 'embedded' in the price of patented products are both included. In the case of Belgium, most expenses (except licence fees and amortization costs relating to acquired patents) remain deductible at the full 34% rate.

9.70 There is one last interesting side-effect highlighted by the Mirrlees review from the Institute of Fiscal Studies in London. This showed that, in principle, reducing taxes related to mobile assets like those associated with R&D (where companies have a choice of where to create them) enables a higher tax rate to be justified and successfully levied on fixed, immobile assets such as infrastructure, concluding that 'patent boxes may allow governments to maintain a higher tax rate and therefore collect more revenue from other, less mobile, forms of corporate income than would otherwise be the case'.[15]

9.71 Most of the patent boxes have been introduced too recently to be able to reach any firm conclusions on the overall tax consequences, especially given the inconvenient timing of the Global Financial Crisis at or around the same time many of the schemes commenced. Initial research suggests that the additional patenting activity the schemes appear to have encouraged is not, in itself, enough to outweigh the likely reduction in overall tax take. The benefits of the policy are likely to be much more in evidence in increased research, sales, and job creation or enhancement.[16]

R&D tax credits

9.72 First introduced in the United States in 1981, at least thirty countries[17] now provide some sort of tax incentive for the R&D work companies conduct. These tax credits address innovation inputs. Like the patent box described earlier, they provide a means to address the fact that the benefits to society from innovation may significantly outweigh those which can be realized by the firm, and that a decision

---

[15] Griffith, R. and Miller, J. (30 June 2011). 'Patent Boxes: An Innovative Way to Race to the Bottom?' *Vox*. Available at http://www.voxeu.org/index.php?q=node/6706.

[16] Griffith, R., Miller, H., and O'Connell, M. (2010). *Corporate Taxes and Intellectual Property: Simulating the Effect of Patent Boxes* (London, Institute for Fiscal Studies). Available at: http://www.ifs.org.uk/bns/bn112.pdf.

[17] Deloitte Touche Tohmatsu Limited. (March 2014). '2014 Global Survey of R&D Tax Incentives'.

by a company to conduct research comes by definition before there can be any certainty of a commercial benefit. They also seek to acknowledge that, even if a particular company cannot successfully commercialize its research at all, there may be a benefit to other organizations from its activities in having extended the body of knowledge in a particular field.

Alongside the introduction of reliable IP protection regimes and robust, high speed IT infrastructure, R&D tax credits are an important part of national strategies that seek to encourage multinational companies to locate innovation-related activities in their territory. Generally speaking, the nature of what counts as R&D is reasonably consistent across different countries, though the ways in which the benefit is calculated vary widely, and different restrictions apply in some places regarding the type and nature of the activity being conducted, the status of the beneficiary company, and the use to which the resulting IP is put. **9.73**

In the United Kingdom, the primary criterion that must be met is that the R&D activity is directed at resolving some type of 'scientific or technological uncertainty'. As in other countries, the types of activity which qualify for tax relief are those which would typically be expensed annually, such as payroll costs, consumables, other expenses directly linked to the activities such as power, fuel and water, and sub-contracted specialist assistance (subject to limits). **9.74**

The particularly attractive aspect of an R&D tax credit is that, in the United Kingdom as elsewhere, it enables companies to make a claim based on an amount greater than their original expenditure. In the case of the United Kingdom this so-called 'super-deduction' is 225% for small companies and 130% for larger companies. In addition, the UK scheme rules allow loss-making SMEs and large companies without corporation tax liabilities to claim cash credits, which is particularly helpful to early stage R&D-intensive firms. **9.75**

The United Kingdom is not the most generous scheme. In Singapore, for example, R&D is classed as 'any systematic, investigative and experimental study that involves novelty or technical risk carried out in the field of science or technology with the objective of acquiring new knowledge or using the results of the study for the production or improvement of materials, devices, products, or processes'.[18] Its tiered scheme provides a base level deduction of 100% for R&D expenses, augmented by an additional 50% if these activities are conducted within the country. There is then an additional deduction available on the first SD400,000 incurred each year which means that regardless of where the qualifying R&D activity has been conducted, 400% relief on this initial amount can be claimed. **9.76**

[18] ibid. Information drawn from Inland Revenue Authority of Singapore.

9.77 Also, some countries take the view that certain companies are by definition entitled to lower tax rates because of the nature of their activities. In China, companies with high and new technology status have a reduced tax rate of 15% rather than the usual 25%, and remain eligible for a 150% super-deduction for qualifying R&D expenses, though their IP must be located in China, and less than 40% of their R&D expenses can take place outside the country. Technology and software companies can also benefit from tax concessions on technology transfers.

9.78 Not all economically powerful countries offer these types of tax incentives. In Germany, for example, incentives for R&D generally take the form of 50% match-funded, non-repayable grants (the rate can be higher for some SMEs) or R&D loans instead. Qualifying activities have to take place in Germany (which is also where the costs must be incurred) and the exploitation of results must take place principally within the country. However, given other international developments, it appears likely that Germany may well move towards a tax incentive scheme in future.

9.79 Research into the economic returns from R&D tax credit schemes suggests not only that they encourage more activity, but also that they act as an incentive to relocate R&D in favour of territories offering more favourable tax treatments. Different studies have arrived at a variety of research investment to tax cost ratios ranging from 1.1 to 2.9.[19] There also appears to be a beneficial effect on the number of companies engaged in R&D at all, and there are indications that raising the benefits of such tax credits increases the amount of R&D foreign companies invest in a given nation. These incentives therefore look likely to be an enduring feature of the economic landscape.

Other tax planning strategies

9.80 It has now become common practice amongst multinational corporations to use IP in their tax planning. The creative ways in which organizations structure these arrangements are motivated by the desire to do two things: to reduce the overall effective rate of tax that such corporations pay on their profits (not least because high taxes have an adverse impact on earnings per share), and enable them to drive up the deductions that can be claimed on the investments that they need to make, including innovation-related costs.

9.81 In doing so, companies are taking advantage of the fact that while trading income has not historically been very mobile from a tax perspective, a well-engineered 'value chain' can enable commercial opportunities and risks to be centralized in one entity

[19] These studies include Bloom, N., Griffith, R., and Van Reenen, J. (2002). 'Do R&D Tax Credits Work? Evidence from a Panel of Countries 1979–1997' *Journal of Public Economics* 85(1): 1–31.

that can be placed in a favourable tax jurisdiction. Taken to its logical extreme, locally-based activities essentially become support operations, and the limited value they add reduces the returns they make. This enables multinationals still to have an effective presence in high tax territories, but pay less tax.

The differences that exist between policies in different countries go well beyond varying rates of corporation tax, and these variations provide further opportunities for efficiencies. The patent box is one particular IP-specific example, but corporations will also take into account the different policies regarding tax-free payment of dividends, the presence or absence of withholding tax, rules on capital gains, and capital allowances (as examples) into consideration. **9.82**

The strategy of separating out IP ownership from usage is a well established one, enabling its returns to be realised in a different jurisdiction. The main complication with such a move is that the act of separation is a taxable event, because it is regarded as being a sale. This means that separation is generally best done when the value that is attributable to the asset is comparatively low (under certain circumstances it may be possible to claim relief on reorganization, or find other ways of deferring tax). **9.83**

The separation process itself is relatively straightforward; it simply involves placing the IP into a separate company, which then charges royalties to the trading entity under a licensing structure. As noted earlier, this is a highly flexible arrangement (and may be a sensible strategy anyway, for reasons which have nothing to do with tax). It can immediately introduce efficiencies if the 'IP company' pays lower taxes than the trading entity, especially if the trading entity is also able to claim its royalty payments to the IP company as a legitimate business expense. **9.84**

Even if the corporation tax treatment is not particularly positive (or not positive at all), the tax treatment applied to royalty receipts may be beneficially different, as is the case for example in Luxembourg, where a number of IP companies are based. The main issue for the multinational is to avoid any rules that directly attribute incomes to a parent company even when they are not actually repatriated to it. Accordingly, more elaborate structures have been devised to 'disregard' trading entities and the companies which charge them royalties from the IP company, which may itself be placed in a separate tax haven. **9.85**

Whilst such tax planning strategies are most often associated with online retailers based in the United States, there is no reason why companies with a physical high street presence cannot employ similar strategies (and some do). In fact, the relevance of the United States is primarily that the high corporation tax rates levied in that country may provide an additional incentive to exercise 'creativity'. **9.86**

While these strategies have (understandably) attracted strongly negative press, they merely take advantage of tax treatments devised by individual national governments **9.87** to enhance their competitiveness. Put another way, if a trading entity is located in a country which is happy to allow tax deductions for royalty expense, or the parent is based in a territory which allows tax to be deferred on a royalty or a future dividend receipt, the real question is whether any tax would have been payable even without the strategy.

Conclusion

9.88 As has been demonstrated, the range of contexts in which IP delivers real firm value is diverse, including sales, fundraising, licensing, and litigation. IP can also continue to have value even when the business that originated it is no longer in existence; and for trading businesses, it has an increasingly important role to play in management of tax liabilities, and therefore levels of distributable profits. The next chapter goes on to consider whether, in value creation terms, all IP is created equal, or some IP rights are more equal than others.

10

DETERMINANTS OF INTELLECTUAL PROPERTY VALUE

Beyond the obvious point that IP is (or should be) unique, and therefore comparison of any two 'bundles' of IP is at the very least difficult, there are some general conclusions about the principal factors influencing relative value which can be drawn from the study of different successful transactions. Some of these are, to an extent, intrinsic to the IP itself, whereas others are only determined by reference to the context in which it is or should be used or sold (or, more intriguingly, the market which it controls without needing to be used). This latter point is reflected in the generally accepted valuation principle that refers to consideration of the IP's 'highest and best use'. **10.01**

This chapter starts by considering the extent to which the value of any given portfolio is likely to be influenced by the types of IP rights present within it. It then identifies and briefly examines the influence of other factors: rights duration, geographical reach, 'strength', ability to detect infringement, cross-sector applicability, transferability, uniqueness, and the preservation of confidentiality (or ability to keep a secret). **10.02**

After consideration of these influencing factors, and before diving into the detail of how IP valuation is performed (discussed in Chapter 11), further information is provided on the extent to which standards are applicable to this area of valuation practice, and the aspects that make IP valuation different from business valuation. **10.03**

Is There a 'Hierarchy' of IP Rights Value?

One theory that is attractive for its simplicity is that there will be a correlation between the types of IP rights involved and their fair market values. Using this logic, the strong, monopolistic rights associated with patents, and the scrutiny they receive prior to being granted, ought to make them the most valuable IP variant of **10.04** all, with copyright and designs languishing at a distance behind, and trade marks somewhere in the middle.

10.05 Study of the available data does not necessarily bear this theory out, particularly since the value in copyright (automatic, and not subject to any prior scrutiny) can be far greater than most patents, especially if data from the United States, a country in which patenting is a well-established way of seeking to protect ideas, is anything to go by. US estimates[1] indicate that of 2.1 million live patents, 95% of patents are not commercialized and therefore potentially worth nothing, except where some value is derived from their blocking function. An even smaller proportion, potentially as little as 2%, are estimated by the US Patent and Trademark Office to make significant profits for the inventor. Even once a patent is granted, there remains a risk it will subsequently be claimed to infringe another, leading to a costly court battle and/or out of court settlement.

10.06 The ordering of any such hierarchy would also have to include the value of other types of intangible assets. Contracts, licensing agreements, and permissions can all be immensely valuable, as can trade secrets, as examined in Chapter 6 (if appropriately safeguarded). This raises a more fundamental challenge, because as referenced in Chapter 8, while IP rights and intangible assets need to be understood at an individual level, they need to be viewed as a 'bundle' because they tend to add value to each other.

10.07 As an example, the well-known restaurant chain, Kentucky Fried Chicken (KFC), makes a point of taking great care to protect its original 'secret recipe of eleven herbs and spices' as a trade secret. It is stored in a vault; the number of employees that know the recipe is limited to two people; for manufacturing purposes, the mix is split into two parts and its manufacture is sub-contracted to two different companies; the final mix is only combined when KFC restaurants do this during food preparation. However, even if the precise recipe is 'original' and closely guarded,[2] it would be relatively simple to reverse engineer an approximation of it.

10.08 If valuing KFC's IP, it would be inappropriate to seek to consider the secret spice mix without also seeking to quantify the contribution made by the brand, the international distribution network, and the processes used during preparation, to name a few. The same could be said for Coca-Cola, which has managed to maintain its trade secret for over 100 years using similar controls; in view of the large number of imitators which exist, it can be argued that the importance of the trade secret is not

[1] See for example Forbes, at http://www.forbes.com/sites/danielfisher/2014/06/18/13633.

[2] This fact is questionable, as a 1971 version of the recipe that appears to be genuine is easily found on the internet. Further articles suggest that the recipe has changed over time, and that the taste and texture of the chicken is also attributable to the use of pressure fryers which, while not a secret, are not generally used in domestic contexts.

merely that it makes the 'exact' taste more difficult to copy, but that it enables the owner to claim that it has the 'original' (which can be marketed in such a way as to imply that it is also the best).

Notwithstanding the importance of the 'bundling' approach, the following half dozen factors are likely to influence the assessment of value in any given situation, positively or negatively. **10.09**

Duration of protection

For IP rights and intangible assets that are time-bound, the remaining validity period is an important starting point when considering value, especially in the context of a sale, purchase, or licensing agreement, because it governs the period over which an acquirer or licensee has the potential to obtain economic benefits from the use of the asset. After this period, it may still be able to derive value from an asset whose IP protection has expired, but its vulnerability to competitor activity will increase substantially, as the legal barriers preventing imitation will no longer be present. **10.10**

It is important to bear in mind that the remaining economic life of an asset may be quite different from its legal life, especially when the most commonly used methods of IP valuation are concerned with future value generation. A patent may be rendered obsolete by competing technical advances long before it expires, and any acquirer or licensee will want to satisfy itself that this commercial lifespan is sufficiently long-lived to make the asset of interest. **10.11**

Conversely, the income streams built up during the life of a patent may continue for some time after the patent itself has expired. When this happens, however, it is likely to be not only the formulation or technology that is delivering value but also the brand and the associated contracts and supply relationships. Accordingly, when valuing a patent, it is usual to regard the legal lifespan as the end point for its first phase of value generation, but also to consider whether attributing some residual or terminal value at this time is justified. **10.12**

Particular care is required when assessing the likely lifespan of trade marks, as a valid mark is capable of being renewed indefinitely. However, as with the patent example above, this does not mean that a trade mark's value will necessarily keep accumulating over the long term. **10.13**

Geographical extent of protection

Linked to the above point, the territories covered by any IP protection may also be a material consideration for a valuation. This is one reason why it is very important for companies to consider carefully where to apply for protection, to ensure future options are preserved. **10.14**

10.15 When it comes to patents, US coverage is generally regarded as delivering the most value, despite US patents not necessarily being of world-leading quality. Their popularity reflects the fact that the United States represents a large addressable market for many businesses, and the comparatively more acquisitive nature and greater patent awareness of US corporations increase the likelihood that a buyer can be found there.

10.16 However, a more important question for any valuer will be the extent to which the IP protection that exists covers all the markets that are demonstrably important for the company's present and future trading activities. The treaties and protocols which exist to facilitate the obtaining of IP rights outside a company's home markets make it relatively straightforward to extend protection, provided that decisions to do so are made at the right time, though of course this is not without cost.

Strength of protection

10.17 An individual patent seldom carries a very significant amount of value in isolation. Aside from the question of whether supporting intangibles like the necessary accompanying know-how are present and available, single patent families carry the risk that if successfully challenged, all the protection on which a company may be reliant can fall away. In more mature businesses, it is usual to file additional patents in order to protect subsequent development and enhancements and create something of a 'fence' around the core technology. In this respect, the practice that arose in the late 2000s of calculating the 'average value per patent' based on the comparison of large technology company portfolios is of very limited use.

10.18 The value of designs may also benefit from being registered as a series. Recording a number of 'variations on a theme' may help to reduce the risk of a competitor designing around a key styling feature, and increase a company's options for licensing where relevant. Unfortunately, the biggest threat to effective design protection does not necessarily come from competitor activity, but from a company's own processes of continuous improvement, which have a tendency to render existing designs obsolete. This can also be a problem when a company is reliant on image marks to protect its brands if its registrations do not keep pace with the company's marketing activity.

10.19 Strength, however, is a complex concept that has quite a lot to do with just how unique and well-differentiated a technology or other invention really is, a point considered in more detail below.

Ability to detect infringement

10.20 An important consideration when dealing with any IP right is whether the owner will be able to enforce it in practice. This not only concerns the inherent uniqueness, or otherwise, of the right, but also is a question of whether it is possible to detect infringement.

Where a patent deals with subject matter such as the fundamental properties of a new material, the functionality of a product, or the formulation of a chemical compound, infringing goods are not particularly difficult to spot. However, if patents covering process innovation are being infringed behind closed doors, it may not be possible to detect this fact merely from the existence of the finished goods. This matters because such infringement undermines the state-backed monopoly that the patent is supposed to confer on an owner or licensee. **10.21**

This does not mean, of course, that process patents cannot be very valuable, especially where such innovations have applications across a range of industries and can be successfully licensed. It does mean, though, that selection of patenting as a protection strategy carries more risk in this context than in others, before considering whether the owner has sufficient resources to be able to defend the patent if challenged, or pursue infringers. **10.22**

Cross-sector applicability

It follows from the previous point that, 'everything else being equal', a patent covering a technology with applications across many markets is likely to be more valuable than one that is highly specialized. When conducting a patent assessment, it is possible to explore this point by looking for similarities between a patent under scrutiny and other related technologies. Another technique which can be used (also helpful in identifying prospective buyers or licensees) is to examine the International Patent Classification (IPC) codes that have been applied to a patent, and compare these with those that accompany subsequent citations. Quite often, it will be found that at least some of the 'overlapping' IP rights are being used for applications entirely unrelated to those for which the original patent application was first envisaged. **10.23**

This technique is useful when IP value needs to be underwritten, because consideration has to be given to the potential for a future sale. Since it is a well-established principle that a better price can be achieved for almost anything when there are buyers competing to own it, being able to identify who these buyers might be, assessed according to their current technology usage, will tend to lend confidence to the idea that there will be a realizable value, and if they appear to exist across more than one market sector, this confidence will be strengthened. **10.24**

The problem, however, is that the 'everything else' reference point is seldom equal. In practice, the answer on comparative value will depend on how lucrative any specialist application is, and whether a company has the ability and capacity to penetrate possible wider markets. **10.25**

10.26 To take a simple example, what may appear to be a niche invention offering a modest incremental operational benefit for one specific manufacturer's design of silicon chip could turn into a blockbuster patent (or family of patents) because of the volume and variety of needs such chips now fulfil. By contrast, a new and beneficial method of drug delivery that could be used for a wide variety of treatments may prove to have little actual transfer potential if it cannot be produced to the required price point.

10.27 Care also needs to be taken with the identification of similar applications because it does not follow that any third parties identified in this manner are necessarily active buyers—indeed, they may be active litigants.

Transferability between businesses

10.28 If a patent or series of patents is inextricably linked to its parent company's products or services or its particular operating practices, this can pose a challenge for valuation. The concept of transferability or separability is important in post-acquisition accounting, dealt with in Chapter 12, because of the idea that the value allocated to identifiable intangible assets should have some connection with their fair market value via the price being paid for them. This is a difficult principle to apply if there is in reality no market for the IP rights because no one else can use them. In such circumstances, it may be argued that the value of the IP is not separable from the value of the business.

10.29 Some types of IP and intangibles can have restrictions placed on their transferability. For example, in the defence industry, governments have certain pre-emptive rights that can be exercised where inventions are believed to have a national security implication; these may limit the markets to which they can be sold, or even confer exclusive rights to their use in favour of the government. Similarly, commercial contracts may contain clauses preventing IP rights from being assigned, or may place restrictions on the involvement of any sub-contractors. Also, in more general terms, it is frequently the case that patents and trade secrets require accompanying specialist know-how to be transferred in order for them to have any 'real-world' utility to a buyer.

10.30 This is not a problem that affects most designs or copyright materials. Assigning a publication or a photograph is very straightforward, and because assets of this nature are generally in some sense 'finished', the recipient does not need to know how they were created and will not need to maintain them (beyond tackling any infringement) in order to enjoy the economic benefits they generate. Even works such as recorded music or computer games libraries are relatively straightforward to transfer (though due to the complex blend of rights contained within them, films do not fall into this category). Trade marks, too, are regularly transferred to new owners (with or without the sale of the underlying business), and it is only if the link is broken between the brand and the underlying product that difficulties typically arise.

'Genuine' uniqueness

As explored in Chapter 3, a key economic reason for having a patent regime at all is (in summary) to grant a state-backed monopoly to a company that has invented something with a unique and original technical effect, to give them an opportunity to recoup their investment whilst ensuring that the benefits will subsequently pass to society at large. It follows that a patented asset that is genuinely distinctive and has significant exploitation potential is likely to be considerably more valuable (at least for a given period of time) than an asset that does not have this protection. **10.31**

The complication is that the granting of a patent (or a whole family of patents) is not of itself a guarantee that the owner of an asset can relax safe in the knowledge that his or her investment is safely protected. There are a number of features that are present in the way in which the patenting system operates which can affect the protection, and, therefore, the value, that a granted patent affords. These go beyond the fact (already discussed) that patenting is a negative right, and are worth summarizing here. **10.32**

First, it is the job of a patent agent or attorney to serve their customers' interests by obtaining for them the protection they are seeking. In order to do this, it is essential to be able to demonstrate a degree of novelty in the invention, to the satisfaction of a patent examiner. It is perhaps unsurprising that on some occasions, particularly where a substantial amount of prior art exists, language to suggest novelty is used very creatively, whilst descriptions of functionality are kept at as obscure a level as possible in order to protect the client's commercial interests. As an example, whilst it will be necessary to disclose the ingredients in a novel formulation for, say, a lubricant, it may not always be necessary to specify the exact proportions in which the ingredients are combined (or the way in which they are combined) in order to obtain patent protection. **10.33**

Secondly, it may be surprising to those less well-acquainted with the patenting process to learn that comprehensive searches to establish the novelty of patentable ideas are often not conducted in advance of making an application. Sometimes, this important step is omitted because the inventor is already convinced that their application relates to something genuinely original (which, if they are particularly well-versed in the area in question, they may be better able to determine than a patent examiner). On other occasions, it is because the budget needed for searching is unavailable or a decision is made to expend funds on patent drafting instead. The logic here is that when the patent reaches the examination stage it will be submitted to searches anyway, so the client could otherwise end up paying twice for the process. **10.34**

10.35 The consequence of these two factors is that patents get granted which are not in fact novel. Two degrees of severity can be characterized: sometimes claims that have been granted are found to duplicate rights already owned by other organizations (rendering them effectively valueless because they are not enforceable). On other occasions, claims that have been granted have significant overlaps with existing assets.

10.36 Estimates of the seriousness of this problem vary. The US House of Representatives Judiciary Committee took evidence on the issue of patent enforceability in 2001. Submissions made included analysis by M-CAM which estimated that, based on its own proprietary patent matching and analytical software, one-third (33%) of US patents issued at that time shared claims with patents that had already been granted and in addition, almost a further half (47%) were 'commercially impaired'. This latter description meant that overlaps were found with other rights covering the same exclusionary space and the patents would, therefore, most likely prove unenforceable were they ever to be tested.[3]

10.37 As a related but separate point, it is also the case, as many patent applicants will testify, that examiners may find it difficult to grasp the significance of an inventive step and will draw parallels with pre-existing granted patents which may in practice have little in common with the new technology. As well as complicating or even frustrating the standard examination process, this can also lead to patents being incorrectly classified.

10.38 Sophisticated mapping tools now exist which can express the position of a patent spatially in respect of its prior art. Naturally, these are only as good as the data on which they are built, so if classification errors exist, most such maps will reflect them.

10.39 Examination of these patent maps confirms that real uniqueness can be a mixed blessing. Whilst a patent which is not closely hemmed in by prior art is less likely to be the subject of unwelcome attention from litigants claiming that their rights are being infringed, and might represent a truly disruptive technology, the greatest commercial opportunity is more likely to be located in the map's 'hot spots'.

Ability to keep a secret

10.40 Whilst the monopolistic rights of patents are often the focus for discussions on IP value, it is possible for some businesses to generate equal or greater value by virtue of

[3] See transcript from Congress at: http://commdocs.house.gov/committees/judiciary/hju72305.000/hju72305_0f.htm.

keeping their inventions secret (which also has the advantage that their novelty does not have to be proven in order to be protected).

The question in relation to the value of trade secrets is the extent to which it is possible to keep them secret in the long term. As with the point above on enforceability, if a process innovation becomes obvious when examining its end product, or if it can be reverse engineered without significant difficulty, the value that can be attributed to the secret will be limited. A question will also arise in relation to the procedures in place at the company in terms of whether these are adequate to ensure the secret does not 'leak out' (as discussed in reference to KFC above). **10.41**

It is still necessary for a company relying on secrecy to understand whether it may be infringing the patent rights of other firms, given that ignorance of a patent is no defence against its enforcement. **10.42**

In conclusion, then, there are a substantial number of factors which may determine the perceived quality and utility of any given set of intangible assets, which an IP valuation needs to take into account. **10.43**

IP Valuation Standards

There is at present no single set method for IP valuation, a process that has traditionally been conducted by specialist consultants and large accounting firms. There are, however, a number of generally accepted approaches, set out in Chapter 11, and there are a few specific contexts in which particular methods are starting to emerge as having 'preferred' status. **10.44**

The primary factors preventing the adoption of a single standard, outside some specific contexts, are the (supposedly) unique nature of IP (discussed earlier in this chapter) and the absence of transparent markets where it is regularly bought and sold, which give confidence to assist valuation of other assets that change hands such as real property and vehicles. These two factors compound each other: since IP assets should by definition be unique, it is difficult to be confident that such data as is available (or could be made available) will necessarily be applicable in any other set of circumstances. They also create the further complication that because there are not open and transparent markets, the number of contexts in which a 'fair market value' can be used to record a balance sheet value (rather than simply a cost) for the assets is very limited indeed. **10.45**

Apart from international accounting standards, discussed in detail in Chapter 12, the professional body most closely associated with IP valuation generally is the International Valuation Standards Council (IVSC). This is an independent, **10.46** not-for-profit organization established to improve the quality and reputation of valuation practice with operations in the United Kingdom and the United States. Whilst its activities cover a wide range of valuation contexts, IVSC has produced, and recently revised, its International Valuation Standard 210 on intangible assets and the standards and accompanying guidance notes reference the three overall approaches to valuation and many of the specific variants explained in Chapter 11. UK organizations which are members of IVSC include the Institute of Chartered Accountants in England and Wales (ICAEW) and the Royal Institute of Chartered Surveyors (RICS).

10.47 Some of the emerging contexts for IP value realization have found it necessary to establish and promote 'preferences' for certain approaches to its valuation. For example, the schemes that now exist in a number of countries to assist in leveraging the collateral value of IP for fundraising purposes face a particular challenge in overcoming the lack of familiarity and outright scepticism of banks and other lending institutions when asked to place any specific value on IP and intangible assets. As an example, bearing in mind the need to adopt a relatively conservative view of IP value, the Malaysian Intellectual Property Office (MyIPO) developed a set of guidelines for IP valuation in the context of its own funding scheme, described in its 'IP Valuation Model Salient Features' document.

10.48 Having studied the guidance issued by IFRS, IVSC, and ISO, this concluded that 'the generally accepted method and the one selected for the IPVM is the income method, specifically the valuation on a relief-from-royalty (RFR) basis'. It goes on to state that:

> The real economic substance of the RFR approach, including its reliance on transaction-based market evidence, provides strength to conclusions of value derived on this basis. It is also a rational approach which can be readily explained and understood. When used in conjunction with secondary valuation approaches, including transaction multiples for comparable businesses, it provides a reliable estimate of the fair value of the IP assets.

10.49 As the Malaysian model points out, this valuation draws on the fact that 'both IFRS and IVS discuss the concept... that the fair value of a non-financial asset (including IP) is the value to a market participant putting the asset to its highest and best use.' Accordingly, it should be noted that this approach is only likely to generate a value indication for IP in the context of a business which is a going concern and that the true collateral value of such assets (i.e. the amount that might reasonably be expected to be achieved in the context of an arm's length sale with no business left to support and deliver them) would be significantly lower.

10.50 Nevertheless, any approach that moves towards wider acceptance and understanding of the fact that IP has value under such circumstances can be regarded as progress.

Business vs. IP Valuation

Finally, before examining the various methods of IP valuation, it may be helpful briefly to discuss the difference between business and IP valuation techniques, especially since many of the contexts in which IP needs to be valued may also have a wider business impact. In some cases, it may appear that IP ought to be the chief (or even only) contributor to a company's value, whilst in other cases, other factors may appear substantially to outweigh it. 10.51

The first observation is that, depending on the context for the business valuation, a figure may be derived from a 'top down' view (i.e. one that is based on overall sales or earnings), a 'bottom up' value build-up approach (which considers the assets available to the business), or a combination of the two. Also, in the case of an acquisition or merger, there is often a focus on the synergies or opportunities that it is believed can be exploited when two businesses are combined; under such circumstances, the purchase price (and thus the value being attributed) may appear to bear very little relation to the business cash flows or the underlying assets of whatever type. Further, it should be noted that price is always likely to be influenced by a number of external factors such as the presence or absence of competition. 10.52

The 'top down' approach

A favourite, traditional starting point when valuing a trading business from the 'top down' has been to look at the earnings (profits) it delivers after deducting any exceptional items that would be subject to change if it were acquired, and then apply a market-derived multiple. It is usual to take out interest payments and tax aspects, to which are often added depreciation and amortization charges that are to some extent discretionary or a consequence of a current structure or strategy that will fall away. Sometimes, the profits base will be purely historical, but since in many contexts the key motivation for the purchase is the achievement of future business benefits, it will be necessary to consider the future prospects of the business in the short and longer term and use these to model assumptions that can be brought back to an equivalent present day value using capitalization techniques.[4] 10.53

Where a business does not have an established profit stream, another indicator is required to form a basis for negotiation. This may be its turnover, to which a reduced 10.54

[4] Defined by Investopedia as a 'method of determining the value of an organisation by calculating the net present value (NPV) of expected future profits or cash flows. The capitalisation of earnings estimate is done by taking the entity's future earnings and dividing them by the capitalisation rate (cap rate). This will take into account the risk that earnings will stop or be lower than the estimate'. See http://www.investopedia.com/terms/c/capitalization_of_earnings.asp.

multiple will generally be applied; however, it can also be a multiple of a value attributed to non-financial performance indicators, such as the number of users or the size of the network it has successfully accumulated.

10.55 Where the main attraction to an acquirer is the number of user relationships, as in the case of a young business such as Instagram referenced in Chapter 8, an assessment will be made not only of the cost of reproducing those relationships, but also whether (given the level of market traction already achieved by the business under examination) it is likely that the acquirer could replicate the success already achieved, regardless of budget. In such instances, the value is not necessarily being driven by registered IP (though branding is very likely to be a factor) but may be heavily dependent on other intangible assets.

10.56 Valuation of IP and intangibles can therefore be expected to be particularly useful when seeking to support the view that a company that is yet to deliver substantial turnover or profits (or may not even be trading) nevertheless contains value. This view can be helpful when seeking to raise investment, for example. The difficulty, as will be apparent from the following chapter, is that many of the methods that can be applied to IP nevertheless require some consideration of future income generation and that unless these have been secured by way of a binding contract, they may be regarded with a degree of scepticism.

The 'bottom up' approach

10.57 Once a price for a business has been agreed, post-acquisition accounting rules require the price paid to be analysed using a 'bottom up' method divided into tangible assets, identifiable intangibles, and goodwill. These are explained in more detail in Chapter 12.

10.58 Under usual circumstances, any value attributed to the identifiable IP and intangible assets owned or controlled by a company can be expected to be a subset of the overall value of that business. This is because IP valuation is likely to miss out a significant number of potentially important value-producing aspects. The most obvious of these, which would not usually be included in an IP valuation, is any value attributable to tangible assets, such as bricks and mortar, plant and machinery, computer equipment, and vehicle fleets. However, it is important to acknowledge that the dividing lines between these two types of asset are not always clear-cut.

10.59 One particular aspect concerns software, which is necessary to run any computer equipment and derive value from it (whether the code is standard commercially available software or something much more specialist). Where this is purchased alongside the machinery in question, it is often regarded as not being separable from the hard asset and is depreciated using the same principles. However, if the software is developed or customized by the company using the equipment, it creates an intangible asset that may prove to have independent value (for example, it may prove to be capable of being sold or licensed to other businesses with a similar requirement). If this is recognized on a balance sheet at all, it will usually be because the company has elected to capitalize it.

Intangible value can even be a consideration when valuing the 'hardest' of tangible assets—real estate. If a building associated with a particular hotel or retail chain is being valued, for example, its worth may look quite different depending on whether it is assessed simply on an arm's length, open market basis (as a bare shell) or with all its associated assets in place, some of which are either branded or feature trade dress or a 'get-up' that is associated with their ownership. **10.60**

In line with the percentages noted in respect of stock market company valuation (referred to in the macro-economic discussion in Chapter 8), around one-fifth of the price paid for a typical business is typically likely to be attributable to its tangible asset portfolio, though substantially more value than this may be found in companies that own large quantities of hard assets (as might be found in manufacturing industries and potentially in retail). **10.61**

Another type of asset unlikely to feature in an IP valuation is a company's workforce. Whilst the staff of a business may 'embody' IP in the form of know-how that is used to create value, and be essential to its operation, any such know-how that resides solely in the heads of employees is by definition difficult to control. Since a company does not 'own' its workforce and individuals have a tendency to change jobs periodically (especially in more knowledge-intensive industries), the benefit of being able to access a skilled and experienced team will generally be regarded as part of a business's goodwill when it comes to post-acquisition value attribution and under international accounting standards is not an identifiable intangible asset. **10.62**

The benefit to a business of having a particular workforce can be valued, and where needed this is often done by making an assessment of replacement cost, a concept explained in more detail as one of the valuation methodologies. **10.63**

Conclusion

From the above analysis it will be clear that while care must be exercised when making assumptions about the relative value of different IP rights, determining a value for them is a feasible and appropriate thing to do. Furthermore, while the approaches for IP and business valuation are not wholly dissimilar, they are separate and distinct. The following chapter sets out in more detail the approaches that have been found to be most satisfactory and effective when considering IP value. **10.64**

11

INTELLECTUAL PROPERTY AND INTANGIBLES VALUATION METHODOLOGIES AND TECHNIQUES

Before diving headlong into IP valuation techniques, a quick précis of the main points covered in this chapter may be helpful. When seeking to understand the present, fair (i.e. 'arm's length') value of the tangible assets owned by a business, the most common starting point will be to examine its balance sheet, where the level of investment made and the current worth attributed to the assets in question can be found. However, as discussed in detail in Chapter 12, accounting rules do not provide the same clarity in terms of intangible asset value. In the absence of an external acquisition event to establish a price, only a select few types of intangibles can be represented in company accounts at their expected market value, and everything else can only be accounted for in terms of development cost, if at all. **11.01**

This appears to fly in the face of the fact that IP value permeates the very being of any knowledge-based, technologically sophisticated or creative enterprise, and is an important instrument of value creation and/or protection in many businesses that rely on their brands to sell their products and services. Simply put, intangible assets are what companies spend the most money on and drive most profit from, and which ultimately contribute the most to their underlying value appreciation. **11.02**

Whilst there are a number of well-established methods used in IP valuation, there is no single, agreed approach for determining the value of a given set of IP and intangibles. This presents an obvious challenge for any commercial negotiation involving IP rights, particularly since the results that are obtained through the use of different legitimate valuation methods can vary widely; a prospective buyer may simply disagree with the basis on which the value has been calculated. **11.03**

Add to this the existence of uncertainties around many of the data sources likely to be available, and it might be concluded that all IP valuations are necessarily imprecise, except where the value of a specific 'bundle' of IP has been determined **11.04** via an actual sale of those rights at a specific point in time. Also, as set out in Chapter 8, even when a price is known and has been validated by market activity, there are often unique situational factors which have led to that particular value being achieved, which may have been positive or negative (such as the perceived likelihood of litigation, the respective strengths of the organizations involved, and/or competitive considerations).

11.05 However, a little further consideration reveals that this lack of absolute precision is also evident in the valuation of tangible assets, such as real estate. Here too, the valuer's view is essentially a guide to price setting, but the final amount is determined by negotiation and by market demand. It is not reasonable to say, therefore, that IP valuations are inherently 'inaccurate'; the problem is more that in an environment largely devoid of transparent and readily available precedents to use as benchmarks, it is difficult to demonstrate just how accurate they are.

11.06 IP valuation practices have gained in credibility over time, and their selection is based on an appreciation of the advantages and drawbacks inherent within each of the methods it is possible to deploy. Whenever it is necessary to determine a value, there will usually be at least one method capable of being used. Where more than one alternative is available, each can be weighted or triangulated to arrive at a conclusion using either a blended figure or an upper and lower range.

11.07 As stated at the outset, it is not the aim of this work to provide a practical guide to the process of valuation (there are already useful reference works available on this subject). Instead, this chapter first explores a couple of underlying concepts used in different valuation approaches, before moving onto the principles behind each of the most commonly used valuation methods. Consideration is given to the applications for which each one is generally regarded as being most and least suitable, and the questions that it answers (and raises); there is also discussion of how challenges around early stage technologies can be addressed, how distinctions can be made between asset 'bundles' and individual assets, and what techniques can be employed when a liquidation value is required.

11.08 This chapter does not attempt to cover all the proprietary branded methods of valuation which exist, particularly in the United States. However, the vast majority represent relatively subtle variations on the central techniques which are discussed here.

Underlying Concepts

Discounted cash flow

11.09 Whenever future turnover or cash flow is used as an input for an IP valuation (or any other kind of valuation, for that matter), it is generally necessary to make adjustments which reflect the fact that income tomorrow is not worth the same amount as it would be today. Discounted[1] cash flow, or DCF, is a popular and well-established approach used to determine the net present value[2] of future expected financial benefits relating to a product, service, or technology (or company). It is a concept that is applicable in many situations, so is worth explaining before looking at individual valuation approaches.

The way in which a DCF model is built up means that cash flows which are closest to the present day will have a stronger impact on the net present value than those which are farther away. The impact of the particular discount rate chosen will vary depending on how long the forecast future cash flows are expected to continue, what growth rates are anticipated for the longer term (which usually need to be determined beyond any period likely to be modelled by the business in the ordinary course of planning), and whether some kind of 'terminal value' is justified, due to the economic life of the asset being indefinite.[3] **11.10**

The DCF calculation process requires a discount rate to be set and used. This is the weighted average cost of capital (WACC) considered to be applicable to the particular situation. This will be a percentage figure, generally built up by considering the returns required from a 'safe' investment option over a given period (being the return that would be anticipated by a provider of debt or equity to the business; usually, a blend of the two is used) and adding a premium to take account of the perceived risk that the forecast gain may not occur. **11.11**

In terms of the base elements, namely the debt and equity costs, the WACC used will normally take into account the size and nature of the organization which controls the intangibles under scrutiny. It is particularly important to consider its capital structure, as this will affect that organization's cost of money (e.g. it is much easier and cheaper for a large multinational quoted on the London stock exchange to raise either equity or debt finance than it is for a small enterprise to do so). In the absence of client-specific insights, it is customary to assume a split between equity and debt of 80/20 or 70/30. The equity return can then be built up using typical rates of return, and debt costs can be predicted using published borrowing rates. **11.12**

In some instances, it is possible to use DCF as a method of IP valuation on its own, provided that net cash flows (i.e. additional profits) are available as an input. For example, where a company does not have any operating activities, but simply acts as an IP 'holding company' and earns all its money through licensing, it is possible to establish the net present value of that future licensing income by applying a DCF calculation to it over a given period of time (which may or may not include **11.13**

[1] In this context, the word 'discounted' refers to the difference between the value of a sum that arises in the future compared with its value if it were available today.

[2] Net Present Value = what something is deemed to be worth today.

[3] Note that 'indefinite' when applied in this context means 'indeterminate', not 'infinite'.

attributing some sort of 'terminal value' to it). Depending on the level of certainty associated with the future income streams, the discount rate used in such cases may be quite low—not much more than the expected returns from other 'safe' investment routes—and where this is the case, such IP may be a good candidate for securitization. In fact, if future cash flows are very safe, then a seller of such an IP portfolio may argue for a multiplier on present value to be applied to reflect this perceived certainty of a return.

11.14 DCF is also sometimes used with default values which are not based on close scrutiny of IP assets. One such valuation approach, sometimes called the venture capital method and more commonly practiced in the United States, simply applies a flat discount rate of between 40 and 60% to future cash flows to compensate for the uncertainties and risks likely to be present. More often, however, DCF is incorporated within other valuation approaches that involve tailored assessment of the risks associated with the IP and the markets in which it is used, such as the relief from royalty method explained below.

'Rules of thumb'

11.15 Over time, certain assumptions have been formulated that appear to reflect the way in which commercial arrangements (particularly licensing deals) are generally constructed. The starting point is to consider why a deal between two parties, such as an inventor of a technology and a company that incorporates the invention in its products, should *not* use a 50/50 distribution of future identifiable (net) proceeds. The answer to this, generally, is that there are significantly greater levels of risk and expenditure in taking an idea from bench-top to end product than there are in the research that has led to its discovery or creation. Thereafter, once a product is on sale, the purchaser or licensee will carry most if not all of the costs of delivery.

11.16 Licensing arrangements also have to bear in mind that the licensee needs to maintain adequate profits to promote the goods properly, and some consideration of the underlying profitability of the arrangement as a whole is needed in order to produce a mutually acceptable agreement regarding royalties. For example, there is no point in trying to agree a 10% royalty on sales if margins are less than 20%—even if a 50/50 distribution were deemed to be fair under the circumstances.

11.17 This has led to the popularization of a 25/75% theoretical net profit split between inventor/licensor and commercialization partner/licensee. However, it is stretching the point to describe this as a 'rule': in practice, innovations that can be brought to market more swiftly and with less risk, and which command a higher margin (as is often the case with software) tend to command a higher rate than this, and those which have a longer development cycle may attract a lower one.

Where the 25% principle (or some modification of it) does appear appropriate, the key question that immediately arises relates to the set of figures on which it should be based. A typical view is that the starting point for the profit calculation should be the new sales generated by a technology after deducting cost of goods sold (and depreciation/amortization of the relevant overhead costs) plus sales costs and other expenditure directly attributable to the product. In a report investigating the link between profitability and royalty rates,[4] KPMG concluded that the most appropriate figure was likely to be earnings before interest, tax, depreciation, and amortization (EBITDA). 11.18

However, licensees are not always known for the transparency of their profit accounting methods (and in practice, even when there is no desire to obfuscate, it is difficult for a licensor to gain access to the licensee's full management accounts for reasons of commercial confidentiality). Accordingly, given the difficulty of obtaining accurate insights into, or agreement on, profitability, an accompanying 'rule of thumb' is sometimes referenced which simplifies matters to a straight 5% royalty on sales, based on the typical averages that are achieved in licensing deals. 11.19

Whilst this number is not without some foundation (not least because the 5% figure has been used for a large number of licensing arrangements), any analysis of actual royalties achieved also shows that much more granular data is available. The range of royalties commanded in the market is in fact quite diverse, with some sectors entering into licensing agreements at significantly lower rates, and others much higher, linked to timescales for introduction, profitability, and lifespan, among other factors. Accordingly, while rules of thumb may serve some purpose in the management of expectations, and the principles on which they are based are not inherently unreasonable, they are of rather limited use in reaching a fair agreement. 11.20

Market Comparables as a Valuation Method

In theory, apart from placing the assets on a real market (by way of auction or otherwise) and seeing how much buyers are prepared to pay for them, the best way to form a view on the fair market value of intangible assets (individually or collectively) is to identify sales and purchases of comparable items, under similar circumstances. A corresponding value can then be determined, probably after making adjustments for any intrinsic or situational differences. 11.21

This method of valuation, reliant on prior factual transactions, is basically the same one normally used to assess tangible assets offered for sale. In some contexts, it can 11.22

[4] KPMG International Global Valuation Institute. (2012). 'Profitability and Royalty Rates Across Industries: Some Preliminary Evidence'.

be achieved with a high degree of sophistication, as in the case of motor vehicles (an example used in Chapter 1). When previously owned cars are bought and sold, data aggregated from recent similar transactions can be called upon to set pricing. This data is deemed sufficiently predictive that it can be used as a basis for calculating future asset values upon which reliance is placed.

11.23 This pricing data also forms a basis for new product development. To give one example, an expected residual value makes it possible for asset finance to be provided to a customer with confidence that it only has to cover the depreciation and profit elements of a transaction rather than the total (hard) asset purchase cost. As another example, maintenance can be added into a financing agreement, enabling the lender to leverage its buying power to pass on cost savings, while helping to safeguard the future value of its asset.

11.24 Such approaches can create significant economic benefits for customers (assuming their main interest is to obtain trouble-free use of the asset than ultimately own it). Unfortunately, the qualities that make this market-based approach such a suitable method for cars mitigate against its use for IP and intangible assets.

11.25 There is an obvious point that intangible assets are supposed to be unique, whilst cars are commodities that are largely the same as each other. Whilst this is an oversimplification,[5] markets have decided that identical models of car are *sufficiently* similar to each other that price comparisons are valid and methods of adjusting for individual circumstances are sufficiently robust.

11.26 The more important and fundamental problem with market-based valuation of IP and intangibles is that the essential input data on comparable transactions is scarce and very difficult to obtain. Most companies' IP and intangible assets are not created with the intention of re-selling them, and if they do change hands, it will generally occur as an unspecified part in a sale of the whole business. In fact, the prevailing absence of clarity over the exact portfolio of intangibles owned by companies makes this an attractive option for buyers, since they can then (depending on the terms of the transaction) be more confident of securing not only the IP but also access to the surrounding know-how.

11.27 Where IP is sold separately from the business that owns it, the transaction is often conducted under conditions of commercial confidentiality. Whilst open sales (such as auctions) have the potential to achieve higher prices for assets that are in demand, there are often reasons why it suits the seller (and/or the buyer) to keep both their

[5] New cars when first produced are not necessarily identical to each other since (for example) they may use components sourced from different suppliers. Once a car is then sold, the manner in which it is used can make a substantial difference to its condition, in ways that are not always apparent to a prospective future buyer.

own identities secret, and the existence and nature of the IP that is changing hands, in order not to provide valuable strategic insights to their competitors. This is especially popular given the rise of non-practising entities in the United States (referred to in Chapter 3 on patents) and it is noteworthy that the leading IP auctioneer, ICAP Patent Brokerage, has taken to conducting a significant proportion of its business behind closed doors.

When IP transactions are publicly reported, the IP has often been sold under unique circumstances, undermining comparability. One well-known example is where a very particular set of market pressures, leading to a bidding war, was responsible for the price of USD 12.5 billion paid to acquire Motorola's Mobility business in 2011.[6] This is an example of a price paid by a patent purchaser, but not necessarily of a fair market value being determined. **11.28**

It is equally likely that assets may become available and be sold when a business has run into difficulties. The overall trading performance of the 'distressed' company that owns these assets will normally have the effect of depressing value, even when this is not attributable to any deficiency in the quality of the underlying technology. **11.29**

Even where there are 'baseline' transactions which look promising as reference points, making adjustments to cater for the remaining differences is not straightforward. For example, when seeking to compare different patent portfolios, these typically involve different technological specialisms, territorial spreads, and durations. They are also likely to vary in terms of their enforceability (which might be termed 'strength'), comprehensiveness of coverage of a particular area ('spread'), and the scale of the market opportunity they may enable a company to exploit ('potential'). They may also be subject to different legal or contractual restrictions, and expire at different points in time. **11.30**

For all these reasons, it is not feasible to expect the type of market comparison exercise typically conducted for tangible asset sales or transfers to be usable in isolation. However, that is not to say that market reference points are completely absent. There are several areas in which market data does have a positive contribution to make towards IP valuation, three of which are briefly set out below: **11.31**

- First, the presence or absence of transactions involving similar types of assets in related markets can lend a degree of confidence in determining whether there is demand for the portfolio under examination. Whilst there will still be questions to be asked (most importantly, has the previous transaction eliminated the one possible buyer for this technology?), it is generally preferable to be able to reference some activity rather than none. These reference points do not necessarily

[6] Widely refererenced, for example at http://spectrum.ieee.org/tech-talk/at-work/innovation/google-highlights-value-of-patents-in-motorola-sale-to-lenovo.

have to be 'pure' IP sales, as merger and acquisition activity which is driven by the desire to obtain access to know-how and technologies may be equally relevant.

- Secondly, it may be the case that transactions in other sectors where similar technologies are in use might present alternative exploitation routes. By studying the underlying properties of an invention, a design, or even a brand, it is possible to find new and potentially more profitable applications for it than those originally intended.
- Thirdly, in terms of available data, there is not a complete vacuum. It is possible to augment valuation activity with insights derived from surveys, price lists, and other databases. The most commonly used reference point is the royalty information derived from licensing agreements which have to be registered in the United States[7] as a matter of course (but which records US dealings with other organizations wherever they are located).

11.32 Whilst a detailed comparison with one or more specific precedents may still not be possible or appropriate, a sufficient volume of information is available to create confidence that a range of royalty values is likely to be applicable to a given company in a particular sector. These data sets form the basis for the relief from royalty income-based method of valuation discussed in more detail below and do at least allow a 'market dimension' to be added.

Cost as a Valuation Method

11.33 In certain contexts, cost—whether of reproduction (exact copying of the finished item) or replacement (with something else that has the same utility or properties)—is used as a means to determine IP value. The starting point to find inputs for reproduction will often be the actual historical costs of creation, though once established, these calculations may well need to be adjusted in order to compensate for the time period since they were incurred (to express a figure at today's costs), and further adjusted to account for obsolescence (which might be functional, physical, or economic as well as legal).

11.34 The use of the cost method has a certain logical appeal: why would a buyer pay more to acquire a set of assets than it would cost to reproduce or replace them? It also has some practical attractions, principally its apparent simplicity. It should normally be possible to develop a fairly good estimate of initial costs from historical data, without recourse to external sources which, as explained earlier, are neither numerous nor immediately applicable. It may be possible to determine cost simply

[7] Licensing agreements are routinely filed with the US Securities and Exchange Commission (SEC). Data is aggregated and analysed by a number of providers including RoyaltyStat (http://www.royaltystat.com) and RoyaltySource (http://www.royaltysource.com).

by reference to payroll data and external contractor/consultant records, plus direct expenses (including IP protection measures and raw materials) and an apportionment of overheads. Under some circumstances, advertising and marketing costs may be included also.

Consideration of the ways in which assets are typically represented in accounts provides some parallels for this practice. After all, tangible fixed assets are shown at their cost after adjustments (for amortization and/or depreciation) and are used as a guide to the underlying collateral value retained in the business. In addition, when seeking to value assets that are part of the wider intellectual capital of a business (as opposed to assets it legally owns), the cost may prove to be the only convenient method available. If it is necessary to determine the value of a workforce, for example, the current annual payroll data is perhaps as good a place to start as any, plus the costs of recruitment and training. There are also occasions when the costs of building networks (such as distribution networks) and non-business critical software or websites may form a reasonable basis for their valuation. **11.35**

However, the limitations of the cost method are quickly apparent when it is applied to 'strong' IP. If protection is in place, it is not possible (or at least, not permissible) to reproduce these assets at any price. Accordingly, applying a cost-based calculation explicitly fails to recognize the most important aspect in any IP rights transaction, which is the economic benefit of having the rights themselves (which may include a reduction in commercial risk as well as a revenue uplift). **11.36**

Clearly, delivering a benefit that exceeds cost is germane to the whole rationale of seeking IP rights. However, it is also apparent that on some occasions, very large sums can be invested in creating IP that turns out to have very little value because there is no market for it or it does not work at scale. It would, therefore, be unwise to assume that cost is necessarily a good predictor of IP value. **11.37**

Using cost as a negotiating tactic is also fraught with difficulties, for several reasons. First, there can be legitimate reasons why a buyer might think that its cost of reproducing or replacing the assets in question may not be the same as those originally incurred. Some of these may relate to cost efficiencies which a buyer can bring to the table, but a more fundamental issue is that the initial development activities have proved that a particular outcome is possible (and may also have provided access to data relating to successful approaches which are not protected by IP). Simply put, when a certain result is known, reproducing it does not require the same level of trial and error (this may have generated valuable 'negative know-how',[8] but it may not be commercially useful). Second, whilst the concept of 'reproducing' cost ought to **11.38**

[8] This is a term used to refer to lines of enquiry that have proven not to be productive (things that did not work as desired). As such it can have significant value because it enables a firm to learn from its mistakes.

include all prototyping and other necessary stages, a 'replacement' might not need to take into account the costs of any interim step or line of enquiry that ultimately proved non-productive.

11.39 Another question that arises is the small matter of which costs are genuinely attributable to a particular IP asset or portfolio. In addition to the differences between buyer and seller cost levels, there may be debate over whether it is legitimate to include certain categories of cost (such as allocated overheads) at all. It is also problematic, particularly in a research-intensive environment such as a university where innovation is occurring continually, to allocate known costs between individual projects, and to divide the costs of new 'foreground' IP that has been created from all the 'background' IP that has preceded it.

11.40 Clearly, much IP is not technical in nature. Whilst brand value depends to an extent on the characteristics of the product or service being offered for sale, it is reasonable to assume that the amount of money spent building awareness and reputation through marketing and sales activity could be a consideration when valuing a brand. As with other forms of development, however, marketing is an area in which it is possible to spend large amounts of money for minimal returns, and it is likely that an easier justification for arguing that value has accumulated will be found in the sales or usage figures than in the marketing budget.

11.41 In summary, cost has its attractions as a sense-check, and can sometimes be a factor in evidencing to a buyer that significant time and effort has been spent in developing IP. If a product has not reached the market, but would be relatively simple to copy without risk of infringement, then prospective buyers will almost certainly have reproduction in their mind as an alternative and the costs associated with this may well influence how much they will be prepared to pay. However, cost has many inadequacies if used in isolation and is particularly counter-intuitive whenever enforceable IP rights are in place.

Income as a Valuation Method

11.42 The normal focus for valuation in business is to use current and future profits or turnover, viewed in the light of historical past performance (where applicable), to determine worth. This also tends to be the case with IP valuation, where the most commonly used techniques also focus on income (because of the non-availability of sufficiently robust data to conduct a market comparison, and the shortcomings of using cost calculations).

11.43 Given that valuation activity is normally prompted by some kind of transaction, where the rights and benefits of a set of assets are going to be shared or transferred, this focus on cash and profit is sensible. It is usually the case that the incoming party expects to benefit by way of cost saving or turnover and profit generation. The future potential of the IP to contribute to business performance is therefore central to their motivation for entering into any such transaction, and means that it will often be necessary for the two parties to agree what this potential looks like. Where this is the case, it is logical to use this 'agreed' (or, at least, shared and consistently derived) data as the basis for determining the price to be paid.

This is not to say, however, that an income valuation is necessarily straightforward. The main difficulty to be overcome is that the future is seldom certain (e.g. even where a set of income streams is governed by a signed contract, there is generally a possibility that the contract in question may not be honoured). Therefore, within many income-based methodologies, steps have to be taken to compensate for uncertainties in any set of forecasts that are used. These uncertainties may go well beyond the control of the IP owner (e.g. competitor activity may have a strong effect on a market in ways that may not be foreseeable; a business may also be strongly affected by cyclical macro-economic factors whose timing can be very hard to predict). **11.44**

The past performance of a company is an important consideration in assessing the future. Most valuation methods look at the growth or profit trend in a business to see whether these provide any comfort in terms of future cash and profit generation. Assessment will also need to be made of whether there are good grounds for thinking that the future may be different to the past for internally-related reasons (such as new investments that have been made, or innovations that are at an early stage of being brought to market). **11.45**

Occasionally, historical income is used as the benchmark for determining value. Except where the business is young, there may be a number of years' worth of data that can be used as a basis for calculation, raising the question of which set is likely to be most representative. This is traditionally overcome by creating a weighted average, with more recent numbers given a higher weighting. **11.46**

Use of historical data has the obvious attraction that the past is 'fact' while the future is not (yet). However, reliance on past performance can present particular difficulties for the seller or sharer. Leaving aside the manner in which past accounting techniques and management practices may have influenced profitability, the problem here is that the motivation for acquisition or access is often that the incoming party sees an opportunity to realise value from the IP that is *not* available to the seller, which may translate into new and larger income streams that will not be reflected in the basis for valuation. **11.47**

11.48 There are a substantial number of variations on the income-based valuation theme. The principal ones that are most often used are set out below, separately followed by some of the more 'esoteric' variants used to address early stage valuation risks.

Relief from royalty

11.49 Relief from royalty is one of the most commonly adopted mechanisms for determining IP value. This makes the assumption that a royalty, or licence fee, would be payable by any third party seeking to use the IP and intangibles in question under a licensing arrangement. By applying a suitable royalty rate to the cash generated by sales of the product or service, and discounting the results back to a present-day equivalent value in the manner explained earlier, the financial benefit to the assets' owner from not having to pay the royalty can be determined. This calculation is generally done on the basis of turnover, not profit, because the latter is too easy for a licensee to 'massage', though it has to be clear *which* turnover (or proportion of it) would in fact be attributable to the IP.

11.50 Apart from being one of the easier constructs to understand, the appeal of relief from royalty is that it is focused on data that is, in part, independently sourced (from databases and public records of royalty rates actually paid in licensing transactions), giving it a market dimension. Also, the possible distorting effect of tangible assets and other factors such as human capital are largely addressed because a licensing arrangement normally relates solely to the IP and intangibles, not a business's other assets. Add to this the fact that it can be driven from the same financial data that will be used to negotiate a prospective transaction (be it investment, bank lending, a licensing deal, or an IP sale) and it is easy to see why this method has become very popular, particularly for finance.

11.51 However, relief from royalty has to be used with care. Royalty rate selection is critical (because as discussed earlier, rates can vary substantially according to the activity sector chosen, the stage of development of the IP, and the terms of the licence, particularly in terms of exclusivity). Quite often, the royalty agreements used as a benchmark include other commercial terms such as up-front payments, and it is also important to note that unlike a licensee, the owner of the IP retains full control over the asset, which is an extra benefit.

11.52 Using this method, future royalty streams have to be brought back to a net present value using DCF. As discussed earlier, selection of an appropriate discount rate that takes risks associated with the forecasts into account is critical. Lastly, whilst cash flow or turnover sound attractively simple as a basis for calculation, the position becomes much more complicated when products feature (for example) patented components from a range of suppliers; in these instances a cash figure has to be agreed which represents the value of that component or element within the whole, and this can give rise to a lot of debates (and sometimes litigation).

Capitalization of profits

There are three other commonly used methods. Perhaps the simplest of these is capitalization[9] of profits associated with a 'bundle' of IP. This may be historic, in which case it involves multiplying the proportion of the assets' past economic contribution that is deemed to be maintainable by a suitable factor that reflects the IP's relative strength, which in turn has been determined by an assessment of its scope, protectability, market position, and profit trend. Alternatively, the calculation may use the net present value of future earnings, and may be called income capitalization or occasionally technology factor capitalization. **11.53**

This technique is perhaps most effective when the future earnings are already virtually assured by way of contract (such as royalties derived from a licensing agreement) and long-lived (i.e. based on brands or copyright materials). Here the use of a factor, or multiple, is justified by the level of certainty that the cash flows will materialize. It is easiest to perform if the IP assets are generating their own revenue stream and for obvious reasons, it is necessary to have sufficient data to be able to isolate a profit element. **11.54**

While the concept of using a multiplier has much in common with company valuation methods, the challenge is to ensure that the value to which the multiplier is applied genuinely reflects the contribution made by the assets or technology. There may be some correlation between the factor used and the types of earnings multiples present in the sector in which the company operates, though adjustments will need to be made, for example, to account for the relative illiquidity of an unquoted company's shares. **11.55**

Excess earnings

Another technique that is applied quite frequently by valuation professionals is to apply an excess earnings calculation. This is based on the principle that the value of the intangibles in a business can best be determined by subtracting from its overall worth the current market value attributable to the net tangible assets. A variation on this theme is first to determine the value of the net tangible assets, then add a rate of return to estimate the profits required to encourage investors to participate. If the actual return is higher than this minimum level, it is considered to be attributable to the business's intellectual capital. **11.56**

[9] Defined by the International Valuation Standards Council as 'the conversion of income into a capital sum through the application of an appropriate discount rate'. See International Valuation Standards. (2013). 'Framework and Requirements'.

11.57 In both cases there is often a 'multi-period' emphasis, which refers to the fact that more than one financial year is likely to be used for calculation purposes (and may then be used to determine a weighted average). It may be a calculation based on future or on historical earnings, in which case balance sheet entries may make the fixed asset base look deceptively easy to calculate. However, since the aim of the method is not to apply book value, but to determine what economic contribution the assets make, an adjustment may need to be made by applying a charge for the use of all of the assets that are not the subject of the valuation.

11.58 In some instances, it may not be feasible to draw a line between the returns delivered by tangible and intangible assets in this way. Nevertheless, as a means to value contracts, customer relationships and the expected benefits arising from product developments, the excess earnings method has proved quite popular.

Profit premium or differential

11.59 A third method is to think about the profit premium that a business earns by virtue of having the intangible asset(s) in question, by virtue of additional income or cost efficiencies compared with its competitors. Sometimes, it is possible to use financial benchmarks within an industry to consider what the business as a whole is worth with the benefit of the IP, and what it would be worth without it. In other cases, and particularly where fast-moving consumer goods operating in highly competitive markets are being assessed (and generic equivalent items exist), this may take the form of valuing the profit differential.

11.60 This works by estimating the difference in the profit generated between a particular branded asset and a generic item, as a means of isolating the value attributable to it. This can be done at an individual product level, referencing comparative information on retail (or wholesale) pricing, with an adjustment for the difference in marketing costs. It can also be done at a consolidated whole brand level (covering several products).

11.61 This approach is quite often used in brand valuation, as it seeks to focus on the difference that the brand is making; it can also be applied both to historical and to expected future profits provided that adequate account is taken of industry trends. However, it is rare that detailed insights are available on the cost base applicable to the point of comparison, or even whether the sales volumes are truly comparable, and difficult to estimate what relative levels of price elasticity may exist. Perhaps the biggest difficulty, though, is that the underlying assumption is that the branded and generic products are otherwise comparable in terms of quality and other characteristics—which may not be the case.

11.62 An alternative way of considering profit differential, as with capitalization of profits, is to measure the cost savings which are attributable to ownership of a particular bundle of IP. These might be operational savings arising from (for example) greater process efficiencies or access to superior materials, or they might be reductions in the amount of capital required to operate a business that has the benefit of the IP compared with one that does not. These cost reductions, where quantifiable, may potentially be applied in place of profit calculations in any of the above methods; they may be calculated from a weighted average of past performance, or by determining the net present value of expected future savings.

From this brief overview it will be apparent that each income valuation method is **11.63** seeking to arrive at a view on intangible asset contributions via a slightly different route: by thinking about what someone else would pay to license the IP (relief from royalty), capitalizing the profit contribution it makes, subtracting the benefits of the tangible asset portfolio in achieving profit, or determining how much more profitable the IP makes a product, brand, or business. All of these, however, rely on there being historical and/or future financials on which to base a calculation approach. This raises the question of what happens to IP valuation when neither of these is present.

Techniques Applied to Early Stage Technologies: 'Probabilistic' and Option-based Methods

A high proportion of IP valuation activity involves an established company and **11.64** takes place in the context of a larger (i.e. whole business) transaction. However, there is sometimes a need to understand how much value exists in ideas that have not yet been commercialized, not least because of the need to prioritize them and/or raise investment for them. This early stage environment is very different, especially when long lead times to market are involved and there are significant barriers to overcome. Here, the current earnings are generally minimal or nil, and while future earnings may have the potential to be very considerable, they may also be quite uncertain, and/or a long way from being realized.

In this environment, the established methods explained earlier can be difficult to **11.65** apply. Market comparisons may be helpful in drawing broad parallels with other novel ideas that have successfully raised finance, but are unlikely to yield relevant insights about the present value of a potentially disruptive new technology. Relevant costs will be difficult to isolate (especially if the idea has emerged from 'pure' research) and will provide a very incomplete picture of the total investment required to get to market, the point at which cash generation becomes possible. Even when forecasts exist which show the future incomes that might be generated, there may be no historical parallels within the business that can be used to test their reasonableness.

11.66 There are at least five areas of uncertainty in these early stage opportunities for which valuation approaches need to compensate. To illustrate these, the example below is based on the risks that might be encountered in bringing a novel pharmaceutical to market, but the same headings can be applied to most other areas of technology:

- *Development risk:* a future proof of concept may not function as intended, or feasibility tests may fail. Even if everything works exactly as expected, a technology may prove to be too complex or costly to be commercially viable.
- *Manufacturing risk:* laboratory results can prove difficult to duplicate in a 'lower-tech' production environment. For example, some batches may not work, and/or yields may be unacceptably low.
- *Marketing risk:* it is often difficult to predict what companies or individuals will want to buy in the future. There is always the possibility of 'backing the wrong horse', and this risk increases the further the technology is from market (in terms of time and/or the hurdles that need to be overcome before it is saleable).
- *Competitor response:* the introduction of a new technology may affect competitor behaviour in ways that are hard to anticipate.
- *Legal risks:* in addition to the need to overcome regulatory hurdles, changes to the legislative or policy environment can also have a significant impact on market dynamics, above and beyond the risk of legal challenges to the underlying IP rights, especially as these may not yet be granted.

11.67 A number of models have therefore emerged to try to take account of the many possible outcomes that there may be for an early stage technology, and the fact that they are not all equally probable.[10]

11.68 In terms of probabilistic modelling, the model most often quoted in the valuation context is the one known as Monte Carlo. This uses repeated, randomized sampling to address questions of uncertainty, calculating possible values based on an underlying mathematical expression, and generating a probability-based distribution of potential answers. Depending on the formula used, these answers may be distributed uniformly across the range of possible values; they may peak at a 'most likely' value; or they may use a 'bell' curve to show a mean, with some variation around it.

11.69 In the valuation context, Monte Carlo's range of answers—the spread of possible values—can then be used as a series of inputs to perform DCF exercises. These, in turn, provide a set of results that can be compared and analysed in order to understand

[10] For an interesting discussion and useful worked examples of the techniques applied to early stage technologies, see Razgaitis, R. (2003). *Valuation and Pricing of Technology-Based Intellectual Property* (USA, Wiley).

which variables have the most decisive effect (positive or negative) on the net present value the model calculates, enabling subsequent iterations to be refined.

As well as being used as DCF modelling inputs, simulations of this nature can be useful in helping to determine the probability of individual events during an IP development process. However, Monte Carlo (and its derivatives) is best used where there is uncertainty around the right core values to use; it does not lend itself particularly well to cases in which there are a series of binary outcomes (as is quite often the case with early stage developments). Where these 'go/no-go' stages are a feature of the development path, probability trees and option-based models may be preferable. These seek to cater for situations where there are defined points at which different outcomes may arise, and where potentially large sums of development expenditure may be required in order to reach a given goal. **11.70**

In effect, probability trees perform DCF in a different way by enabling the risk element of the discount rate to be broken up into its individual constituent parts. A tree diagram is constructed (often by working back from the point at which the technology is successfully commercialized), with a junction at each point where different outcomes may occur (e.g. at which a patent may or may not be granted). Each 'branch' can then have a weighting applied to it that takes into account the fact that as the development process progresses, extreme bad outcomes (such as the technology failing) should increasingly be eliminated. The weighting of each alternative outcome should be tailored to suit the specific risks likely to be encountered (which vary according to technology, sector, and distance from market) and should be set with reference to available internal experience or industry statistics in order to make the values used as objective as possible. **11.71**

In recent years, a further approach has been gaining in popularity amongst multinational corporations, based on adopting techniques originally developed for hedging investment risks. As with stock markets, it is possible to hedge against the risks of introducing a new technology if this is regarded as the purchase of one or more 'options'. The most famous such model is the Black-Scholes Method (named after its inventors, but subsequently revised and adapted by many other practitioners). **11.72**

In the IP valuation context, the attraction of this method is that it recognizes investors are essentially viewing a new patentable technology as being a potential opportunity to control an area of a future market. If all the risks involved with such an investment are added together, as is the case in a typical DCF calculation, the opportunity may not appear worthwhile because the discount rate will be high and will nullify the attraction of large returns that are distant and uncertain. By comparison, the option structure enables an investor to determine whether the point at which a large investment needs to be made can be deferred until the outcome is less **11.73** risky and more certain. The points at which such options arise may also be modelled and represented using a decision tree approach.

11.74 Whilst these individual methods are a little complex to explain in detail in a work of this nature, it is important to acknowledge that approaches are evolving to take account of technological and market uncertainties. This means that even those early stage opportunities that do not readily lend themselves to 'conventional' methods of IP valuation can still be subjected to a meaningful form of value assessment. It is also possible to combine methods—for example, by modelling an in-market IP value and then using a probability tree to set an appropriate discount rate for the period until the product, service, or technology is in a position to start generating the returns that have been estimated.

Liquidation Value

11.75 One aspect that all the above methods have in common is an assumption that the IP a business owns will continue to be supported in the future, either by the existing company or by a new owner. Sometimes, however, the IP may need to be sold under circumstances where the business in question will no longer be operating. This is the scenario that makes financiers (especially lenders) reluctant to view IP as a legitimate form of collateral, because of the concern that the value will turn out to be nil, a subject discussed in more detail in Chapter 9.

11.76 Under certain circumstances, this fear may be justified. If for example a company's IP is so specialist that it is only relevant for its own operations, and those operations cease, then the only way forward in terms of value realization will be to sell the whole business (including its IP) to a buyer who believes that this specialism is worth preserving and developing. However, few organizations are so unique as to be the only participants in their particular area of business.

11.77 Whether the IP and intangibles in question are a film or music catalogue, a set of recipes, a brand, a distribution network, a technology, a material, or a manufacturing process, there is normally a potential market for it (and there may be multiple markets, depending on how versatile the assets are). As noted above, however, the fact that the business selling the IP is not trading profitably can be expected to place downward pressure on the achievable value under normal circumstances. In such cases, what is required is a liquidation value—the minimum amount that an arm's length buyer could be expected to pay in order to acquire the IP.

11.78 In the absence of transparent marketplaces for IP disposal, all three sets of 'mainstream' techniques described above can potentially have a role to play, though no one method is likely to provide a complete answer in isolation. If there are any recent market comparators in terms of IP disposals within relevant sectors, and/or involving similar assets, these will be of interest, though all the usual difficulties remain in terms of getting an understanding of the detailed terms, making appropriate adjustments, and most crucially of all, establishing that there are other similar buyers out in the market (i.e. that the comparable transaction has not exhausted the only possible exit route). In addition to IP sales, business mergers and acquisitions activity may also be a useful indicator of appetite, though probably not a price guide.

Cost may also have a role to play, on the basis that if substantial investment has been made in developing a product, process, technology, or service offering, a buyer might be willing to pay a proportion of that cost rather than incur it from scratch. Here the biggest issue may be for a buyer to be convinced of the utility of the assets in question, given that they have not (by implication) turned the business that currently owns them into a commercial success. **11.79**

There may also be a role for income analysis, though the relevance of this technique is likely to depend on whether the seller is in a position to hand over assets with a long-established cash flow and/or relationships which are already generating substantial income streams (which it may be contractually prevented from doing). Whilst brokers may be able to construct models for prospective purchasers indicating how they would be able to make additional returns from the IP in question (e.g. via cost savings), the easiest assets to sell will be those which can readily be accommodated within the portfolio of a buyer, such as literary or artistic works protected by copyright, or products and services that complement an existing offering. **11.80**

The ability to set a reliable liquidation value is a subject of considerable interest in business financing, though as has been well-documented elsewhere, it is likely to require the availability of specialist underwriting and insurance and/or access to more transparent markets to dispose of and purchase IP, neither of which are well established in the United Kingdom. **11.81**

Valuing All or Part of a Company's IP and Intangibles

Frequently, the requirement in a valuation exercise is to determine how much all the IP and intangible assets associated with a business are worth. Sometimes, however, the focus will be on valuing one or more specific assets within a larger portfolio, for example when one specific item (such as a patent or trade mark) is to be used as security. **11.82**

Under these circumstances, whichever valuation methodology is adopted, care needs to be taken in order to ensure that the value being placed on a single asset is not being overstated and that inherent dependencies on other intangibles are acknowledged. Whilst it may be reasonable to argue, for example, that the main source of value within a patented prescription drug lies in its formulation, it is often **11.83** the case that such drugs will be branded and trade marked in order to increase familiarity and simplify marketing, and value accrues to these assets also. Under these circumstances, how much value lies in the company's patent(s) as opposed to its trade mark(s)?

11.84 When a transfer or licence to a new, 'arm's length' party is in prospect, rather than an assessment of the value contribution being made by assets already *in situ*, this dilemma is heightened, particularly if aspects of specialist know-how are involved. Will the know-how needed to extract value from a particular process or trade secret be made fully available to the recipient?

11.85 The ease or difficulty with which individual assets within a portfolio can be valued chiefly depends on the extent to which the costs, cash flows, and profits associated with them can be separated with accuracy. In many cases the input data is simply not available at the required level of granularity and so the initial assessment is made on the whole 'basket' of rights that exist (as explained earlier, separating the tangible assets from the intangible ones can generally be done with an acceptable degree of confidence). Therefore it is usual to start from an assessment of total IP and intangible asset value and then consider how individual elements contribute to that overall amount, rather than try to build from the 'ground up' on an asset-by-asset basis.

11.86 In the case of a domain name, for instance, the value might be estimated by assessing the volume of custom that it generates (or the proportion of the sales pipeline for which it accounts). This can then be expressed as a proportion of the overall brand value, if this has already been determined, so where a £10 million value has been placed on a brand as a whole and 20% of the company's business is generated by its website, it may be reasonable to argue that the domain name and the website combined make a contribution towards £2 million of that figure. This calculation becomes more difficult if a company is generating large numbers of users but not significant amounts of income. Even here, though, it can be possible to examine total traffic and activity and derive an indicative percentage.

Conclusion

11.87 This discussion of valuation methods has illustrated that while many different ways exist to estimate and determine IP value, one or more methods can be applied to almost any situation in which such value needs to be realized. This non-exhaustive exploration has shown that few practical impediments exist to determining what IP is worth with a sufficient level of confidence to support a range of transactional activities. Given that the value in question is often material, the final point to consider is why it is routinely hidden.

12

REPORTING AND ACCOUNTING FOR INTELLECTUAL PROPERTY AND INTANGIBLES

The Balance Sheet Issue

A balance sheet has been defined as 'a financial statement that summarises a company's assets, liabilities and shareholders' equity at a specific point in time. These three balance sheet segments provide an idea of what the company owns and owes, as well as the amount invested by the shareholders'.[1] This seems a particularly apt definition, because 'an idea' is just about all that a contemporary balance sheet does provide. Nowhere is this more evident than in its treatment of intangible assets, including all forms of IP. **12.01**

In times past—as recently as the 1970s—it was possible to draw some meaningful conclusions about the worth of a company by examining its balance sheet. However, as the brief macro-economic analysis presented in Chapter 8 has shown, balance sheets are no longer indicative of company value in most cases, and a key contributory factor in this state of affairs is that statutory accounts seldom take intangible value into account. Having demonstrated that the value exists at a macro and micro level, it is, therefore, necessary to examine the reasons *why* these assets are so conspicuously absent from most such accounting documents; additionally, where they are present at all, it is important to understand why they are simply written down in value over time, despite the fact that the amount of value they are contributing to the business may well be moving in the opposite direction. **12.02**

The problem is quite a fundamental one, and not capable of being easily resolved. To understand why the difficulty arises, it may be helpful to delve a little into the accounting mindset and the context in which balance sheets are examined before summarizing the relevant rules to which accountants operate, and how these are beginning to change. **12.03**

1 See http://www.investopedia.com/terms/b/balancesheet.asp.

The role of accounting

12.04 Company accounting has been defined as 'financial information that a company is required to produce at the end of every year, including details of its profits or losses'.[2] Its basic purpose is to 'keep score' by providing a reliable and robust indication of performance in financial terms, in a standardized format, to make it capable of being useful in a variety of contexts. Also, accounting is fundamentally reliant on transactions because these provide the evidence needed to satisfy the necessary test of reliability. They make it possible to prove that value has been given and been received, and enable an overview to be generated that shows where a company's trading activity leaves it in terms of its credits and debits.

12.05 A balance sheet is an important element of this scorekeeping process. By definition, it needs to balance. In a nutshell, and continuing with the earlier definition,[3] 'This makes sense: a company has to pay for all the things it has (assets) by either borrowing money (liabilities) or getting it from shareholders (shareholders' equity).'

12.06 Determining the content of a balance sheet can be a rather complex process since detailed lists of transactions must sit underneath each of these sections. Nevertheless, it is revealing that assets have always been very much equated with 'things' that can readily be counted—in most cases, cash, inventory (stock), property, and machinery.

12.07 Tangible assets that are purchased by businesses in order to produce goods nearly always have a clearly identifiable (external) source, usually another business, and will have paid for them on an arm's length basis. They also have an anticipated lifespan (or period of use encompassed by a lease or hire purchase agreement) and an associated depreciation[4] curve,[5] which can be predicted with a high degree of confidence based on known disposal values.

12.08 An obvious example is a car or van, of the sort many businesses need in order to trade. As explained in Chapter 11, there are well-established resale markets that

---

[2] See http://www.markets.ft.com/research/lexicon.

[3] See n 1.

[4] As set out in the Oxford Dictionary, depreciation is 'a reduction in the value of an asset over time, due in particular to wear and tear', while amortization, (referred to elsewhere below) means to 'gradually write off the initial cost of (an asset) over a period of time'—normally the period associated with its useful life. See http://www.oxforddictionaries.com.

[5] 'Curve' refers to the fact that the realizable value of tangible assets seldom reduces in a linear fashion. Returning to the car or van example, such vehicles are generally assumed to lose a substantial proportion of their new value (typically 20–30%) the moment they are no longer 'new'. However, they may only lose the same amount again over the following three years. Such a curve will therefore drop steeply at first and then level out over time. Depending on how the asset has been paid for, a company's accounts may or may not reflect this pattern.

make it easy to predict with an acceptable degree of accuracy what an asset like this will be worth after thirty-six months of use under average conditions—and if the usage has not been average, to adjust appropriately for this fact. It is therefore not difficult for a firm, its accountants, or auditors to work out not only what tangible assets cost, but what they are worth on the open market at any given point in time (for instance, when someone else wants to buy the company).[6]

In some cases where an identifiable intangible asset that has a long-term benefit is purchased outright, such as a new software platform, it could be added to the balance sheet and have a value placed against it commensurate with the amount paid. This will be accounted for over its estimated useful life (or, in certain cases, subjected to an annual test for impairment). This accounting treatment is fairly straightforward, but two sets of circumstances conspire against its use. The first issue is that, in the everyday course of business, most intangible assets that are bought in are not characterized in this way and are simply shown as expenses in the profit and loss account, at which point they disappear from view. **12.09**

The second problem is that the circumstances described above are seldom applicable, because most intangible assets are internally generated. Where another business has a piece of IP or technology that an acquisitive company requires, it will generally buy the whole business, not just the IP (because this is the easiest way to be certain it will obtain access to all relevant assets, including supporting know-how) or it will license the technology, in which case there will be no entry on its balance sheet relating to this fact. And if the whole business is bought, smaller firms have usually been able to use simpler merger accounting rules which perpetuate these assets' invisibility (though this has changed in the latest version of UK Generally Accepted Accounting Principles, or UK GAAP).[7] True, IP is sometimes transferred between companies within a group, but this raises an entirely different set of issues, being generally done for the purposes of tax efficiency, as discussed in Chapter 9. **12.10**

The challenge presented by IP and other intangible assets

Since accountants have a long-standing love of tangible assets, it is small wonder that intangibles are a source of puzzlement because their behaviour is different in **12.11**

[6] This is not to say that such assessments are foolproof; the Global Financial Crisis (GFC) provides the ultimate demonstration of what can happen when genuinely realizable asset values get buried under too many layers of complexity. However, what the GFC also demonstrates is that not even meltdown can shake the underlying belief in tangible assets. Financiers may have become more conservative in their assessment of individual ability to repay debts relating to these assets, but despite the inescapable conclusion that the assets' values turned out to be significantly less than originally thought, their underlying worth as security is still lurking on bank balance sheets (and ironically, being used to provide a degree of reassurance on the overall resilience of these institutions).

[7] UK GAAP now includes Financial Reporting Standard 102 (FRS 102), dealt with later in this chapter.

almost every respect. Intangibles are not usually bought from anyone, but rather (as mentioned above) are internally generated; there is no payment, let alone an arm's length one (though subsequent merger/acquisition activity points to the fact that the intangibles do exist, as set out in Chapter 8); they can just as easily rise in value as fall over time, as they do not get worn out through use (in many cases value increases with use, depending on how 'use' is defined); and if a company tries to sell its intangibles they may be worth billions of pounds... or nothing at all.

12.12 Each of these differences creates its own problems. The issue of internal generation is the most thorny (even though the internal nature of a process is not necessarily a difficulty for accounting in other respects) and warrants closer examination.

12.13 When tangible assets are generated by a company, there will typically be an input of raw materials (and their associated transactions), which will be processed using labour and machinery (with a known value, shown on the balance sheet). This results in clearly identifiable outputs—most importantly, the products a company sells or holds in stock in the expectation of selling them (which can also be put on a balance sheet as an asset value).

12.14 The value added by this endeavour can readily be established by summing the cost elements and subtracting them from the sales price. There is a limitation, since if the goods are not sold, their realizable (and therefore 'true') value may vary according to market demand. In the event of a company going into administration it will often be the case that the stock shown on the balance sheet is not worth its book value (or not there at all, or both). However, this is not a particular concern in the routine preparation of company accounts for a 'going concern'.[8]

12.15 When intangibles are created within businesses, the corresponding 'raw material' inputs are ideas or requirements (perceived or actual). These may have a high potential value, but money seldom changes hands to acquire them. Labour (and possibly some machinery—which might be on the balance sheet, but may simply be computer equipment of fairly nominal value than is soon written down to nothing) will be applied to these inputs and produce an output, but it may not be a product as such; it may be a service, a process improvement, or simply a new area of know-how.

12.16 Such an asset probably will not form part of a company's stock unless it has a tangible output such as a book, a software package, or computer game. Even if it relates to something that is very 'high-tech' like a new drug, it will in the first instance be

[8] This is defined by Investopedia as a 'term for a company that has the resources needed in order to continue to operate indefinitely. If a company is not a going concern, it means the company has gone bankrupt.' See http://www.investopedia.com/terms/g/goingconcern.asp.

a formulation, not a neatly packaged bottle of pills, and as a research output, this will not be on the balance sheet (for the reasons set out in the analysis which follows later in this chapter).

To the accountant, the main element that can be counted here is the cost of the labour, not the assets that result, as these are variable (as well as invisible). The human capital element will initially be expensed through the payroll, and it is only if the company can show that an alternative accounting treatment is justified (for example, because the company is in the process of developing the assets for a known market opportunity) that outputs of this kind can end up as intangible assets on the balance sheet. And even where they do qualify, as explained below, such assets can only be added at cost—not value. **12.17**

However, even this description understates the depth of the problem. Often, intangibles are created without it being possible to attribute any direct cost to them at all. As one example, the absence of a ready means of recognizing the value of 'blood, sweat, and tears' expended in bringing an idea to a realizable and potentially investable form is a source of particular frustration to entrepreneurs who have not been able to pay themselves during the creative process. Attempts are usually made to translate this 'sweat equity' into a financial equivalent value via a calculation of salary payments that have been foregone, but without compelling evidence to underpin them, this attempt to 'visualize' sweat as an asset seldom proves acceptable to business angels and other private investors. What they see is a substantial value being placed on a business that does not appear to have had any money spent on it at all, but now wants theirs.[9] **12.18**

Accounting and Reporting Rules

IAS 38: bringing (some) intangibles onto the balance sheet (sometimes)

The consequence of all the above is that in the ordinary course of business, accountants have not sought actively to record intangibles because the usual signals that something of value is being created are not present. It is therefore fairly common to find no 'pulse' for IP or other intangible assets in the balance sheet, where one would expect to find other assets. **12.19**

---

[9] It is, of course, possible for an entrepreneur to create an 'artificial' transaction and thereby an identifiable cost by selling an idea to his or her own business, at which point it will be recognizable as an asset, as previously explained. However, this has pitfalls too, because it is very difficult to determine and then justify a 'fair value' for an intangible asset of this kind. It may look very much like an attempt to prop up an insubstantial balance sheet or lay claim to an excessive amount of money that a company cannot afford. It can also create some interesting personal tax liabilities, though that aspect is not within the scope of this book.

12.20 If an accountant is minded to seek to recognize intangible assets like IP, he or she will consult the relevant accounting standards. These are easiest to study at their internationally agreed level, where they are at their most stable. National policies tend to follow in most material respects (and from 2015/16 onwards, FRS 102 applies to small as well as large businesses as part of UK GAAP, creating increased alignment with the international standards set out below).

12.21 International Accounting Standard (IAS) 38 was originally introduced in 1998.[10] Whilst it is not the only accounting standard that touches on intangible assets, this particular document is important because it sets out principles for the types of intangible asset that can be recognized under most circumstances outside the acquisition context (to which IFRS 3, covered separately later, applies). It applies to a number of important categories of expenditure likely to create intangibles, including advertising, training, start-up and research and development (R&D) activities (IAS 38.5)—the types of business spending that economists Corrado, Hulten, and Sichel pinpoint as behaving in a similar manner to tangible investments, as referenced in Chapter 8.

12.22 In order to be clear about its intended scope, IAS 38.8 defines an intangible asset as *an identifiable non-monetary asset without physical substance.* IAS 38.9 then sets the parameters of the assets that require consideration as follows:

> Entities frequently expend resources, or incur liabilities, on the acquisition, development, maintenance or enhancement of intangible resources such as scientific or technical knowledge, design and implementation of new processes or systems, licences, intellectual property, market knowledge and trademarks (including brand names and publishing titles). Common examples of items encompassed by these broad headings are computer software, patents, copyrights, motion picture films, customer lists, mortgage servicing rights, fishing licences, import quotas, franchises, customer or supplier relationships, customer loyalty, market share and marketing rights.

12.23 Excellent, so can the costs associated with all these go on the balance sheet? If only it were that straightforward. IAS 38.10 goes on to state that:

> Not all the items described in paragraph 9 meet the definition of an intangible asset, i.e. identifiability, control over a resource and existence of future economic benefits. If an item within the scope of this Standard does not meet the definition of an intangible asset, expenditure to acquire it or generate it internally is recognised as an expense when it is incurred.

12.24 In other words, as well as being identifiable (which poses its own challenges), there has to be an element of control, and there must be future economic benefits. Otherwise,

[10] The full text of IAS 38, from which subsequent extracts are taken, can be found at: http://www.ec.europa.eu/internal_market/accounting/docs/consolidated/ias38_en.pdf.

the asset must continue to remain anonymous on the profit and loss account. In fact some assets which companies would identify as being valuable assets are explicitly prohibited from ever making it onto balance sheet (at IAS 38.63):

> Internally generated brands, mastheads, publishing titles, customer lists and items similar in substance shall not be recognised as intangible assets.

So, what can be recognized? The principles in determining whether an asset is identifiable, set out at IAS 38.12, are as follows: **12.25**

- It is separable, i.e. capable of being separated or divided from the entity and sold, transferred, licensed, rented, or exchanged, either individually or together with a related contract, identifiable asset, or liability (regardless of whether or not the entity intends to do so); or
- It arises from contractual or other legal rights, regardless of whether those rights are transferable or separable from the entity or from other rights and obligations.

All IP meets the first criteria, along with many other important types of intangible assets like trade secrets. Patents, trade marks, designs, and copyrights can all be separated from the company that created them. As IP, they would also satisfy the second condition. **12.26**

IAS 38.21 then states that an intangible asset should be recognized (i.e. shown as an asset of the company rather than just an expense) initially at cost, but if and only if: **12.27**

- it is probable that the expected future benefits that are attributable to the asset will flow to the entity; and
- the cost of the asset can be measured reliably.

By definition, research activities do not meet the first of these tests, and IAS 38.56 specifically states that no asset created in the course of research can be recognized. So if a patentable invention or a new design is created as a result of a company's activities, it cannot be put on the balance sheet unless and until the company has embarked on the journey of commercializing it, at which point it can be called 'development'. **12.28**

Considering the perceived importance of the 'knowledge economy' to the future prosperity of most Western economies, it may be a little surprising that the list of balance sheet exceptions provided by IAS 38 includes many of the kind of activities that are most associated with innovation, such as: **12.29**

> a) Activities aimed at obtaining new knowledge;
> b) The search for, evaluation and final selection of, applications of research findings or other knowledge;
> c) The search for alternatives for materials, devices, products, processes, systems or services; and

d) The formulation, design, evaluation and final selection of possible alternatives for new or improved materials, devices, products, processes, systems or services.

12.30 Any asset that does not meet these criteria has to be expensed (i.e. put through the profit and loss account) as and when it is incurred. Furthermore (in case there was still any scope for doubt), there is also a stringent list of requirements a company must satisfy if it is to recognise any development assets, at IAS 38.57:

a) The technical feasibility of completing the intangible asset so that it will be available for use or sale.
b) Its intention to complete the intangible asset and use or sell it.
c) Its ability to use or sell the intangible asset.
d) How the intangible asset will generate probable future economic benefits. Among other things, the entity can demonstrate the existence of a market for the output of the intangible asset or the intangible asset itself or, if it is to be used internally, the usefulness of the intangible asset.
e) The availability of adequate technical, financial and other resources to complete the development and to use or sell the intangible asset.
f) Its ability to measure reliably the expenditure attributable to the intangible asset during its development.

12.31 The Standard is not prescriptive about the types of intangible assets that can be recognized, although at IAS 38.119 it advocates that a suitable process of disclosure should be conducted and that this should be separate for internally generated and 'other' assets. In doing so it provides the following illustration:

A class of intangible assets is a grouping of assets of a similar nature and use in an entity's operations. Examples of separate classes may include:

a) Brand names;
b) Mastheads and publishing titles;
c) Computer software;
d) Licences and franchises;
e) Copyrights, patents and other industrial property rights, service and operating rights;
f) Recipes, formulae, models, designs and prototypes; and
g) Intangible assets under development.

The classes mentioned above are disaggregated (aggregated) into smaller (larger) classes if this results in more relevant information for the users of the financial statements.

12.32 Having established a fairly stringent approach on what can and cannot be put on a balance sheet, IAS 38 goes on to state how assets can be valued. The answer is fairly straightforward—it is at cost—and once intangible assets have been initially recognized in this way, they can only be re-valued if there is an 'active market' in that particular asset, which is seldom the case (IAS 38.78 suggests that the only likely exceptions are assets that are known to be regularly traded, like taxi licences, fishing licences, and production quotas).

It goes on to specifically exclude some assets: **12.33**

> An active market cannot exist for brands, newspaper mastheads, music and film publishing rights, patents or trademarks because each such asset is unique. Also, although intangible assets are bought and sold, contracts are negotiated between individual buyers and sellers, and transactions are relatively infrequent. For these reasons, the price paid for one asset may not provide sufficient evidence of the fair value of another. Moreover, prices are often not available to the public.

While it may not be what the innovative company with a relatively 'thin' balance **12.34** sheet wants to hear, this is not an unfair analysis. The whole point of IP is that each item is unique, and establishing comparability with other transactions is far from straightforward (as demonstrated in the preceding analysis of market methods of valuation in Chapter 11).

Where this leaves IP and intangibles

Quite apart from the frustration that assets can only be accounted for at their cost, **12.35** at best, there is a further issue raised by accounting treatments based on IAS 38. The process of moving eligible development assets onto the balance sheet arguably offers little proof of anything, except that the company in question knows how to spend money. Returning to the earlier example of tangible assets: where a balance sheet entry exists for plant and machinery, it indicates that there will (or should) be some identifiable 'things' on a shop floor somewhere that the business is likely to need in order to trade, and which will have some sort of disposal value. By comparison, in and of itself, an intangible entry on a balance sheet is not traceable back to any specific assets—it simply reflects a judgement made by an accountant that a certain level of expenditure met the necessary criteria.

This partly explains the time-honoured tradition practised by almost every lender, **12.36** which is to draw a 'red line'[11] through any such sums they see. This sounds unreasonable, but it is rational, given that banks are still interested in balance sheets. One particular aspect deserves a further brief explanation here.

Unlike an equity investor,[12] a bank (or any other organization or individual provid- **12.37** ing debt facilities, i.e. loans, to a business) normally has little or no opportunity

[11] Such 'red lines' used to be literal (i.e. traditionally, items were struck out with a red pen if the bank did not feel they were admissible in support of a lending application). Nowadays the actual lines are metaphorical, but the practice of actively setting information of this nature to one side remains alive and well.

[12] 'Equity' refers to the purchase of share capital in a business. Its significance here is that only equity (i.e. a shareholding) enables the holder to benefit from a business's overall performance through an appreciating share value and/or the payment of dividends.

to benefit from the upside that good performance can generate. Whilst a business angel will seek to gauge the possibility that company X could be the 'one in ten' which delivers an outstanding return[13] (and puts right the damage done to their wallets by the other nine investments made), the best a bank can do is to avoid experiencing the effects of the downside.

12.38 As a consequence of this, a bank is obligated to consider two aspects that make balance sheets useful. The first, from a credit underwriting perspective, is that it wants to understand how far a business's underlying profit performance is being influenced by accounting charges like depreciation rather than actual outgoings, because this is important in determining whether a company is generating sufficient cash to service debt. As a related point, a lender will also wish to assess what the annual capital expenditure[14] profile looks like (in terms of replacement equipment and other similar costs that need to be budgeted for). The movement in assets on the balance sheet provides useful information on this point, though of course it is likely to be silent on the investment needed in intangibles required to keep the business competitive (which is still hidden in the profit and loss account).

12.39 The second and more fundamental point is that a bank wants to know what recourse it may have to other assets of value should the borrower default.[15] Its obligation to do this arises both in the interests of its own protection, and also in its need to comply with regulatory requirements concerning capital adequacy, which have been on an ever-tightening trajectory in the wake of the GFC.

12.40 Setting aside for a moment the fact that IP often represents a set of assets in which management has a close personal interest,[16] and therefore is well-suited to fulfil one of the primary purposes of security—namely, to bring the borrower to the table if something goes wrong—there are clear attractions to fixing a value on a piece of commercial property found on a company balance sheet. Even if market conditions change and it transpires that the value of such tangible assets turns out to have been over-estimated, there will generally be a price at which a buyer can be found, and as illustrated above, there are ratios that can be applied with a reasonable degree of confidence to determine what

---

13 For an exploration of the returns which equity investors may expect, see 'Siding with Angels' Wiltbank, R. (2009), Nesta, available at: http://nesta.org.uk/publications/siding-angels.

14 Capital expenditure is generally associated with 'funds used by a company to acquire or upgrade physical assets such as property, industrial buildings or equipment'. See Investopedia at http://www.investopedia.com/terms/c/capitalexpenditure.asp.

15 Default is defined by the Oxford Dictionary as 'failure to fulfil an obligation, especially to repay a loan or appear in a law court'. Here (and elsewhere in this book) it means that a company has failed to meet its repayment obligations on a loan. See http://www.oxforddictionaries.com.

16 This aspect of lending motivation is discussed in more detail in Brassell, M. and King, K. (2013). *Banking on IP?*,(Newport, UK Intellectual Property Office), Ch. 3.

the 'distress value'[17] of, for example, commercial property may be (and which, therefore, can contribute to capital adequacy).

IP is an entirely different 'ball game'. The absence of comparable transactions and ready markets for IP is clearly an issue, but the immediate practical problem is that most lenders have no real visibility of the assets a business owns at the time of entering into a lending arrangement, and, therefore, attach no importance to them, let alone any value. Since study of the balance sheet cannot draw a lender's attention to the true *identity* of the underlying assets and their possible market value, a bank is unlikely to be predisposed to allocate any value at all; hence the red lines referred to earlier, where even the cost/investment aspect is liable to get ignored, except in more specialist asset-backed lending approaches which are starting to emerge. **12.41**

IFRS 3: creating value from thin air?

To complete the picture on intangible assets and balance sheets, it is necessary to highlight one important exception that brings intangible asset value into the spotlight, and onto the balance sheet. This occurs when a company engages in merger and acquisition activity. Under the international standards applied to 'business combinations', a fair value has to be determined for tangible and intangible assets which have been bought, with any unidentified intangibles and additional price premium being allocated to 'goodwill'. This is the process which produced the research results summarized in Chapter 8. **12.42**

This has a couple of interesting implications. First, post-acquisition, as a result of this treatment, value appears on the purchaser's balance sheet that was never present in the acquired company's accounts. This makes it look as if this value has appeared from nowhere, which is, of course, impossible (and only goes to show how counter-intuitive the intangible asset recognition process is). **12.43**

Secondly, there is an important technical distinction between goodwill and identified intangibles. Under current rules, any value attributed to goodwill merely has to be subjected to an annual impairment test to see whether it has reduced in value. By contrast, most (not quite all) identified intangible assets need to be amortized[18] **12.44**

[17] A 'distress sale' or 'fire sale' is a term commonly applied to any situation when property, stocks, or other assets need to be sold quickly, such as when funds are needed urgently to repay debt. Sometimes IP may be referred to as 'distressed' if the company that owns it has got into difficulties; this raises a further complication, in that financiers have a tendency to conflate business failure with IP failure (though the two may be entirely unrelated). See also Liquidation value (Chapter 11).

[18] According to the Financial Times Lexicon, amortization is 'the practice of reducing the value of assets to reflect their reduced worth over time. The term means the same as depreciation, though in practice amortisation tends to be used for the write-off of intangible assets, such as goodwill, while either term is used for the write-off of fixed capital.'

over their useful life. This amortization creates an impact on the acquirer's profit and loss account that it would rather avoid, especially given the uncertainties inherent in any acquisition scenario, and it is arguable that incentives have therefore existed not to try too hard to identify intangible assets and simply bundle everything into goodwill. This looks like an excellent strategy until a GFC hits, company share prices go into free-fall, and auditors are obliged to revisit all such calculations, resulting in a much bigger 'hit' to the profit and loss from one-off goodwill impairment charges than would ever have been incurred from intangibles amortization.

12.45 The relevant accounting standard for business combinations, as mergers and acquisitions are collectively known, is International Financial Reporting Standard (IFRS) 3[19] (the revised UK GAAP provisions discussed below have now moved to a substantially similar position, particularly in respect of post-acquisition accounting).[20] Whilst IFRS 3 only applies to listed and quoted companies, and only in the context of a 'business combination', it is an important reference point because it sets out approaches and provides examples of how intangible assets can be separately identified with sufficient rigour to show them in statutory accounts.

12.46 Introduced in 2003, and applicable from April 2004, IFRS 3 brings aspects of international standards into line with US GAAP treatment of intangible assets, especially SFAS 141. It was last updated in 2008 (with effect from 2009). Under IFRS 3, intangible assets are no longer simply bundled up in 'goodwill', as was previously the case. Goodwill in this context becomes a means of accounting for the premium paid once the value of all identifiable assets (tangible and intangible) has been taken into account.

12.47 When businesses are combined, IFRS 3 states that *all* the identifiable intangible assets need to be accounted for, including those which were previously not eligible because (for example) they were internally generated, research-related, or not separable. The intriguing effect of this is that a business that has been reporting under IAS 38 or any of its compatible standards will suddenly appear to have a much broader intangible asset portfolio, and a lot more value in its IP and other intangibles, simply by virtue of having been acquired.

12.48 Helpfully, to assist with interpretation, IFRS 3 (and SFAS 141) includes illustrative examples to propose a way of approaching the identification of intangible assets

[19] The full text of IFRS 3 can be found at http://ec.europa.eu/internal_market/accounting/docs/consolidated/ifrs3_en.pdf, from which all following extracts are taken.

[20] A summary can be found on the website of the Institute of Chartered Accountants for England and Wales. Available at: http://www.icaew.com/en/technical/financial-reporting/new-uk-gaap.

that have been acquired. It suggests five main headings and a representative set of contents for each, as shown in Table 12.1:

Before getting too enthused by this positive recognition of many different types of intangible assets and IP, it is important to observe that some qualifiers **12.49**

Table 12.1 Illustrative examples of intangible asset types provided with IFRS 3

Marketing-related
Trade marks, trade names, service marks, collective marks, and certification marks
Internet domain names
Trade dress (unique colour, shape or package design)
Newspaper mastheads
Non-competition agreements
Contract-related
Advertising, construction, management, service, delivery and supply contracts
Licences, royalties, standstill agreements
Lease agreements (as a lessee or lessor)
Construction permits
Franchise agreements
Operating and broadcasting rights
Use rights such as drilling, water, air, mineral, timber-cutting, and route authorizations
Servicing contracts such as mortgage servicing contracts
Employment contracts that are beneficial contracts from the perspective of the employer, because the pricing of those contracts is below their current market value
Customer-related
Customer lists
Order or production backlog
Customer contracts and related customer relationships
Non-contractual customer relationships
Technology-related
Patented technologies
Computer software and mask works
Unpatented technologies
Databases, including title plants
Trade secrets such as secret formulas, processes, and recipes
Artistic-related
Plays, operas, and ballets
Books, magazines, newspapers, and other literary works
Musical works such as compositions, song lyrics, and advertising jingles
Pictures and photographs
Video and audiovisual material, including motion pictures or films, music videos, and television programmes

remain.[21] For example, IFRS 3 only provides a means of recognizing rights that are separable or arise out of contracts or other legal agreements. Therefore, it does not pick up assets that are intrinsic to, and not separable from, a particular business and which add value to it as a going concern. In addition, IFRS 3 sensibly does not require accountants to arrive at an arbitrary separate value for each asset, because along with IAS 38, it recognizes that it may be very difficult to identify individual values for (by way of example) a customer relationship and a technology that is used to support it, as one would not exist without the other. It, therefore, permits the assets to be combined for reporting purposes. However, both remain distinct intangible assets (especially since the technology may have additional applications, and the customer may have additional requirements), which resonates with the important basic principle stated at the commencement of this discussion on value, that intangible assets including IP are best understood individually but valued collectively.

12.50 While the acquirer's balance sheet may still not explain what all these underlying assets are, there will at least be a schedule showing them, which represents progress. IFRS 3 is also clear about the distinction between separable, identifiable assets like IP and the value of human capital more generally; whilst people may indeed be an organization's greatest asset, the fact that a business has valuable employees does not make its workforce 'intellectual capital'. The Standard says (at IFRS 3 B.27):

> An acquirer may attribute value to the existence of an assembled workforce, which is an existing collection of employees that permits the acquirer to continue to operate an acquired business from the acquisition date. An assembled workforce does not represent the intellectual capital of the skilled workforce—the (often specialised) knowledge and experience that employees of an acquiree bring to their jobs. Because the assembled workforce is not an identifiable asset to be recognised separately from goodwill, any value attributed to it is subsumed into goodwill.

12.51 Appraisal of the headings used for intangible asset discovery reveals that they are not the most user-friendly ones which could have been created. The main problem when seeking to build an asset inventory is that the legal form of the different IP assets likely to be found is not taken properly into account (e.g. copyright assets can and will fall under several different headings). This criticism notwithstanding, a major contribution made by IFRS 3 is the fact that it establishes the basis for a more meaningful set of descriptions of the types of assets often created and owned by a business. The fact that it then attributes value to individual elements within this inventory is clearly a bonus.

12.52 The outcomes of a selection of real IFRS 3 assessments have been shown in Chapter 8. Purists might justifiably argue that value is being back-calculated from a known

[21] For a more detailed discussion of this point see (among others), Grant Thornton International Ltd. (May 2008). 'Intangible Assets in a Business Combination'.

answer (the total purchase price), rather than necessarily being worked out from the ground up. As explained earlier, the value found cannot be an 'absolute' figure because judgements will need to be made as to what is and is not identifiable, how long the useful economic life of the assets is likely to be, and what the most appropriate (or preferred) outcome may be in terms of goodwill vs. identified intangibles. But at the very least, it confirms what is instinctively known to be true, that IP is a significant driver of value that is capable of being recognized objectively.

FRS 102 and the new UK GAAP

A new Financial Reporting Standard 102 (FRS 102) came into effect in the United Kingdom from the end of 2015 (where a company's accounting year is the calendar year) and April 2016 (where it is the financial year). It updates the previous UK GAAP standards with changes that are closer to the concepts established in international financial and accounting standards, and makes them relevant not just for listed companies but for all small and medium-sized businesses, particularly if they buy another company. **12.53**

FRS 102 provides greater certainty about the approach that needs to be taken when one company buys another. Under the old rules, it might be permissible to use merger accounting (which simply requires the two companies' existing balance sheets to be combined) rather than acquisition accounting (which requires a fair value to be placed on all the target company's assets, regardless of how they have been accounted for in the past). Now, acquisition accounting must be used in nearly all cases, the main exception being group reorganizations. **12.54**

A further change, compared with previous UK GAAP rules on acquisition accounting, is that any excess paid over and above the fair value of the assets and liabilities can no longer simply be characterised as an amorphous lump of 'goodwill'. It now needs to be broken down into its constituent intangible assets, in a very similar manner to IFRS 3 as set out in detail earlier (though there are some minor wording differences). **12.55**

UK GAAP also permits this 'goodwill' to have an indefinite life, as long as the value is tested annually for impairment. Under FRS 102, this concept of an indefinite life falls away and a lifespan has to be specified for amortization purposes: if the lifespan cannot be determined reliably, a 'default' figure of five years must be used, which is much shorter than UK GAAP where it would have been customary to amortize assets whose lifespan was uncertain over a much longer period (up to twenty years). **12.56**

FRS 102 preserves the option, previously available under SSAP 13 (which it also replaces), of either capitalizing qualifying development expenditure or expensing it during the year in which it is incurred. Given the reducing reliance of companies on tangible assets, and the fact that capitalization does not necessarily prevent R&D **12.57** tax credits (discussed in Chapter 9) from being claimed, the number of businesses looking to use this approach and place intangibles on their balance sheet looks set to rise.

Integrated reporting: Into the future?

12.58 Clearly, it would be a bad idea if accounting statements were not based on 'real' transactions, especially when it comes to asset valuation. Unfortunately, the absence of liquid markets for intangible assets to which current Standards refer means that there are few real transactions to act as reference points. As a consequence, their cost ends up being used, and understatement of true value results. However, the accounting profession also recognizes the importance of ensuring that those responsible for managing businesses are adequately equipped to focus on the assets that drive growth, and able to explain these drivers to shareholders and investors.

12.59 As a result, there have been a number of international initiatives aimed at making intangible assets and their value contribution more visible. Some notable ones include work in Germany on the development of intellectual capital statements, leading to the creation of a 'Wissensbilanz' (or knowledge capital) toolkit,[22] and the working group set up in France in 2011, which derived twelve principles aimed at encouraging companies to monitor the performance of their intangible assets so they can be correctly measured and reported to markets.[23]

12.60 A further international initiative recently incorporated into UK training courses run by the Association of Chartered Certified Accountants (ACCA) is that of integrated reporting (IR). This framework was launched by the International Integrated Reporting Council (IIRC) in 2013, IIRC being a global coalition of regulators, investors, companies, standard setters, the accounting profession, and non-governmental organizations (NGOs) with an interest in encouraging value creation for the long term. The framework document[24] describes the role of IR as follows:

> The primary purpose of an integrated report is to explain to providers of financial capital how an organisation creates value over time.... Integrated thinking takes into account the connectivity and interdependencies between the range of factors that affect an organisation's ability to create value over time, including:
>
> - The capitals that the organisation uses or affects, and the critical interdependencies, including trade-offs, between them;

[22] Fischer, T. and Wulf, I. (eds). (2013). *Wissensbilanzen im Mittelstand—Kapitalmarktkommunikation, Immaterielle Werte, Lageberichterstattung, Integrated Reporting* (Schaeffer-Poeschel).

[23] GTMI (Groupe de Travail Mesure de l'immaterial). (October 2011). 'Principles of Measurement of Intangibles: 12 Proposals for the Provision of Competitiveness and the Sustainable Development of Businesses'.

[24] Available at http://www.theiirc.org/wp-content/uploads/2013/12/13-12-08-the-international-ir-framework-2-1.pdf.

- The capacity of the organisation to respond to key stakeholders' legitimate needs and interests;
- How the organisation tailors its business model and strategy to respond to its external environment and the risks and opportunities it faces;
- The organisation's activities, performance (financial and other) and outcomes in terms of the capitals – past, present and future.

The significance of this approach is that the 'capitals' include headings that specifically reference IP and more generally include consideration of training, branding, and organizational improvements, all of which are among the categories regarded as being intangibles-related investments by the Organisation for Economic Co-operation and Development (OECD) and others based on the pioneering work by Corrado, Hulten, and Sichel referred to in Chapter 8. Specifically, the six capitals that feature in IR are financial capital, manufactured capital, intellectual capital, human capital, social and relationship capital, and natural capital. **12.61**

Intellectual capital, the most obviously relevant, is defined in the framework document as 'organisational, knowledge-based intangibles, including: intellectual property, such as patents, copyrights, software, rights and licences [and] "organisational capital" such as tacit knowledge, systems, procedures and protocols'. However, there are also knowledge-based elements in other capitals, with human capital including aspects of organizational development and training, and social and relationship capital explicitly including 'intangibles associated with the brand and reputation that an organisation has developed'. **12.62**

The integrated thinking model is that these capitals are 'stocks and flows'; they act as inputs for the company and are then transformed through the business's activities into outputs and outcomes. These strengthen the capitals over time, but also cause movements in value to occur between them. For example, if a company makes a strategic decision to innovate, this might well lead to a reduction in short-term financial capital (namely, some additional cost) in the interests of achieving improvements to other capitals (such as intellectual, human, social, and relationship capital) that deliver benefit in the longer term. **12.63**

Conclusion

Whilst IR does not provide a particular reporting template and is not set to supersede or replace traditional accounting standards, the fact that it exists at all is a reflection of the growing importance of intangibles in generating competitive advantage through innovation, and a recognition that these assets are not simply costs, but also investments. **12.64**

CONCLUSION

The economic and financial considerations of IP question the status quo, highlight the benefits and costs of IP systems, and suggest potential solutions. However, the challenges unearthed by these analyses are far from resolved. Indeed, as this book outlines, the economic and financial analysis itself is only just beginning. The future of this analysis is promising and should further illuminate weaknesses and strengths of the modern incarnation of IP.

The Importance of Economics of IP

The book aims to introduce the economics of IP and to equip readers with the tools and knowledge to critically assess economic and financial interpretations of IP. In doing so, the book highlights the weaknesses and strengths of economics and IP. Where economics are strong, the analysis provides insights that more traditional approaches to IP may not uncover. Where economics is weaker, the book has identified areas for improvement.

The chapters developing economic analysis of individual IP rights suggest there is a balance to be found between IP's role in incentivizing innovation and protecting existing rights. At the same time, economics highlights that the role of IP in both innovation and protection is less clear than a *prima facie* analysis suggests. The section of the practical use of IP in business sheds a light on the challenges of transforming intangible rights into financial assets. Again, this is an emerging area and one that will continue to evolve.

The Future of Economics of IP

Further advancements in the economics of IP are likely to stem from the following: improved data, macroeconomic analysis, and development of markets and accounting practices for IP.

Globally, we are in the midst of a data revolution that is already transforming all aspects of personal lives and economies. As data and data availability develop, analysis of IP will advance. This is likely to happen on two fronts: first, on the construction and analysis of economic evidence for policy and second, on the development of markets for IP. As the gaps in empirical evidence and data are slowly filled in, current economic interpretations of IP may be further evidence, called into question, or entirely new paradigms could develop. Improved data, which is the basis of financial calculations, will bolster the development of IP markets and improve decision-making. The impact of data on economics of IP cannot be understated.

Another area of further exploration is that of the macroeconomic aspects of IP. This book has deliberately focused more on microeconomic concepts as being most immediately relevant to readers. The book considers key concepts of IP in relation to innovation, economic performance, and growth, and the wider macroeconomic perspective will provide further information on the success or failure of IP for economies. Given the decades that have passed since the introduction of the Agreement on Trade-Related Aspects of Intellectual Property Rights (TRIPS), the future of this research is promising. It is likely that the economic analysis of IP will move further in this direction in coming years as data becomes more readily available and a clearer picture develops.

As the final section on financial and practical aspects of IP demonstrates, there are still great passes to be made in this area. In addition to the potential impact of data noted above, the convergence of international standards for IP valuation and the development of best practices in the use of IP rights as intangible assets, will serve to mature the practical role of IP. The progression of valuation should also reduce uncertainties in both day-to-day business and disputes over IP.

Concluding Remarks

Economic approaches to IP form a key part of the complex interpretations of IP systems and practices globally. As economics delves further into this area, and the economic approach is further accepted in IP, IP systems and practices should benefit from the critical perspectives economics provides. Economics offers much to enrich IP.

Finally, we hope this book has proved as enjoyable to read, as it was to write, and that you now share our enthusiasm for IP seen through the lens of economics and finance.

BIBLIOGRAPHY

Adams, S. (2010). 'Intellectual Property Rights, Investment Climate and FDI in Developing Countries' *International Business Research* 3(3); 201.

Agarwal, S. and Barone, M. J. (2005). Emerging Issues for Geographical Indication Branding Strategies. Midwest Agribusiness Trade Research and Information Center (MATRIC) at Iowa State University, 2005.

Aglionby, J. and Ward, A. (2015). 'David Cameron Calls for Action to Fight Antibiotic Resistance'. FT.com.

Almeling, D. S. (2012). 'Seven Reasons Why Trade Secrets are Increasingly Important' *Berkeley Tech. Law Journal* 27: 1091.

Amine, L. (2008) *Coke and Pepsi Learn to Compete in India* (Burr Ridge, IL, Irwin).

Andenas, M. and Andersen, C. (2012). *Theory and Practice of Harmonisation* (Cheltenham, Edward Elgar Publishing). Available at http://public.eblib.com/choice/publicfullrecord.aspx?p=881389.

Anton, J. J. and Yao, D. A. 'Little Patents and Big Secrets: Managing Intellectual Property' *RAND Journal of Economics* 35: 1–22.

Arundel, A. (2001). 'The Relative Effectiveness of Patents and Secrecy for Appropriation' *Research Policy* 30(4): 611–24.

Association, A. I. P. L. (2013). 'Report of the Economic Survey'. American Intellectual Property Law Association.

Atkinson, R. (2009). 'Effective Corporate Tax Reform in the Global Innovation Economy' (Technical report, ITIF, Washington D.C.). Available at http://www.itif.org/files/090723_CorpTax.pdf.

Atkinson, R. and Andes, S. (2011). *Patent Boxes: Innovation in Tax Policy and Tax Policy for Innovation* (The Information Technology & Innovation Foundation).

Babbage (17 April 2011) 'Doing the Maths' *The Economist,* Available at http://www.economist.com/blogs/babbage/2011/08/valuing-patents.

Bain, J. S. (1959). *Industrial Organization* (New York, Wiley).

Bakhshi, H., Hargreaves, I., and Mateos-Garcia, J. (2013). *A Manifesto For The Creative Economy* (London, NESTA). Available at http://www.nesta.org.uk/publications/manifesto-creative-economy.

Barnett, J. M. (2005). 'Shopping for Gucci on Canal Street: Reflections on Status Consumption, Intellectual Property, and the Incentive Thesis' Virginia Law Review 91(6):1381–1423.

Barton, J. H. (2003). 'New International Arrangements in Intellectual Property and Competition Law | Stanford Law School'. In Granstrand, O. (ed.), *Economics, Law and Intellectual Property: Seeking Strategies for Research and Teaching in a Developing Field* (Boston; Dordrecht; London, Kluwer Academic Publishers) 109–21.

Bender, D. (1985). 'Protection of Computer Programs: The Copyright/Trade Secret Interface' *U. Pitt. L. Rev.* 47: 907.

Bessen, J. (2005). 'Patents and the Diffusion of Technical Information' *Economics Letters* 86(1): 121–8.

Blackman, M. (1995). 'Provision of Patent Information: A National Patent Office Perspective' *World Patent Information* 17(2): 115–231. Available at http://www.sciencedirect.com/science/article/pii/017221909500012O.

Bloom, N., Griffith, R., and Van Reenen, J. (2002). 'Do R&D Tax Credits Work? Evidence from a Panel of Countries 1979-1997' *Journal of Public Economics* 85(1): 1-31.

Bloomberg. (2014). 'Tesla Sued by Businesseman Claiming China Trademark Right'. Available at http://www.bloomberg.com/news/articles/2014-07-07/tesla-sued-in-china-for-trademark-infringement.

Bramley, C. and June, I. (2011). 'A Review of the Socio-economic Impact of Geographical Indications: Considerations for the Developing World' WIPO Worldwide Symposium on Geographical Indications, Lima, Peru.

Bramley, C. and Kirsten, J. F. (2007). 'Exploring the Economic Rationale for Protecting Geographical Indicators in Agriculture' *Agrekon* 46(1): 47–71.

Brassell, M. and King, K. (2013). 'Banking on IP? The Role of Intellectual Property and Intangible Assets in Facilitating Business Finance' (IPO).

Briggs, K. (2013). 'Does Patent Harmonization Impact the Decision and Volume of High Technology Trade?' *International Review of Economics & Finance* 25: 35–51. Available at http://www.sciencedirect.com/science/article/pii/S1059056012000408.

Callmann, R. (1940). 'Style and Design Piracy' *J. Pat. Off. Soc'y* 22: 557.

Carter-Silk, A. and Lewiston, M. (2012). 'The Development of Design Law. Past and Future: From History to Policy' *Newport: The Intellectual Property Office.*

Caves, R. E. (2000). *Creative Industries: Contracts Between Art and Commerce* (Cambridge, Mass., Harvard University Press).

Chaffin, J. (4 February 2013). 'Fresh Accusations in China Dumping Case' FT.com.

Chu, B. (2015). 'Bill Gates: Why Do We Care More About Baldness Than Malaria?' *The Independent*. Available at http://www.independent.co.uk/news/world/americas/bill-gates-why-do-we-care-more-about-baldness-than-malaria-8536988.html

Chun, D. (2011). 'Patent Law Harmonization in the Age of Globalization: The Necessity and Strategy for a Pragmatic Outcome' *J. Pat. & Trademark Off. Soc'y* 93: 127.

CLM. (2015). 'Common Language in Marketing Dictionary'. Available at http://www.commonlanguage.wikispaces.net/Marketing.

Cohen, W. M., Nelson, R. R., and Walsh, J. P. (2000). 'Protecting Their Intellectual Assets: Appropriability Conditions and Why US Manufacturing Firms Patent (or Not)'. National Bureau of Economic Research.

Commission, E. (2013). 'Study on Trade Secrets and Confidential Business Information in the Internal Market'. Brussels, Belgium: European Commission . MARKT/2011/128/D Available at http://ec.europa.eu/internal_market/iprenforcement/docs/trade-secrets/130711_final-study_en.pdf.

Corrado, C. A., & Hao, J. X. (2014). 'Brands As Productive Assets: Concepts, Measurement, and Global Trends' *Geneva, World Intellectual Property Organization-Economics and Statistics Division*, 13.

Corrado, C., Hulten, C., and Sichel, D. (2005). *Measuring Capital and Technology: An Expanded Framework* (Washington D.C., University of Chicago Press).

de la Potterie, B. v. P. (2011). 'The Quality Factor in Patent Systems' *Industrial and Corporate Change* 20(6): 1755–93.

De Rassenfosse, G. and Van Pottelsberghe de la Potterie, B. 2013. 'The Role of Fees in Patent Systems: Theory and Evidence' *Journal of Economic Surveys* 27: 696–716.

Degusta, M. (2011). 'The *Real* Death of the Music Industry' *Business Insider*, Feburary 18. Available at http://www.businessinsider.com/these-charts-explain-the-real-death-of-the-music-industry-2011-2

Denicolo, V. and Alberto Franzoni, L. (2004). 'Patents, Secrets, and the First-Inventor Defense' *Journal of Economics & Management Strategy* 13(3); 517–38.

Dignan, L. (2014). 'Netflix: Comcast is Charging Us for Access to Our Subscribers'. Available at http://www.zdnet.com/article/netflix-comcast-is-charging-us-for-access-to-our-subscribers/.

Dorvee, S. M. (1981). 'Protecting Trade Secrets Through Copyright' *Duke Law Journal* 30(6): 981–98.

Drexl, J., Nérisson, S., Trumpke, F., and Hilty, R. (2013). 'Comments of the Max Planck Institute for Intellectual Property and Competition Law on the Proposal for a Directive of the European Parliament and of the Council on Collective Management of Copyright and Related Rights and Multi-Territorial Licensing of Rights in Musical Works for Online Uses in the Internal Market COM (2012)372' Max Planck Institute for Intellectual Property & Competition Law Research Paper No. 13-04. Available at SSRN: http://ssrn.com/abstract=2208971

Duhigg, C. (2012). 'How Companies Learn Your Secrets' *The New York Times* 16: 2012.

Dutfield, G. (May 2005). 'Harnessing Traditional Knowledge and Genetic Resources for Local Development and Trade'. In *International seminar on intellectual property and development. WIP–UNCTAD–UNIDO–WHO–WTO, Geneva* (Vol. 8).

Economides, N. S. (1988). 'Economics of Trademarks' *Trademark Rep.* 78: 523.

Economist. (2010). 'Busting the Cartels'.

economist.com. (2013). 'Money, Money, Money'. Available from: http://www.economist.com/blogs/graphicdetail/2013/05/daily-chart-1?fsrc=scn/tw/te/bl/ed/moneymoneymoney.

Economist (2014). 'If You Can't Beat Them, Buy Them' *The Economist*, 22 November 2014. Available at http://www.economist.com/news/finance-and-economics/21633883-fear-being-displaced-startups-turning-firms-venture-capitalists-if.

Economist. (2015). 'Economics A-Z Terms Beginning with E | The Economist'. Available at http://www.economist.com/economics-a-to-z/e#node-21529488.

Evans, G. (1997). *Economic Models* (self-published), Ch 1. Available at http://www2.hmc.edu/~evans/chap1.pdf.

Evans, G. (2010). 'The Comparative Advantages of Geographical Indications and Community Trade Marks for the Marketing of Agricultural Products in the European Union'. *International Review of Industrial Property and Copyright Law* 41(6): 645.

Evers, L., Miller, H., and Spengel, C. (2013) 'Intellectual Property Box Regimes: Effective Tax Rates and Tax Policy Considerations' (Centre for European Economic Research). Discussion Paper 13-070.

Feeley, J. (2000). 'Nine West to Pay $34 Million to Settle FTC Claims'. *Los Angeles Times.*

Fink, C. Helmers, C., and Ponce, C. (2014). 'Trademarks Squatters: Evidence from Chile'. World Intellectual Property Organization-Economics and Statistics Division.

Fischer, T. and Wulf, I. (eds). (2013). *Wissensbilanzen im Mittelstand - Kapitalmarktkommunikation, Immaterielle Werte, Lageberichterstattung, Integrated Reporting* (Schaeffer-Poeschel).

Forbes. (2015). 'The World's Most Valuable Brands'. Available at http://www.forbes.com/powerful-brands/list/.

Friedman, D. D., Landes, W. M., and Posner, R. A. (1991). 'Some Economics of Trade Secret Law' *The Journal of Economic Perspectives* 5(1): 61–72.

FTC. (2008). 'FTC Modifies Order in Nine West Resale Price Maintenance Case | Federal Trade Commission'. *Federal Trade Commission Press Release*, 6 May 2008. Available at https://www.ftc.gov/news-events/press-releases/2008/05/ftc-modifies-order-nine-west-resale-price-maintenance-case.

Gallini, N. T. (1992). 'Patent Policy and Costly Imitation' *The RAND Journal of Economics* 23(1): 52–63.

Gantchev, D. (2004). 'The WIPO Guide on Surveying the Economic Contribution of the Copyright Industries' *Review of Economic Research on Copyright Issues* 1: 5–15.

Gerardi, C.P. (2014). 'Inside The Busiest Patent Court in America' *FTI Journal* February 2014. Available at http://ftijournal.com/uploads/pdf/FTI_Journal-Inside_The_Busiest_Patent_Court_In_America.pdf.

Gervais, Daniel. (2014) 'A Cognac After Spanish Champagne? Geographical Indications as Certification Marks' (Cambridge University Press, Cambridge Books Online). Available at http://dx.doi.org/10.1017/CBO9781139524070.011.

Gleick, J. (12 March 2000). 'Patently Absurd'. *New York Times*.

Goodridge, P., Haskel, J., and Wallis, G. (2012). 'UK Innovation Index: Productivity and Growth in UK Industries'. Nesta Working Paper 12/09.

Goodridge, P., Haskel, J., and Wallis, G. (2014). 'Estimating UK Investment in Intangible Assets and Intellectual Property Rights' (IPO).

Goolsbee, A., Levitt, S. D., and Syverson, C. (2013). *Microeconomics* (New York, Worth Publishers).

Gosline, R. A. R. (2009). *The Real Value of Fakes: Dynamic Symbolic Boundaries in Socially Embedded Consumption* (Cambridge, Mass. Harvard University Press).

Greenhalgh, C. et al. (2011). 'Trade Mark Incentives' *Intellectual Property* 1.

Griffith, R., Miller, H., and O'Connell, M. (2010). Corporate Taxes and Intellectual Property: Simulating the Effect of Patent Boxes (London, Institute for Fiscal Studies). Available at: http://www.ifs.org.uk/bns/bn112.pdf.

Grimes, D. (2002). 'Reflections on the Women's Health Initiative Trial of Postmenopausal Hormone Therapy' *World Health Organisation (WHO)*, Available at http://apps.who.int/rhl/Reflections_on_Womens_Health_Initiative_Trial.pdf.

Hall, B. et al. (2012). 'A Study of Patent Thickets'. *UK Intellectual Property Office*, Available at https://www.gov.uk/government/uploads/system/uploads/attachment_data/file/311234/ipresearch-thickets.pdf.

Haskel, J. and Pesole, A. (2011). 'Productivity and Innovation in UK Financial Services: An Intangible Assets Approach'. *Imperial College London Business School*, Discussion Paper 2011/02.

Hiskey, D. (2012). 'The Pharmaceutical Company Bayer Coined the Name "Heroin" and Marketed the Drug as a Non-Addictive Cough Medicine'. Available at http://www.todayifoundout.com/index.php/2012/02/the-pharmaceutical-company-bayer-coined-the-name-heroin-and-marketed-the-drug-as-a-non-addictive-cough-medicine/.

Hovenkamp, H. (1984). Technology, Politics, and Regulated Monopoly: An American Historical Perspective. Texas Law Review 62(7): 1263–131.

INTA. (2005). 'Report and Recommendations: Relative Examination Systems vs. Absolute Examination Systems: Whether INTA should endorse one system or the other,' Emerging Issues Committee Relative Examination Subcommittee, International Trademark Association, October 2005, available at http://www.inta.org/Advocacy/Documents/INTARelativeAbsoluteExamination2005.pdf

IPO. (2014). 'Unified Patent Court Implementation: Alignment of Exceptions to Infringement'. In IPO (ed.) Consultation ed. 25 July 2014. Available at https://www.gov.uk/government/publications/impact-assessment-unified-patent-court-implementation-alignment-of-exceptions-to-infringement.

ITU. (2014). Understanding Patents, Competition & Standardization in an Interconnected World'. WIPO.

Jarboe, K. and Furrow, R. (2008). *Intangible Asset Monetization: The Promise and the Reality* (Athena Alliance). Available at http:// www.athenaalliance.org/ pdf/ IntangibleAssetMonetization.pdf.

Johnson, P., Gibson, J., and Freeman, J. (2013). 'The Impact of Lookalikes Similar Packaging and Fast-moving Consumer Goods (IPO).

Josling, T. (2006). 'The War on Terror: Geographical Indications as a Transatlantic Trade Conflict' *Journal of Agricultural Economics* 57(3): 337–63.

Kappos, D. J. (2010). 'Patent Law Harmonization: The Time is Now' *Landslide* 3: 16.

Kazmin, A. (15 May 2013). 'India: Patents and Precedents'. *Financial Times*.

Kerstetter, J. (5 April 2012). 'How Much is That Patent Lawsuit Going to Cost You?', *CNET.* Available at http://www.cnet.com/news/how-much-is-that-patent-lawsuit-going-to-cost-you/.

Kirzner, I. M. (1979). Perception, Opportunity, and Profit: Studies in the Theory of Entrepreneurship (Chicago: University of Chicago Press).

Kiss, J. (2010). 'Newport State of Mind: Songwriters Pulled the Video from YouTube'. *The Guardian*.

Klerman, D. M. and Reilly, G. (2014). 'Forum Selling'. USC CLASS Research Paper, 14–35: 14–44.

KPMG International Global Valuation Institute. (2012). 'Profitability and Royalty Rates Across Industries: Some Preliminary Evidence'.

Kramer, A. (2007). 'After Long Dispute, A Russian Starbucks' *New York Times*. Available at http://www.nytimes.com/2007/09/07/business/worldbusiness/07sbux.html?_r=0.

Kretschmer, M., Derclaye, E., Favale, M., and Watt, R. (2010). 'The Relationship Between Copyright and Contract Law'. A Review commissioned by the UK Strategic Advisory Board for Intellectual Property Policy (SABIP), 2010. Available at SSRN: http://ssrn.com/abstract=2624945.

Kristensen, S. D., Knuuti, J., Saraste, A., Anker, S., Bøtker, H. E., De Hert, S., Ford, I., Gonzalez-Juanatey, J. R., Gorenek, B., and Heyndrickx, G. R. (2014). '2014 ESC/ESA Guidelines on Non-cardiac Surgery: Cardiovascular Assessment and Management' *European Heart Journal* 35: 2383–2431.

Krugman, P. (2011). 'Economics and Morality'. *The New York Times*. January 10, 2011. Available at http://krugman.blogs.nytimes.com/2011/01/10/economics-and-morality/.

Kur, Annette, et al. (2006) 'First Evaluation of Directive 96/9/EC on the Legal Protection of Databases-Comment by the Max Planck Institute for Intellectual Property, Competition and Tax Law, Munich.' IIC-international review of intellectual property and competition law 37.5: 551-558.

Lacey, M. (2010). 'From Cartel to Corporation: Drug Trade Economics'. *The New York Times*, 7 January 2010. Available at http://economix.blogs.nytimes.com/2010/01/07/from-cartel-to-corporation-the-economics-of-the-drug-trade/.

Landes, W. M. and Posner, R. A. (1989). 'An Economic Analysis of Copyright Law' *The Journal of Legal Studies* 18(2): 325–63.

Landes, W. M. and Posner, R. A. (1987). 'Trademark Law: An Economic Perspective' *Journal of Law and Economics* 30(2): 265–309. Available at http://www.jstor.org/stable/725498.

Lantagne, S. (2014). *Sherlock Holmes and the Case of the Lucrative Fandom: Recognizing the Economic Power of Fanworks and Reimagining Fair Use in Copyrigh.* (self-published). Available at SSRN: http://ssrn.com/abstract=2402951.

LegalFlip. (1990). 'Otis Elevator Company Inventor Trademarks "ESCALATOR". LegalFlip.com—This Day in the Law. Available at http://www.legalflip.com/ThisDayInTheLaw.aspx?id=156.

Lee, I. K. (1999). 'Non-cooperative Tacit Collusion, Complementary Bidding and Incumbency Premium' *Review of Industrial Organization* 15: 115–34.

Liebeler, L. H. (1986). 'Trademark Law, Economics and Grey-Market Policy' *Ind. LJ* 62: 753.

Lerner, J. (2006). 'Using Litigation to Understand Trade Secrets: A Preliminary Exploration'. Working paper. Available at SSRN: http://ssrn.com/abstract=922520.

Lines, S.-A. P. (2012). 'Drug Patent Expirations and the "Patent Cliff"' *US Pharm* 37(6): 12–20.

Lippoldt, D. C. and Schultz, M. F. (2014). 'Uncovering Trade Secrets—An Empirical Assessment of Economic Implications of Protection for Undisclosed Data'. *OECD Trade Policy Papers*, No. 167, OECD Publishing, Paris. DOI: http://dx.doi.org/10.1787/5jxzl5w3j3s6-en.

Lipsey, R. G. and Courant, P. N. (1996). *Microeconomics* (New York, HarperCollins College Publishers).

Mancusi, M. L. (2008). 'International Spillovers and Absorptive Capacity: A Cross-Country Cross-Sector Analysis Based on Patents and Citations' *Journal of International Economics* 76(2): 155–65.

Mankiw, N. G. (2012). 'Competition Is Good for Governments, Too—Economic View'. *The New York Times*, 14 April 2012. Available at http://www.nytimes.com/2012/04/15/business/competition-is-good-for-governments-too-economic-view.html.

Markt, D. (2014). 'Assessing the Economic Impacts of Adapting Certain Limitations and Exceptions to Copyright and Related Rights in the EU' (European Union). Available at http://ec.europa.eu/internal_market/copyright/docs/studies/140623-limitations-economic-impacts-study_en.pdf.

Masnick, M. (2008). 'EU Again Thinks About Extending Copyright, Despite Earlier Rejection'. Available at https://www.techdirt.com/articles/20080715/0101411681.shtml.

Mazziotti, G. (2013). 'Copyright in the EU Digital Single Market'. CEPS Task Force Reports (2013). Available at SSRN: http://ssrn.com/abstract=2307855

Mazzucato, M. (2014). *The Entrepreneurial State: Debunking Public vs. Private Sector Myths* (New York, NY, Anthem Press).

McCall, T. (2013) 'Michael Kors Sues Costco' *Fashionista*. Available at http://fashionista.com/2013/07/michael-kors-sues-costco.

McCreevy, C. (2008). 'Performing Artists-No Longer the Poor Cousins of the Music Business' *DG Internal Market Press Release, IP/08/240* 14.

Menell, P. S. and Scotchmer, S. (2007). 'Intellectual Property'. In A. Mitchell Polinsky and Steven Shavell (eds.), *Handbook Of Law And Economics* (North Holland, Elsevier), ch. 19, 1473–1570.

Millot, V. (2009). 'Trademarks as an Indicator of Product and Marketing Innovations'. OECD Science, Technology and Industry Working Papers, OECD Publishing 2009(6).

Mirghani, S. (2011). 'The War on Piracy: Analyzing the Discursive Battles of Corporate and Government-Sponsored Anti-Piracy Media Campaigns' *Critical Studies in Media Communication* 28(2): 113–34.

Mitton, T. (2007). *Read Me Out Loud!: A Poem to Rap, Chant, Whisper or Shout for Every Day of the Year* (London, Macmillan).
Montague, G. H. (1927). 'Anti-Trust Laws and the Federal Trade Commission, 1914–1927' *Columbia Law Review* 27: 650–78.
Morikawa, M. (2014). 'Innovation in the Service Sector and the Role of Patents and Trade Secrets'. Centre for Applied Macroeconomic Analysis, Crawford School of Public Policy, The Australian National University. CAMA Working Papers 2014-48.
Morin, J. F. (2009). 'Multilateralizing TRIPs-Plus Agreements: Is the US Strategy a Failure?' The Journal of World Intellectual Property 12(3): 175–97.
Moschini, G. and Yerokhin, O. (2007). 'The Economic Incentive to Innovate in Plants: Patents and Plant Breeders' Rights' (CABI, Wallingford): 190–203.
Moultrie, J. and Livesey, F. (2011). 'Design Right Case Studies'. In *The Economics of Design Rights* (UK Intellectual Property Office), ch 3. Available at https://www.gov.uk/government/publications/the-economics-of-design-rights.
Moy, R. C. (1992). 'History of the Patent Harmonization Treaty: Economic Self-Interest as an Influence' *J. Marshall L. Rev.*26: 457.
Mueller, M. (2004). Toward an economics of the domain name system. In M. E. Cave, S. K. Majumdar, and I. Vogelsang (eds). *Handbook of Telecommunications Economics: Technology Evolution and the Internet* (North Holland, Elsevier), Volume 2.
Nolo. (2015). *Nolo's Plain-English Law Dictionary.* Wex Online Dictionary Legal Information Institution. Available at https://www.law.cornell.edu/wex/cartel.
NSF. (2006). *Survey Says?: Questionable Future.* National Science Foundation, Special Reports, 17 March 2006 Available at http://www.nsf.gov/news/special_reports/survey/index.jsp?id=question.
O'Grady, J. D. (2013). 'Report: iTunes Owns 74 Percent of the Digital Music Market'. ZDNET, 21 June 2013. Available at http://www.zdnet.com/article/report-itunes-owns-74-percent-of-the-digital-music-market/.
OECD. (1989). 'Predatory Pricing' (Paris, OECD). Available at http://www.oecd.org/competition/abuse/2375661.pdf.
Office, U. C. (2013). 'Copyright in Derivative Works and Compilations'. Washington, D.C., United States Copyright Office, 14:1013. Available at http://copyright.gov/circs/circl4.pdf.
OHIM. (2015). 'Trade Mark Definition' CTM. Available at https://oami.europa.eu/ohimportal/en/trade-mark-definition.
Osterwalder, A., Pigneur, Y., and Clark, T. (2009). *Business Model Generation: A Handbook for Visionaries, Game Changers, and Challengers* (Amsterdam, Alexander Osterwalder & Yves Pigneur).
Ozeke, H. B. (2014). 'Trademark Squatting: Why Registration Of Your Trademark In Turkey Matters—Intellectual Property—Turkey'. Available at http://www.mondaq.com/turkey/x/356880/Trademark/Trademark+Squatting+Why+Registration+Of+Your+Trademark+In+Turkey+Matters.
Page, W. and Gandelman, M. (2010). 'Economics & Understanding Brazil's Unique Model of Collective Rights Management'. PRS for Music. *Economic Insight 21.* Available at https://www.prsformusic.com/creators/news/research/Documents/Page,%20Gandelman,%20Dickinson%20(2010)%20ECADonomics.pdf.
Paine, L. S. (1991). 'Trade Secrets and the Justification of Intellectual Property: A Comment on Hettinger' *Philosophy & Public Affairs* 20(3): 247–63.
Passman, D. S. (2009). *All You Need to Know About the Music Business* (New York: Free Press)
Peoples, U. P. F. o. I. (2015). 'Indigenous Peoples'. Indigenous Voices Factsheet. Online.

Piketty, T. (2014). *Capital in the Twenty-first Century* (Cambridge, MA, Harvard University Press).

Png, I. P. (2012). 'Law and Innovation: Evidence from State Trade Secrets Laws'. Available at SSRN 1755284, 2012.

Porter, M. E. (2001). 'Strategy and the Internet' *Harvard Business Review* 79: 62–79.

Qian, Y. (1 November 2008). 'Impacts of Entry by Counterfeiters' *The Quarterly Journal of Economics* 123(4): 1577–1609. Available at http://qje.oxfordjournals.org/content/123/4/1577.abstract.

Razgaitis, R. (2003). *Valuation and Pricing of Technology-Based Intellectual Property* (USA, Wiley).

Rai, R. K. (2008). 'Effect of the TRIPS-Mandated Intellectual Property Rights on Foreign Direct Investment in Developing Countries: A Case Study of the Indian Pharmaceutical Industry' *The Journal of World Intellectual Property* 11(5–6): 404–31.

Richards, M.-A. (2008). 'Cultural and Economic Importance of Traditional Knowledge, Traditional Cultural Expressions and Genetic Resources for Caribbean Countries'. WIPO.

Saunders, L. (2007). 'Educational Research Commissioned by/for Policy Audiences' (London, TLRP).

Schumpeter, J. A. *Business cycles*. Vol. 1. New York, McGraw-Hill, 1939.

Schumpeter, J. A. (1934). *The Theory of Economic Development: An Inquiry into Profits, Capital, Credit, Interest, and the Business Cycle* (Piscataway, NJ, Transaction Publishers).

Schwarzkopf, S. (2008) 'Turning Trade Marks into Brands: how Advertising Agencies Created Brands in the Global Market Place, 1900–1930', Queen Mary, University of London, School of Business and Management, Centre for Globalisation Research, Working Papers, No 18. Available at http://webspace.qmul.ac.uk/pmartins/CGRWP18.pdf.

Scotchmer, S. (2006). *Innovation and Incentives* (Cambridge, Mass., MIT Press).

Scott-Morton, F., and Shapiro, C. (2014). 'Strategic Patent Acquisitions'. *Antitrust Law Journal* 79(2): 463.

Searle, N. (2011). 'Changing Business Models in the Creative Industries: The Cases of Television, Computer Games and Music' *UK Intellectual Property Office*. Available at https://www.gov.uk/government/publications/changing-business-models-in-the-creative-industries.

Searle, N. (2012). 'The Criminalization of the Theft of Trade Secrets: An Analysis of the Economic Espionage Act' *IP Theory* 2(2): 2.

Searle, N. C. (2010). 'The Economics of Trade Secrets: Evidence from the Economic Espionage Act. PhD Thesis, University of St Andrews.

Shapiro, C. (2001). 'Navigating the Patent Thicket: Cross Licenses, Patent Pools, and Standard Setting'. In A. Jaffe, J. Lerner, and S. Stern (eds). *Innovation Policy and the Economy*, Volume 1 (Cambridge, Mass, MIT Press) 119–50.

Shy, O. (1995). *Industrial Organization: Theory and Applications* (Cambridge, Mass, MIT Press).

Smith, A. (1759). *The Theory of Moral Sentiments* (New York, NY, Cambridge Univeristy Press).

Stender, N., Stark, J., and Ye, F. (2010). 'China Income Tax Preferences for High/New-Tech Enterprises (HTNE)' (Technical report, Orrick, Herrington & Sutcliffe LLP, Wheeling, WV). Available at http://www.orrick.com/fileupload/2420.pdf.

Stigler, G. J. (1993). *The Organization of Industry* (Chicago, University of Chicago Press).

Strowel, A. and Dussolier, S. (1999). Workshop on Implementation Issues of the WIPO Copyright Treaty (WCT) and the WIPO Performances and Phonograms

Treaty (WPPT): Legal Protection of Technological Systems. WCT-WPPT/IMP/2. Geneva: WIPO. Available at http://www.wipo.int/edocs/mdocs/copyright/en/wct wpptimp/wet wppt imp 2. doc.

Stucke, M. E. (2013). 'Is Competition Always Good?' *Journal of Antitrust Enforcement* 1: 162–97.

Sundara Rajan, M. (2012). 'At the Frontiers of Law-making: Copyright and the Protection of Culture in India' *World Intellectual Property Organisation Journal* 4: 111–20.

Swanson, T. and Göschl, T. (2000). 'Property Rights Issues Involving Plant Genetic Resources: Implications of Ownership for Economic Efficiency' *Ecological Economics* 32(1): 75–92.

Tewkesbury, J., Crandall, M., and Crane, W. (1980). 'Measuring the Societal Benefits of Innovation' *Science* 09/1980:658-62.

Towse, R. and Handke, C. (2007). 'Regulating Copyright Collecting Societies: Current Policy In Europe'. Society for Economic Research on Copyright Issues (SERCI) Annual Congress. Available at http://www.gbz.hu-berlin.de/downloads/pdf/SERCIACPapers/towsehandke.pdf.

UPOV. (2015). 'Getting the Most Out of Your New Plant Variety'. International Union for the Protection of New Varieties of Plants. Available at http://www.wipo.int/sme/en/documents/upov_plant_variety_fulltext.html.

USPTO. (2013). 'USPTO Publishes Final Rules and Guidelines Governing First-Inventor-to-File.' United States Patents and Trademarks Office, Press Release: 13-10. Available at http://www.uspto.gov/about-us/news-updates/uspto-publishes-final-rules-and-guidelines-governing-first-inventor-file.

Van Kempen, L. (2007). 'Status Consumption and Ethnicity in Bolivia: Evidence from Durables Ownership' *International Journal of Consumer Studies* 31(1): 76–89.

Vigen, T. (2014). 'Number of People Who Drowned By Falling in a Pool Correlates With Films Nicholas Cage Appeared in'. Available at http://www.tylervigen.com/spurious-correlations.

von Graevenitz, G. et al. (2012). 'Trade Mark Cluttering: An Exploratory Report'. Intellectual Property Office UK.

Voyer, B. (2014. 'Coca Cola's Secret Formula: An Ancient Creative Marketing Recipe'. Creative Marketing Centre (ESCP) Blog. Available at http://www.creativitymarketing.org/posts/2014/february/20/coca-cola%E2%80%99s-secret-formula-an-ancient-creative-marketing-recipe.aspx.

Wall, P. K. (April 2012). 'A Bitter Pill to Swallow' *Intellectual Property Magazine*. 31 August 2012. Available at http://directory.intellectualpropertymagazine.com/ipwo/doc/view.htm?id=282410&searchCode=SEC&channelID=design&sectionID=features.

Watt, R. (2010). 'Fair Copyright Remuneration: The Case of Music Radio' *Review of Economic Research on Copyright Issues* 7: 21–37.

Wex Law Dictionary (2015a). *Antitrust: An Overview* (Legal Information Institute, Cornell University Law School). Available at https://www.law.cornell.edu/wex/antitrust.

Wex Law Dictionary (2015b). 'Joint venture'. (Legal Information Institute, Cornell University Law School.) Available at https://www.law.cornell.edu/wex/joint_venture.

Wex Law Dictionary (2015c). *Unfair Competition Law: An Overview* (Legal Information Institute, Cornell University Law School). Available at https://www.law.cornell.edu/wex/unfair_competition.

Wikimedia. (7 July 2015). 'Supplementary Protection Certificate'. Available at https://en.wikipedia.org/wiki/Supplementary_protection_certificate.

Wiltbank, R. (2009). *Siding with the Angels* (Nesta). Available at https://www.nesta.org.uk/sites/default/files/siding_with_the_angels.pdf.

WIPO. (2013). 'World Intellectual Property Report Brands—Reputation and Image in the Global Marketplace'. WIPO.

WIPO. (2015). Industrial Designs. WIPO. Available at http://www.wipo.int/designs/en/.

WIPO. (2015). 'Traditional Knowledge'. Available at http://www.wipo.int/tk/en/tk/. World, J. (2015). *Elephant and the Blind Men*. Available at http://www.jainworld.com/literature/story25.htm.

Yar, M. (2005). 'The Global "Epidemic" of Movie "Piracy": Crime-Wave or Social Construction?' *Media, Culture & Society* 27(5): 677–96.

Zou, X. (2009). 'On Unification of Functionality and Aesthetics of Design Art'. *Asian Social Science* 5(10): 144.

Zou, X. (2003). *The Economic Structure of Intellectual Property Law* (Cambridge, Mass., Harvard University Press). Available at http://site.ebrary.com/id/10328824.

CASES AND LEGISLATION

UK STATUTES

UK STATUTORY INSTRUMENTS

EU PRIMARY LEGISLATION

EU SECONDARY LEGISLATION

EU Directives

EU Regulations

NATIONAL LEGISLATION IN OTHER JURISDICTIONS

Indian Legislation

US Legislation

INDEX